He says it's love, but does he really mean it . . . ?

The age-old question that women pose again and again is "Why does he say one thing and then do another?" The answer is very simple. Men often do not say what they really feel. They say what is convenient and easy. In their defense, though, men are also often confused and cannot clearly understand *themselves* what they really feel. Therefore, how can we understand our men when so much of their deeper emotional makeup remains in shadow? In astrology, to get a trenchant insight into that mysterious realm of male feeling, one must look to the sign of the moon. . . .

WHY DOES HE SAY ONE THING AND DO ANOTHER?

UNDERSTANDING MEN THROUGH THEIR MOON SIGNS

ROBIN MACNAUGHTON

POCKET BOOKS

New York   London   Toronto   Sydney   Tokyo   Singapore

An *Original* Publication of POCKET BOOKS

 POCKET BOOKS, a division of Simon & Schuster Inc.
1230 Avenue of the Americas, New York, NY 10020

Copyright © 1997 by Robin MacNaughton

ISBN: 0-671-00207-4

First Pocket Books printing February 1997

10 9 8 7 6 5 4 3 2 1

POCKET and colophon are registered trademarks of Simon & Schuster Inc.

Printed in the U.S.A.

To Amelia, my extraordinary editor. With deep gratitude for your immense involvement, efficiency, and for being uniquely you.

Contents

Contents

WHY DOES HE SAY ONE THING AND DO ANOTHER?

Introduction

An astounding number of women are terribly confused by men and have a deep desire to better understand them. These women live their lives on hold, hoping that something positive "will mysteriously happen" with men on whom they are misplacing their time and affection. They do not understand men at all because they look at them completely from the outside and are often thrown by their contradictory and ambivalent behavior. The age-old question that these women pose again and again is "Why does he say one thing and then do another?" The answer is very simple. Men often do not say what they really feel. They say what is convenient and easy. In their defense, though, men are also often confused and cannot clearly understand *themselves* what they really feel. So how can we understand our men when so much of what drives their actions remains in shadow? In astrology, to get a trenchant insight into that mysterious realm of male feeling, we must look to the sign of the moon.

While the sun sign represents our reason, our con-

1

scious ego, our will, our sense of power, and need for recognition, the moon sign represents our deeper feelings. It shows how we tend to respond emotionally to a given situation as well as how profoundly we are capable of being moved. It also shows the way we tend to interact and defines the extent to which we *need* to relate. For instance, a man who has a moon sign in the element of air, which governs the realm of thinking, relates through talking, humor, and intellect. This sort of man has a strong need for space and can easily be suffocated. However, because he thinks rather than feels, he may not be able to actually say this. Therefore, his reaction to a woman who demands closeness and commitment too soon would be flight— even though he may be very attracted to her and actually encouraged such a response from her. Men with air sign moons are emotionally detached and feel comfortable with women who are more cerebral than emotional. On the surface these men can be very charming and engaging. However, if they get caught up in a demanding relationship, they can also become emotionally remote. This behavior is puzzling until we see that it's demonstrated by the man with the air sign moon. Then it all begins to make sense. The moon sign reveals the true story of what is happening under the surface as well as the sort of emotional behavior that will become evident over a period of time.

In psychological terms, the moon is associated with the man's anima, also known as his feminine side. When a man is completely unconscious of his feminine side, he has problems with relationships. He has trouble being caring and nurturing. Although he may be charming in his persona, which is the face he shows to the world, emotionally he is stunted or immature. Therefore, he would tend to project his anima or feminine side onto a woman who lives it out for him. Over time, of course, the woman will become deeply frustrated because not only is she living with someone who is incomplete, in turn, he is treating her as incomplete. Those who have experienced a relationship with a man who does this know that. To live as someone's projection is to live only as a facade and to have one's authenticity ignored.

The psychoanalyst Loren Pedersen says, "In trying to understand some of the deeper aspects of a man's relationship to women, we need to understand that his conscious ideas of women represent only one facet of what he experiences with actual women. The anima is a conditioner of his personal relationships. Whether or not a man is conscious of it, the inner struggle with the masculine/feminine polarity is one of his life's greatest issues. Among other things, behind every man *is* a woman and the inner woman eventually helps to clarify his relationship with the outer woman."

On a positive note, Pedersen adds, "The anima specifically allows him access to his capacities for interpersonal relatedness, differentiating feeling, creativity, spirituality, and further development of his consciousness." On the other hand, "when a man becomes overidentified with his persona (the face he tries to show to the world), he is left with a constricted and shallow view of himself. Paradoxically, he develops an overinflated view of his conscious sense of ego since so much value is placed on his outer personality."

When we understand how the moon sign operates, we can understand a great deal about how the anima functions and what might be done to allow it a more conscious expression. When a woman is aware of how a man tends to feel in many situations she can more easily open the lines of communication to improve the overall quality of a relationship. The moon sign is a remarkable key that helps decipher the deep emotional motives that affect our men's behavior and allows us then to make connections with them based on compassion and tolerance instead of confusion, destructive criticism, and too many unrealistic expectations. In explaining how the moon influences the man in your life, I hope to provide you with a unique approach to an age-old problem—how to know what he is feeling and why. I hope it will help you gain some new and significant insights.

Man, Woman, the Moon, and the Anima

In a man the moon sign corresponds to what in Jungian psychology terms is called the anima. The anima is the feminine part of the man, his feeling side. Many men are uncomfortable with this part of their psyche.

Generally speaking, a man tends to live through the masculine part of his consciousness, which is based on achievement, competition, logic, and ego values. Sometimes the feminine part of him is completely repressed or suppressed and experienced only through his relationship with women.

Most men develop their feminine side gradually and begin by projecting their own feminine nature onto a female with whom they fall in love. This is never mature love, for they are not seeing the entire character and personality of the girl but rather their own anima, the profound emotional side of themselves that they have not yet found a way to consciously express. The girl becomes a vision of what the masculine mind wants her to be. If he were to see her as a total person,

5

she may be quite different from what he is projecting upon her.

As a man matures emotionally, the feminine part of his personality more consciously integrates into his life. He comes in touch with his feelings, he values them, and he is not afraid to express them. The more that the feminine is consciously integrated into his personality, the more he will be capable of loving a woman as a whole person instead of as a psychological projection of his own psyche. He will then consciously treat her as a complex individual instead of a completion of a missing part of himself.

The immature man, however, will go through life projecting his anima onto the woman who becomes the object of his infatuations. A woman can often sense this in a man in this state through her highly developed intuition. She can also use it to her own ends to gain power over him, playing various female roles from seductress to mother to enhance her own sense of ego. In doing so, she becomes an anima figure and her importance to the man to whom she plays her part can assume mythic proportions at the expense of her own individual psychological and emotional development. An obvious example of such an anima figure and the dangers that can befall a woman committed to a man in this role can be seen in the life of Marilyn Monroe, a woman who related to herself only through the eyes of the men she was attracting.

The age-old battle of the sexes is actually the struggle in consciousness between the feminine principle and the masculine principle. Traditionally, women have accused men of being self-centered (the masculine principle). Men, in turn, accuse women of being dependent and overly emotional (the feminine principle). Men want women to be more rational (the masculine principle), and women want men to be more caring and nurturing (the feminine principle). Both sides of this conflict are born of a male and female consciousness that needs more developing.

The man with a poorly developed feminine side is interested in little outside of himself. He relates poorly to other people and to his own feminine feelings, which are borne out in empathy, nurturance, intuition, care, and love. He sees sex as an erotic rather than passionate, loving act and believes that reason is his superior faculty. He is competitive, egotistical, emotionally shallow, and does not really value women or values them only as instruments of momentary gratification or pleasure. Because he is so frightened of his own feelings, this sort of man is also often frightened of women and of women's feelings. Therefore, his behavior with women is usually either controlling or ambivalent, the latter pattern being one of hot-cold, hot-cold, stop-go, stop-go.

This sort of man usually never consciously realizes his feeling of fear until he undergoes some serious life crisis, like the end of a marriage, and his old way of life starts to fall apart, engulfing him in a sea of intense emotional pain. This rupture can be an opportunity for him to transform and begin to live in a positive way through his feminine side. Often therapy or analysis at this time can provide a man with some objective help as he becomes familiar with handling and identifying his feelings.

As sex roles are changing, both feminine and masculine consciousness is changing. Gradually, more and more men are living through their feelings, moving toward becoming people who are more emotionally integrated, while women are moving away from passive dependency and developing more as strong, independent individuals.

Ideally, both men and women should strive for greater consciousness and balance of the feminine and masculine principles within themselves. The payoff is a less fearful and more fulfilled experience of life and its many offerings that can generate a deep, powerful, truly loving connection with others.

The Emotional Range of the Four Elements: Fire, Air, Earth, and Water

The universe is made up of four basic elements: fire, air, earth, and water. Each of the twelve signs of the zodiac falls into one of these categories, and each of these elements determines different personality traits. The elements also show the kind of instinctual needs we have, our habitual behavior patterns, and in what ways we try to nourish ourselves. The following sections illustrate some basic personality traits of the moon sign in each of the four elements.

The Fire Sign Moon Type (Aries, Leo, Sagittarius)

The fire sign moon type is restless, impatient, impulsive, and adventure-oriented. There is a strong need for exploration, excitement, and challenges of all kinds. This type of person is easily bored with a mundane routine and can lose interest when things fall into predictable patterns that he finds confining. Fire moon signs are freedom-oriented, thrill-seeking, passionate, and romantic. However, they are not known for their staying power. Their deepest need is to feel fully alive in the moment, which can lead to affairs, should their long-standing relationship start to seem stale.

Fire sign moon types are highly pleasure-oriented and, in the extreme, can be very self-centered. They seek immediate gratification and have a hard time with frustrations that obstruct the path to their goals. Optimistic, outgoing, and always ready to have a good time, they can be a lot of fun to be with, especially if everything is going their way.

The Air Sign Moon Type (Gemini, Libra, Aquarius)

The air sign moon type is emotionally detached, cerebral, and uses his mind to process feelings. Air sign moon types seek mental stimulation through conversation, humorous exchanges, or learning. They need a lot of emotional space, are easily suffocated, and find it necessary to communicate well with their partner. At times they may appear to be cold. Certainly, they don't have the deep, lingering emotional reactions to life that characterize many of the other moon signs. Their strength is an emotional objectivity that potentially gives them a wide perspective when analyzing a situation. They are weak in compassion and have a tough time achieving a deeper understanding of the complexities of other people.

The Earth Sign Moon Type (Taurus, Virgo, Capricorn)

The earth sign moon type is highly security-conscious, grounded, and practical. Work, responsibility, order, and organization are top priorities for them. This type needs to feel the ground underneath his feet, know where he's going, and have a good sense of how all plans will work out. Stability, reliability, and dependability are extremely important to earth moon people. Tangibility is also a priority. Earth moon people have the most conventional attitudes of the four elements and put a high price on loyalty, fidelity, and trust.

The Water Sign Moon Type (Cancer, Scorpio, Pisces)

The water sign moon type experiences feelings stronger than all other moon signs. The water signs are emotional, subjective, and sometimes moody. They are the most emotionally sensitive, sometimes too much for their own good. Water sign moons can inflate the emotional value of situations and can also hold on to negative feelings for such a long time that everything becomes distorted. They can also be introverted, irrational, fantasy-oriented, and tend to get lost in a mysterious inner world of their own making. On the positive side, they can be compassionate, sympathetic, empathetic, and highly intuitive. Water moon people prefer close relationships that are sensual, intimate, and meaningful. Their most essential desire is for a soul mate with whom they can share the deepest part of themselves.

Moon Tables

The following tables will help you find the sign of the moon when you know the date of birth, place of birth, and ideally the time of birth. These tables are easy to use and are based on Greenwich Mean time in England. These tables are needed because the moon moves so fast, changing signs every two days. The tables indicate at exactly what time the moon changed signs, so that a moon sign on a marginal birth date falling between two signs can be accurately determined. However, even if you don't know the exact time of birth, just look up the date of birth. In many instances the moon sign will be clear. When it appears to be marginal, with the birth time starting around 1:00 A.M. or close to midnight, read the next closest sign. One of the two will be an obvious fit.

The basic formula for the moon tables is: for someone born in Eastern Standard Time, add five hours to the time of birth, Central Standard Time, six hours, Mountain Standard Time, seven hours, and Pacific Standard Time, eight hours. Subtract one hour for Daylight Savings Time or, for someone older, War Time. For instance for someone born at 5:15 A.M. under Daylight Savings Time, the real birth time would be 4:15 A.M. If the time zone was Eastern Standard Time, then add five hours for the Greenwich Mean time adjustment, which would give you 9:15 A.M. This means that at the moment this person was born it was 9:15 A.M. under Greenwich Mean time in Greenwich, England, the worldwide central time determinant. It's that simple. So simply add and/or subtract your hours and go straight to the tables!

January 1935		February 1935		March 1935		April 1935	
2nd 4:23 am	Sagittarius	2nd 6:23 am	Aquarius	2nd 5:14 am	Aquarius	2nd 3:32 pm	Aries
4th 6:41 am	Capricorn	4th 5:48 pm	Pisces	4th 5:12 am	Pisces	4th 4:23 pm	Taurus
6th 7:04 am	Aquarius	6th 5:53 pm	Aries	6th 4:43 am	Aries	6th 7:39 pm	Gemini
8th 7:20 am	Pisces	8th 8:26 pm	Taurus	8th 5:48 am	Taurus	9th 2:52 am	Cancer
10th 9:08 am	Aries	11th 2:59 am	Gemini	10th 10:18 am	Gemini	11th 1:55 pm	Leo
12th 1:31 pm	Taurus	13th 12:29 pm	Cancer	12th 6:55 pm	Cancer	14th 2:48 am	Virgo
14th 8:45 pm	Gemini	16th 0:37 am	Leo	15th 6:50 am	Leo	16th 3:00 pm	Libra
17th 6:40 am	Cancer	18th 1:33 pm	Virgo	17th 7:52 pm	Virgo	19th 1:10 am	Scorpio
19th 6:28 pm	Leo	21st 2:03 am	Libra	20th 8:07 am	Libra	21st 9:05 am	Sagittarius
22nd 7:19 am	Virgo	23rd 1:01 pm	Scorpio	22nd 6:44 pm	Scorpio	23rd 3:11 pm	Capricorn
24th 7:57 pm	Libra	25th 9:39 pm	Sagittarius	25th 3:23 am	Sagittarius	25th 7:42 pm	Aquarius
27th 6:42 am	Scorpio	28th 3:03 am	Capricorn	27th 9:46 am	Capricorn	27th 10:41 pm	Pisces
29th 2:04 pm	Sagittarius			29th 1:39 pm	Aquarius	30th 0:26 am	Aries
31st 5:43 pm	Capricorn			31st 5:13 pm	Pisces		

May 1935		June 1935		July 1935		August 1935	
2nd 2:11 am	Taurus	2nd 8:46 pm	Cancer	2nd 2:15 pm	Leo	1st 9:08 am	Virgo
4th 5:30 am	Gemini	5th 6:22 am	Leo	5th 2:10 am	Virgo	3rd 9:54 pm	Libra
6th 11:56 am	Cancer	7th 6:26 pm	Virgo	7th 2:51 pm	Libra	6th 9:53 am	Scorpio
8th 9:56 pm	Leo	10th 6:58 am	Libra	10th 2:14 am	Scorpio	8th 7:21 pm	Sagittarius
11th 10:27 am	Virgo	12th 5:32 pm	Scorpio	12th 10:22 am	Sagittarius	11th 1:08 am	Capricorn
13th 10:48 pm	Libra	15th 0:57 am	Sagittarius	14th 2:59 pm	Capricorn	13th 3:20 am	Aquarius
16th 8:52 am	Scorpio	17th 5:20 am	Capricorn	16th 4:52 pm	Aquarius	15th 3:19 am	Pisces
18th 4:11 pm	Sagittarius	19th 7:56 am	Aquarius	18th 5:32 pm	Pisces	17th 2:58 am	Aries
20th 9:21 pm	Capricorn	21st 9:58 am	Pisces	20th 6:36 pm	Aries	19th 4:12 am	Taurus
23rd 1:10 am	Aquarius	23rd 12:25 pm	Aries	22nd 9:24 pm	Taurus	21st 8:31 am	Gemini
25th 4:14 am	Pisces	25th 3:57 pm	Taurus	25th 2:46 am	Gemini	23rd 4:22 pm	Cancer
27th 6:50 am	Aries	27th 9:08 pm	Gemini	27th 10:47 am	Cancer	26th 3:02 am	Leo
29th 10:01 am	Taurus	30th 4:29 am	Cancer	29th 9:07 pm	Leo	28th 3:22 pm	Virgo
31st 2:15 pm	Gemini					31st 4:08 am	Libra

Moon Tables

September 1935
2nd 4:21 am Scorpio
5th 2:46 am Sagittarius
7th 10:03 am Capricorn
9th 1:39 pm Aquarius
11th 2:12 pm Pisces
13th 1:22 pm Aries
15th 1:15 pm Taurus
17th 3:52 pm Gemini
19th 10:29 pm Cancer
22nd 8:53 am Leo
24th 9:20 pm Virgo
27th 10:05 am Libra
29th 10:07 pm Scorpio

October 1935
2nd 8:39 am Sagittarius
4th 4:59 pm Capricorn
6th 10:19 pm Aquarius
9th 0:26 am Pisces
11th 0:19 am Aries
12th 11:54 pm Taurus
15th 1:18 am Gemini
17th 6:24 am Cancer
19th 3:38 pm Leo
22nd 2:45 am Virgo
24th 4:30 pm Libra
27th 4:14 am Scorpio
29th 2:16 pm Sagittarius
31st 10:31 pm Capricorn

November 1935
3rd 4:35 am Aquarius
5th 8:17 am Pisces
7th 9:52 am Aries
9th 10:30 am Taurus
11th 11:57 am Gemini
13th 4:01 pm Cancer
15th 11:50 pm Leo
18th 11:13 am Virgo
20th 11:52 pm Libra
23rd 11:33 am Scorpio
25th 9:08 pm Sagittarius
28th 4:27 am Capricorn
30th 9:57 am Aquarius

December 1935
2nd 2:01 pm Pisces
4th 4:52 pm Aries
6th 7:04 pm Taurus
8th 9:38 pm Gemini
11th 1:55 am Cancer
13th 9:10 am Leo
15th 7:34 pm Virgo
18th 7:57 am Libra
20th 8:00 pm Scorpio
23rd 5:41 am Sagittarius
25th 12:24 pm Capricorn
27th 4:44 pm Aquarius
29th 7:42 pm Pisces
31st 10:15 pm Aries

January 1936
3rd 1:12 am Taurus
5th 5:06 am Gemini
7th 10:32 am Cancer
9th 6:04 pm Leo
12th 4:06 am Virgo
14th 4:11 pm Libra
17th 4:36 am Scorpio
19th 3:06 pm Sagittarius
21st 10:17 pm Capricorn
24th 1:60 am Aquarius
26th 3:34 am Pisces
28th 4:37 am Aries
30th 6:40 am Taurus

February 1936
1st 10:43 am Gemini
3rd 5:02 pm Cancer
6th 1:27 am Leo
8th 11:51 am Virgo
10th 11:46 pm Libra
13th 12:23 pm Scorpio
15th 11:54 pm Sagittarius
18th 8:15 am Capricorn
20th 12:40 pm Aquarius
22nd 1:52 pm Pisces
24th 1:36 pm Aries
26th 1:55 pm Taurus
28th 4:35 pm Gemini

March 1936
1st 10:27 pm Cancer
4th 7:23 am Leo
6th 6:20 pm Virgo
9th 6:28 am Libra
11th 7:05 pm Scorpio
14th 7:03 am Sagittarius
16th 4:48 pm Capricorn
18th 10:51 pm Aquarius
21st 0:58 am Pisces
23rd 0:31 am Aries
24th 11:38 pm Taurus
27th 0:32 am Gemini
29th 4:56 am Cancer
31st 1:08 pm Leo

April 1936
3rd 0:08 am Virgo
5th 12:32 pm Libra
8th 1:06 am Scorpio
10th 1:01 pm Sagittarius
12th 11:24 pm Capricorn
15th 6:45 am Aquarius
17th 10:33 am Pisces
19th 11:18 am Aries
21st 10:39 am Taurus
23rd 10:43 am Gemini
25th 1:28 pm Cancer
27th 8:06 pm Leo
30th 6:25 am Virgo

May 1936
2nd 6:44 pm Libra
5th 7:17 am Scorpio
7th 6:55 pm Sagittarius
10th 4:55 am Capricorn
12th 12:44 pm Aquarius
14th 5:50 pm Pisces
16th 8:12 pm Aries
18th 8:49 pm Taurus
20th 9:14 pm Gemini
22nd 11:21 pm Cancer
25th 4:45 am Leo
27th 1:52 pm Virgo
30th 1:39 am Libra

June 1936
1st 2:12 pm Scorpio
4th 1:37 am Sagittarius
6th 11:01 am Capricorn
8th 6:15 pm Aquarius
10th 11:28 pm Pisces
13th 2:46 am Aries
15th 4:49 am Taurus
17th 6:32 am Gemini
19th 9:14 am Cancer
21st 2:11 pm Leo
23rd 10:17 pm Virgo
26th 9:26 am Libra
28th 9:53 pm Scorpio

July 1936
1st 9:24 am Sagittarius
3rd 6:32 pm Capricorn
6th 0:56 am Aquarius
8th 5:10 am Pisces
10th 8:11 am Aries
12th 10:48 am Taurus
14th 1:42 pm Gemini
16th 5:31 pm Cancer
18th 11:00 pm Leo
21st 6:58 am Virgo
23rd 5:33 pm Libra
26th 5:51 am Scorpio
28th 5:54 pm Sagittarius
31st 3:22 am Capricorn

August 1936
2nd 9:21 am Aquarius
4th 12:34 pm Pisces
6th 2:33 pm Aries
8th 4:15 pm Taurus
10th 7:15 pm Gemini
12th 11:53 pm Cancer
15th 6:24 am Leo
17th 2:49 pm Virgo
20th 1:18 am Libra
22nd 1:37 pm Scorpio
25th 2:09 am Sagittarius
27th 12:30 pm Capricorn
29th 7:08 pm Aquarius
31st 10:05 pm Pisces

September 1936
2nd 10:44 pm Aries
4th 11:05 pm Taurus
7th 0:55 am Gemini
9th 5:19 am Cancer
11th 12:17 pm Leo
13th 9:22 pm Virgo
16th 8:16 am Libra
18th 8:34 pm Scorpio
21st 9:24 am Sagittarius
23rd 8:51 pm Capricorn
26th 4:49 am Aquarius
28th 8:35 am Pisces
30th 9:08 am Aries

October 1936
2nd 8:28 am Taurus
4th 8:41 am Gemini
6th 11:34 am Cancer
8th 5:49 pm Leo
11th 3:02 am Virgo
13th 2:21 pm Libra
16th 2:48 am Scorpio
18th 3:38 pm Sagittarius
21st 3:37 am Capricorn
23rd 12:55 pm Aquarius
25th 6:24 pm Pisces
27th 8:06 pm Aries
29th 7:35 pm Taurus
31st 6:52 pm Gemini

November 1936
2nd 8:03 pm Cancer
5th 0:37 am Leo
7th 9:03 am Virgo
9th 8:16 pm Libra
12th 8:51 am Scorpio
14th 9:35 pm Sagittarius
17th 9:19 am Capricorn
19th 7:08 pm Aquarius
22nd 2:03 am Pisces
24th 5:33 am Aries
26th 6:28 am Taurus
28th 6:14 am Gemini
30th 6:44 am Cancer

December 1936
2nd 9:48 am Leo
4th 4:36 pm Virgo
7th 2:56 am Libra
9th 3:28 pm Scorpio
12th 4:06 am Sagittarius
14th 3:24 pm Capricorn
17th 0:43 am Aquarius
19th 7:42 am Pisces
21st 12:23 pm Aries
23rd 3:03 pm Taurus
25th 4:24 pm Gemini
27th 5:37 pm Cancer
29th 8:15 pm Leo

January 1937
1st 1:46 am Virgo
3rd 10:58 am Libra
5th 10:57 pm Scorpio
8th 11:41 am Sagittarius
10th 10:52 pm Capricorn
13th 7:22 am Aquarius
15th 1:26 pm Pisces
17th 5:47 pm Aries
19th 9:06 pm Taurus
21st 11:55 pm Gemini
24th 2:40 am Cancer
26th 6:10 am Leo
28th 11:34 am Virgo
30th 7:51 pm Libra

February 1937
2nd 7:10 am Scorpio
4th 7:57 pm Sagittarius
7th 7:30 am Capricorn
9th 3:55 pm Aquarius
11th 9:08 pm Pisces
14th 0:10 am Aries
16th 2:35 am Taurus
18th 5:24 am Gemini
20th 9:07 am Cancer
22nd 1:54 pm Leo
24th 8:06 pm Virgo
27th 4:29 am Libra

March 1937
1st 3:26 pm Scorpio
4th 4:07 am Sagittarius
6th 4:19 pm Capricorn
9th 1:34 am Aquarius
11th 6:46 am Pisces
13th 8:57 am Aries
15th 9:55 am Taurus
17th 11:22 am Gemini
19th 2:29 pm Cancer
21st 7:38 pm Leo
24th 2:45 am Virgo
26th 11:50 am Libra
28th 10:52 pm Scorpio
31st 11:34 am Sagittarius

April 1937
3rd 0:16 am Capricorn
5th 10:34 am Aquarius
7th 4:54 pm Pisces
9th 7:25 pm Aries
11th 7:39 pm Taurus
13th 7:35 pm Gemini
15th 9:04 pm Cancer
18th 1:12 am Leo
20th 8:18 am Virgo
22nd 5:54 pm Libra
25th 5:22 am Scorpio
27th 6:06 pm Sagittarius
30th 6:56 am Capricorn

May 1937	June 1937	July 1937	August 1937
2nd 6:06 am Aquarius	1st 8:54 am Pisces	3rd 0:35 am Taurus	1st 9:30 am Gemini
5th 1:57 am Pisces	3rd 2:17 pm Aries	5th 2:17 am Gemini	3rd 11:35 am Cancer
7th 5:44 am Aries	5th 4:34 pm Taurus	7th 2:55 am Cancer	5th 1:39 pm Leo
9th 6:31 am Taurus	7th 4:46 pm Gemini	9th 4:03 am Leo	7th 4:59 pm Virgo
11th 5:58 am Gemini	9th 4:34 pm Cancer	11th 7:22 am Virgo	9th 10:59 pm Libra
13th 6:03 am Cancer	11th 5:49 pm Leo	13th 2:09 pm Libra	12th 8:41 am Scorpio
15th 8:33 am Leo	13th 10:04 pm Virgo	16th 0:36 am Scorpio	14th 8:59 pm Sagittarius
17th 2:23 pm Virgo	16th 6:11 am Libra	18th 1:21 pm Sagittarius	17th 9:36 am Capricorn
19th 11:35 pm Libra	18th 5:34 pm Scorpio	21st 1:51 am Capricorn	19th 8:03 pm Aquarius
22nd 11:21 am Scorpio	21st 6:26 am Sagittarius	23rd 12:17 pm Aquarius	22nd 3:27 am Pisces
25th 0:10 am Sagittarius	23rd 6:58 pm Capricorn	25th 8:21 pm Pisces	24th 8:23 am Aries
27th 12:51 pm Capricorn	26th 5:52 am Aquarius	28th 2:15 am Aries	26th 11:57 am Taurus
30th 0:13 am Aquarius	28th 2:35 pm Pisces	30th 6:31 am Taurus	28th 3:03 pm Gemini
	30th 8:50 pm Aries		30th 6:06 pm Cancer

September 1937	October 1937	November 1937	December 1937
1st 9:24 pm Leo	1st 8:31 am Virgo	2nd 7:51 am Scorpio	2nd 2:06 am Sagittarius
4th 1:36 am Virgo	3rd 3:36 pm Libra	4th 7:48 pm Sagittarius	4th 3:07 pm Capricorn
6th 7:53 am Libra	6th 0:57 am Scorpio	7th 8:51 am Capricorn	7th 3:40 am Aquarius
8th 5:03 pm Scorpio	8th 12:47 pm Sagittarius	9th 9:18 pm Aquarius	9th 2:18 pm Pisces
11th 5:01 am Sagittarius	11th 1:47 am Capricorn	12th 7:04 am Pisces	11th 9:53 pm Aries
13th 5:51 pm Capricorn	13th 1:35 pm Aquarius	14th 12:55 pm Aries	14th 1:49 am Taurus
16th 4:48 am Aquarius	15th 10:02 pm Pisces	16th 3:08 pm Taurus	16th 2:42 am Gemini
18th 12:14 pm Pisces	18th 2:32 am Aries	18th 3:09 pm Gemini	18th 2:03 am Cancer
20th 4:28 pm Aries	20th 4:09 am Taurus	20th 2:50 pm Cancer	20th 1:50 am Leo
22nd 6:49 pm Taurus	22nd 4:41 am Gemini	22nd 4:00 pm Leo	22nd 4:01 am Virgo
24th 8:46 pm Gemini	24th 5:49 am Cancer	24th 7:59 pm Virgo	24th 9:58 am Libra
26th 11:26 pm Cancer	26th 8:46 am Leo	27th 3:23 am Libra	26th 7:46 pm Scorpio
29th 3:17 am Leo	28th 2:05 pm Virgo	29th 1:49 pm Scorpio	29th 8:15 am Sagittarius
	30th 9:48 pm Libra		31st 9:17 pm Capricorn

January 1938	February 1938	March 1938	April 1938
3rd 9:29 am Aquarius	2nd 1:57 am Pisces	1st 9:10 am Pisces	2nd 4:41 am Taurus
5th 8:06 pm Pisces	4th 9:53 am Aries	3rd 4:14 pm Aries	4th 7:32 am Gemini
8th 4:26 am Aries	6th 3:56 pm Taurus	5th 9:29 pm Taurus	6th 10:08 am Cancer
10th 10:02 am Taurus	8th 8:07 pm Gemini	8th 1:33 am Gemini	8th 1:06 pm Leo
12th 12:47 pm Gemini	10th 10:25 pm Cancer	10th 4:46 am Cancer	10th 4:52 pm Virgo
14th 1:20 pm Cancer	12th 11:34 pm Leo	12th 7:24 am Leo	12th 10:03 pm Libra
16th 1:11 pm Leo	15th 0:57 am Virgo	14th 10:07 am Virgo	15th 5:24 am Scorpio
18th 2:17 pm Virgo	17th 4:32 am Libra	16th 2:13 pm Libra	17th 3:22 pm Sagittarius
20th 6:32 pm Libra	19th 11:42 am Scorpio	18th 8:56 pm Scorpio	20th 3:33 am Capricorn
23rd 2:57 am Scorpio	21st 10:34 am Sagittarius	21st 7:03 am Sagittarius	22nd 4:09 pm Aquarius
25th 2:52 pm Sagittarius	24th 11:26 am Capricorn	23rd 7:32 pm Capricorn	25th 2:51 am Pisces
28th 3:57 am Capricorn	26th 11:34 pm Aquarius	26th 7:52 am Aquarius	27th 10:03 am Aries
30th 3:57 pm Aquarius		28th 5:48 pm Pisces	29th 1:57 pm Taurus
		31st 0:33 am Aries	

May 1938	June 1938	July 1938	August 1938
1st 3:43 pm Gemini	2nd 2:10 am Leo	1st 12:29 pm Virgo	2nd 6:54 am Scorpio
3rd 4:50 pm Cancer	4th 4:24 am Virgo	3rd 4:14 pm Libra	4th 5:05 pm Sagittarius
5th 6:43 pm Leo	6th 9:40 am Libra	5th 11:49 pm Scorpio	7th 5:33 am Capricorn
7th 10:17 pm Virgo	8th 6:03 pm Scorpio	8th 10:49 am Sagittarius	9th 6:14 pm Aquarius
10th 4:07 am Libra	11th 4:58 am Sagittarius	10th 11:23 pm Capricorn	12th 5:43 am Pisces
12th 12:19 pm Scorpio	13th 5:22 pm Capricorn	13th 12:05 pm Aquarius	14th 3:33 pm Aries
14th 10:41 pm Sagittarius	16th 6:07 am Aquarius	15th 11:56 pm Pisces	16th 11:27 pm Taurus
17th 10:52 am Capricorn	18th 6:01 pm Pisces	18th 9:50 am Aries	19th 4:50 am Gemini
19th 11:38 pm Aquarius	21st 3:38 am Aries	20th 5:28 pm Taurus	21st 7:38 am Cancer
22nd 11:05 am Pisces	23rd 9:44 am Taurus	22nd 9:42 pm Gemini	23rd 8:27 am Leo
24th 7:32 pm Aries	25th 12:21 pm Gemini	24th 10:55 pm Cancer	25th 8:47 am Virgo
27th 0:17 am Taurus	27th 12:26 pm Cancer	26th 10:27 pm Leo	27th 10:33 am Libra
29th 1:51 am Gemini	29th 11:48 am Leo	28th 10:19 pm Virgo	29th 3:33 pm Scorpio
31st 1:52 am Cancer		31st 11:34 pm Libra	

September 1938	October 1938	November 1938	December 1938
1st 0:28 am Sagittarius	3rd 8:57 am Aquarius	2nd 5:09 am Pisces	2nd 0:04 am Aries
3rd 12:31 pm Capricorn	5th 8:27 pm Pisces	4th 2:32 pm Aries	4th 6:57 am Taurus
6th 1:10 am Aquarius	8th 5:20 am Aries	6th 8:40 pm Taurus	6th 10:15 am Gemini
8th 12:26 pm Pisces	10th 11:40 am Taurus	9th 0:03 am Gemini	8th 11:07 am Cancer
10th 9:41 pm Aries	12th 4:09 pm Gemini	11th 1:59 am Cancer	10th 11:20 am Leo
13th 4:54 am Taurus	14th 7:31 pm Cancer	13th 3:52 am Leo	12th 12:42 pm Virgo
15th 10:22 am Gemini	16th 10:20 pm Leo	15th 6:40 am Virgo	14th 4:31 pm Libra
17th 2:08 pm Cancer	19th 1:10 am Virgo	17th 11:06 am Libra	16th 11:14 pm Scorpio
19th 4:27 pm Leo	21st 4:46 am Libra	19th 5:28 pm Scorpio	19th 8:34 am Sagittarius
21st 6:03 pm Virgo	23rd 10:05 am Scorpio	22nd 1:58 am Sagittarius	21st 7:39 pm Capricorn
23rd 8:23 pm Libra	25th 5:59 pm Sagittarius	24th 12:42 pm Capricorn	24th 7:50 am Aquarius
26th 0:59 am Scorpio	28th 4:42 am Capricorn	27th 1:01 am Aquarius	26th 8:42 pm Pisces
28th 9:08 am Sagittarius	30th 5:09 pm Aquarius	29th 1:29 pm Pisces	29th 8:10 am Aries
30th 8:23 pm Capricorn			31st 4:44 pm Taurus

16

Moon Tables

January 1939
2nd 9:18 am Gemini
4th 10:19 pm Cancer
6th 9:33 pm Leo
8th 9:10 pm Virgo
10th 11:12 pm Libra
13th 4:57 am Scorpio
15th 2:13 pm Sagittarius
18th 1:45 am Capricorn
20th 2:16 pm Aquarius
23rd 2:51 am Pisces
25th 2:40 pm Aries
28th 0:30 am Taurus
30th 6:45 am Gemini

February 1939
1st 9:17 am Cancer
3rd 9:05 am Leo
5th 8:06 am Virgo
7th 8:35 am Libra
9th 12:28 pm Scorpio
11th 8:26 pm Sagittarius
14th 7:43 am Capricorn
16th 8:21 pm Aquarius
19th 8:51 am Pisces
21st 8:23 pm Aries
24th 6:17 am Taurus
26th 1:44 pm Gemini
28th 6:04 pm Cancer

March 1939
2nd 7:28 pm Leo
4th 7:17 pm Virgo
6th 7:29 pm Libra
8th 10:01 pm Scorpio
11th 4:26 am Sagittarius
13th 2:38 pm Capricorn
16th 3:00 am Aquarius
18th 3:29 pm Pisces
21st 2:38 am Aries
23rd 11:55 am Taurus
25th 7:13 pm Gemini
28th 0:19 am Cancer
30th 3:14 am Leo

April 1939
1st 4:39 am Virgo
3rd 5:50 am Libra
5th 8:26 am Scorpio
7th 1:52 pm Sagittarius
9th 10:46 pm Capricorn
12th 10:33 am Aquarius
14th 11:04 pm Pisces
17th 10:10 am Aries
19th 6:53 pm Taurus
22nd 1:14 am Gemini
24th 5:41 am Cancer
26th 8:52 am Leo
28th 11:26 am Virgo
30th 2:03 pm Libra

May 1939
2nd 5:39 pm Scorpio
4th 11:11 pm Sagittarius
7th 7:37 am Capricorn
9th 6:42 pm Aquarius
12th 7:08 am Pisces
14th 6:38 pm Aries
17th 3:26 am Taurus
19th 9:02 am Gemini
21st 12:19 pm Cancer
23rd 2:33 pm Leo
25th 4:51 pm Virgo
27th 8:06 pm Libra
30th 0:47 am Scorpio

June 1939
1st 7:18 am Sagittarius
3rd 3:52 pm Capricorn
6th 2:42 am Aquarius
8th 3:05 pm Pisces
11th 3:10 am Aries
13th 12:37 pm Taurus
15th 6:28 pm Gemini
17th 9:04 pm Cancer
19th 9:57 pm Leo
21st 10:56 pm Virgo
24th 1:30 am Libra
26th 6:28 am Scorpio
28th 1:41 pm Sagittarius
30th 10:54 pm Capricorn

July 1939
3rd 9:56 am Aquarius
5th 10:17 pm Pisces
8th 10:47 am Aries
10th 9:25 pm Taurus
13th 4:17 am Gemini
15th 7:12 am Cancer
17th 7:30 am Leo
19th 7:10 am Virgo
21st 8:14 am Libra
23rd 12:08 pm Scorpio
25th 7:12 pm Sagittarius
28th 4:52 am Capricorn
30th 4:16 pm Aquarius

August 1939
2nd 4:42 am Pisces
4th 5:21 pm Aries
7th 4:45 am Taurus
9th 1:01 pm Gemini
11th 5:17 pm Cancer
13th 6:07 pm Leo
15th 5:20 pm Virgo
17th 5:08 pm Libra
19th 7:24 pm Scorpio
22nd 1:15 am Sagittarius
24th 10:36 am Capricorn
26th 10:10 pm Aquarius
29th 10:43 am Pisces
31st 11:16 pm Aries

September 1939
3rd 10:45 am Taurus
5th 8:00 pm Gemini
8th 1:51 am Cancer
10th 4:11 am Leo
12th 4:09 am Virgo
14th 3:42 am Libra
16th 4:47 am Scorpio
18th 9:08 am Sagittarius
20th 5:15 pm Capricorn
23rd 4:24 am Aquarius
25th 4:59 pm Pisces
28th 5:21 am Aries
30th 4:27 pm Taurus

October 1939
3rd 1:38 am Gemini
5th 8:14 am Cancer
7th 12:07 pm Leo
9th 1:44 pm Virgo
11th 2:18 pm Libra
13th 3:22 pm Scorpio
15th 6:40 pm Sagittarius
18th 1:24 am Capricorn
20th 11:44 am Aquarius
23rd 0:06 am Pisces
25th 12:27 pm Aries
27th 11:10 pm Taurus
30th 7:28 am Gemini

November 1939
1st 1:39 pm Cancer
3rd 5:50 pm Leo
5th 8:56 pm Virgo
7th 11:03 pm Libra
10th 1:15 am Scorpio
12th 4:46 am Sagittarius
14th 10:48 am Capricorn
16th 8:04 pm Aquarius
19th 8:02 am Pisces
21st 8:35 pm Aries
24th 7:19 am Taurus
26th 3:05 pm Gemini
28th 8:10 pm Cancer
30th 11:34 pm Leo

December 1939
3rd 2:22 am Virgo
5th 5:23 am Libra
7th 8:00 am Scorpio
9th 1:35 pm Sagittarius
11th 7:54 pm Capricorn
14th 4:47 am Aquarius
16th 4:17 pm Pisces
19th 5:02 am Aries
21st 4:30 pm Taurus
24th 0:37 am Gemini
26th 5:02 am Cancer
28th 7:05 am Leo
30th 8:30 am Virgo

January 1940
1st 10:47 am Libra
3rd 2:40 pm Scorpio
5th 8:14 pm Sagittarius
8th 3:31 am Capricorn
10th 12:46 pm Aquarius
13th 0:04 am Pisces
15th 12:56 pm Aries
18th 1:16 am Taurus
20th 10:27 am Gemini
22nd 3:30 pm Cancer
24th 5:09 pm Leo
26th 5:14 pm Virgo
28th 5:46 pm Libra
30th 8:20 pm Scorpio

February 1940
2nd 1:37 am Sagittarius
4th 9:30 am Capricorn
6th 7:23 pm Aquarius
9th 7:01 am Pisces
11th 7:49 pm Aries
14th 8:33 am Taurus
16th 7:08 pm Gemini
19th 1:47 am Cancer
21st 4:17 am Leo
23rd 4:12 am Virgo
25th 3:31 am Libra
27th 4:17 am Scorpio
29th 7:59 am Sagittarius

March 1940
2nd 3:07 pm Capricorn
5th 1:07 am Aquarius
7th 1:08 pm Pisces
10th 1:00 am Aries
12th 2:44 pm Taurus
15th 1:53 am Gemini
17th 9:53 am Cancer
19th 2:11 pm Leo
21st 3:18 pm Virgo
23rd 2:49 pm Libra
25th 2:38 pm Scorpio
27th 4:36 pm Sagittarius
29th 10:02 pm Capricorn

April 1940
1st 7:15 am Aquarius
3rd 7:11 pm Pisces
6th 8:09 am Aries
8th 8:38 pm Taurus
11th 7:29 am Gemini
13th 4:01 pm Cancer
15th 9:43 pm Leo
18th 0:34 am Virgo
20th 1:23 am Libra
22nd 1:34 am Scorpio
24th 2:50 am Sagittarius
26th 6:54 am Capricorn
28th 2:44 pm Aquarius

May 1940
1st 1:55 am Pisces
3rd 2:51 pm Aries
6th 3:11 am Taurus
8th 1:29 pm Gemini
10th 9:31 pm Cancer
13th 3:20 am Leo
15th 7:15 am Virgo
17th 9:39 am Libra
19th 11:12 am Scorpio
21st 1:03 pm Sagittarius
23rd 4:39 pm Capricorn
25th 11:21 pm Aquarius
28th 9:42 am Pisces
30th 10:18 pm Aries

June 1940
2nd 10:41 am Taurus
4th 8:46 pm Gemini
7th 3:59 am Cancer
9th 8:58 am Leo
11th 12:38 pm Virgo
13th 3:41 pm Libra
15th 6:31 pm Scorpio
17th 9:33 pm Sagittarius
20th 1:45 am Capricorn
22nd 8:19 am Aquarius
24th 5:59 pm Pisces
27th 6:14 am Aries
29th 6:51 pm Taurus

July 1940
2nd 5:11 am Gemini
4th 12:05 pm Cancer
6th 4:09 pm Leo
8th 6:43 pm Virgo
10th 9:07 pm Libra
13th 0:07 am Scorpio
15th 4:06 am Sagittarius
17th 9:19 am Capricorn
19th 4:24 pm Aquarius
22nd 1:59 am Pisces
24th 2:02 pm Aries
27th 2:54 am Taurus
29th 1:59 pm Gemini
31st 9:30 pm Cancer

August 1940
3rd 1:20 am Leo
5th 2:50 am Virgo
7th 3:51 am Libra
9th 5:48 am Scorpio
11th 9:32 am Sagittarius
13th 3:17 pm Capricorn
15th 11:07 pm Aquarius
18th 9:12 am Pisces
20th 9:14 pm Aries
23rd 10:15 am Taurus
25th 10:12 pm Gemini
28th 6:49 am Cancer
30th 11:25 am Leo

Why Does He Say One Thing and Do Another?

September 1940
1st 12:34 pm Virgo
3rd 12:55 pm Libra
5th 1:20 pm Scorpio
7th 3:41 pm Sagittarius
9th 8:47 pm Capricorn
12th 4:53 am Aquarius
14th 3:27 pm Pisces
17th 3:43 am Aries
19th 4:45 pm Taurus
22nd 5:03 am Gemini
24th 2:54 pm Cancer
26th 9:07 pm Leo
28th 11:42 pm Virgo
30th 11:47 pm Libra

October 1940
2nd 11:12 pm Scorpio
4th 11:53 pm Sagittarius
7th 3:31 am Capricorn
9th 10:48 am Aquarius
11th 9:18 pm Pisces
14th 9:50 am Aries
16th 10:49 pm Taurus
19th 10:57 am Gemini
21st 9:17 pm Cancer
24th 4:47 am Leo
26th 9:06 am Virgo
28th 10:35 am Libra
30th 10:26 am Scorpio

November 1940
1st 10:26 am Sagittarius
3rd 12:29 pm Capricorn
5th 6:08 pm Aquarius
8th 3:49 am Pisces
10th 4:14 pm Aries
13th 5:12 am Taurus
15th 4:58 pm Gemini
18th 2:51 am Cancer
20th 10:35 am Leo
22nd 4:07 pm Virgo
24th 7:22 pm Libra
26th 8:45 pm Scorpio
28th 9:20 pm Sagittarius
30th 10:52 pm Capricorn

December 1940
3rd 3:16 am Aquarius
5th 11:41 am Pisces
7th 11:28 pm Aries
10th 12:26 pm Taurus
13th 0:08 am Gemini
15th 9:17 am Cancer
17th 4:14 pm Leo
19th 9:34 pm Virgo
22nd 1:36 am Libra
24th 4:30 am Scorpio
26th 6:37 am Sagittarius
28th 9:02 am Capricorn
30th 1:15 pm Aquarius

January 1941
1st 8:38 pm Pisces
4th 7:38 am Aries
6th 8:29 pm Taurus
9th 8:25 am Gemini
11th 5:31 pm Cancer
13th 11:40 pm Leo
16th 3:46 am Virgo
18th 7:00 am Libra
20th 10:05 am Scorpio
22nd 1:18 pm Sagittarius
24th 5:03 pm Capricorn
26th 10:07 pm Aquarius
29th 5:38 am Pisces
31st 4:05 pm Aries

February 1941
3rd 4:41 am Taurus
5th 5:08 pm Gemini
8th 2:55 am Cancer
10th 9:05 am Leo
12th 12:20 pm Virgo
14th 2:08 pm Libra
16th 3:54 pm Scorpio
18th 6:39 pm Sagittarius
20th 10:55 pm Capricorn
23rd 5:03 am Aquarius
25th 1:21 pm Pisces
27th 11:54 pm Aries

March 1941
2nd 12:24 pm Taurus
5th 1:12 am Gemini
7th 11:59 am Cancer
9th 7:17 pm Leo
11th 10:52 pm Virgo
13th 11:52 pm Libra
16th 0:03 am Scorpio
18th 1:09 am Sagittarius
20th 4:27 am Capricorn
22nd 10:36 am Aquarius
24th 7:32 pm Pisces
27th 6:41 am Aries
29th 7:14 pm Taurus

April 1941
1st 8:05 am Gemini
3rd 7:42 pm Cancer
6th 4:23 am Leo
8th 9:17 am Virgo
10th 10:52 am Libra
12th 10:32 am Scorpio
14th 10:12 am Sagittarius
16th 11:45 am Capricorn
18th 4:36 pm Aquarius
21st 1:07 am Pisces
23rd 12:36 pm Aries
26th 1:21 am Taurus
28th 2:09 pm Gemini

May 1941
1st 1:55 am Cancer
3rd 11:29 am Leo
5th 6:02 pm Virgo
7th 9:10 pm Libra
9th 9:33 pm Scorpio
11th 8:51 pm Sagittarius
13th 9:07 pm Capricorn
16th 0:16 am Aquarius
18th 7:39 am Pisces
20th 6:36 pm Aries
23rd 7:25 am Taurus
25th 8:09 pm Gemini
28th 7:34 am Cancer
30th 5:13 pm Leo

June 1941
2nd 0:37 am Virgo
4th 5:14 am Libra
6th 7:10 am Scorpio
8th 7:23 am Sagittarius
10th 7:36 am Capricorn
12th 9:47 am Aquarius
14th 3:40 pm Pisces
17th 1:32 am Aries
19th 2:04 pm Taurus
22nd 2:43 am Gemini
24th 1:48 pm Cancer
26th 10:54 pm Leo
29th 6:00 am Virgo

July 1941
1st 11:13 am Libra
3rd 2:30 pm Scorpio
5th 4:11 pm Sagittarius
7th 5:22 pm Capricorn
9th 7:38 pm Aquarius
12th 0:43 am Pisces
14th 9:38 am Aries
16th 9:31 pm Taurus
19th 10:08 am Gemini
21st 9:13 pm Cancer
24th 5:45 am Leo
26th 12:00 pm Virgo
28th 4:39 pm Libra
30th 8:08 pm Scorpio

August 1941
1st 10:49 pm Sagittarius
4th 1:16 am Capricorn
6th 4:34 am Aquarius
8th 9:55 am Pisces
10th 6:14 pm Aries
13th 5:33 am Taurus
15th 6:09 pm Gemini
18th 5:34 am Cancer
20th 2:11 pm Leo
22nd 7:51 pm Virgo
24th 11:21 pm Libra
27th 1:49 am Scorpio
29th 4:14 am Sagittarius
31st 7:20 am Capricorn

September 1941
2nd 11:40 am Aquarius
4th 5:54 pm Pisces
7th 2:28 am Aries
9th 1:33 pm Taurus
12th 2:05 am Gemini
14th 2:06 pm Cancer
16th 11:36 pm Leo
19th 5:26 am Virgo
21st 8:14 am Libra
23rd 9:23 am Scorpio
25th 10:27 am Sagittarius
27th 12:48 pm Capricorn
29th 5:19 pm Aquarius

October 1941
2nd 0:17 am Pisces
4th 9:39 am Aries
6th 8:51 pm Taurus
9th 9:22 am Gemini
11th 9:52 pm Cancer
14th 8:25 am Leo
16th 3:31 pm Virgo
18th 6:51 pm Libra
20th 7:24 pm Scorpio
22nd 7:02 pm Sagittarius
24th 7:43 pm Capricorn
26th 11:02 pm Aquarius
29th 5:54 am Pisces
31st 3:40 pm Aries

November 1941
3rd 3:19 am Taurus
5th 3:52 pm Gemini
8th 4:24 am Cancer
10th 3:45 pm Leo
13th 0:29 am Virgo
15th 5:18 am Libra
17th 6:38 am Scorpio
19th 5:54 am Sagittarius
21st 5:15 am Capricorn
23rd 6:52 am Aquarius
25th 12:16 pm Pisces
27th 9:28 pm Aries
30th 9:19 am Taurus

December 1941
2nd 9:59 pm Gemini
5th 10:20 am Cancer
7th 9:41 pm Leo
10th 7:08 am Virgo
12th 1:41 pm Libra
14th 4:47 pm Scorpio
16th 5:08 pm Sagittarius
18th 4:30 pm Capricorn
20th 4:59 pm Aquarius
22nd 8:37 pm Pisces
25th 4:28 am Aries
27th 3:46 pm Taurus
30th 4:27 am Gemini

January 1942
1st 4:40 pm Cancer
4th 3:32 am Leo
6th 12:39 pm Virgo
8th 7:47 pm Libra
11th 0:24 am Scorpio
13th 2:30 am Sagittarius
15th 3:07 am Capricorn
17th 3:54 am Aquarius
19th 6:48 am Pisces
21st 1:14 pm Aries
23rd 11:21 pm Taurus
26th 11:45 am Gemini
29th 0:04 am Cancer
31st 10:35 am Leo

February 1942
2nd 6:56 pm Virgo
5th 1:18 am Libra
7th 5:55 am Scorpio
9th 9:06 am Sagittarius
11th 11:18 am Capricorn
13th 1:30 pm Aquarius
15th 4:55 pm Pisces
17th 10:47 pm Aries
20th 8:01 am Taurus
22nd 7:48 pm Gemini
25th 8:15 am Cancer
27th 7:05 pm Leo

March 1942
2nd 3:06 am Virgo
4th 8:21 am Libra
6th 11:49 am Scorpio
8th 2:29 pm Sagittarius
10th 5:10 pm Capricorn
12th 8:32 pm Aquarius
15th 1:10 am Pisces
17th 7:44 am Aries
19th 4:41 pm Taurus
22nd 4:02 am Gemini
24th 4:32 pm Cancer
27th 4:05 am Leo
29th 12:33 pm Virgo
31st 5:34 pm Libra

April 1942
2nd 7:55 pm Scorpio
4th 9:05 pm Sagittarius
6th 10:43 pm Capricorn
9th 1:58 am Aquarius
11th 7:21 am Pisces
13th 2:51 pm Aries
16th 0:18 am Taurus
18th 11:39 am Gemini
21st 0:10 am Cancer
23rd 12:19 pm Leo
25th 10:01 pm Virgo
28th 3:49 am Libra
30th 5:58 am Scorpio

18

Moon Tables

May 1942		June 1942		July 1942		August 1942	
2nd	6:04 am Sagittarius	2nd	4:05 pm Aquarius	2nd	3:49 am Pisces	3rd	1:49 am Taurus
4th	6:09 am Capricorn	4th	7:18 pm Pisces	4th	9:16 am Aries	5th	12:56 pm Gemini
6th	8:01 am Aquarius	7th	2:14 am Aries	6th	6:25 pm Taurus	8th	1:31 am Cancer
8th	12:48 pm Pisces	9th	12:18 pm Taurus	9th	6:12 am Gemini	10th	1:37 pm Leo
10th	8:32 pm Aries	12th	0:12 am Gemini	11th	6:51 pm Cancer	13th	0:09 am Virgo
13th	6:38 am Taurus	14th	12:49 pm Cancer	14th	7:07 am Leo	15th	8:29 am Libra
15th	6:16 pm Gemini	17th	1:18 am Leo	16th	6:06 pm Virgo	17th	2:35 pm Scorpio
18th	6:49 am Cancer	19th	12:29 pm Virgo	19th	2:50 am Libra	19th	6:32 pm Sagittarius
20th	7:19 pm Leo	21st	9:01 pm Libra	21st	8:56 am Scorpio	21st	8:44 pm Capricorn
23rd	6:04 am Virgo	24th	1:49 am Scorpio	23rd	11:53 am Sagittarius	23rd	10:07 pm Aquarius
25th	1:15 pm Libra	26th	3:06 am Sagittarius	25th	12:36 pm Sagittarius	25th	11:55 pm Pisces
27th	4:26 pm Scorpio	28th	2:30 am Capricorn	27th	12:39 pm Aquarius	28th	3:40 am Aries
29th	4:38 pm Sagittarius	30th	2:02 am Aquarius	29th	1:53 pm Pisces	30th	10:33 am Taurus
31st	3:47 pm Capricorn			31st	5:50 pm Aries		

September 1942		October 1942		November 1942		December 1942	
1st	8:41 pm Gemini	1st	5:04 pm Cancer	3rd	1:18 am Virgo	2nd	6:51 pm Libra
4th	9:00 am Cancer	4th	5:33 am Leo	5th	9:16 am Libra	5th	0:07 am Scorpio
6th	9:14 pm Leo	6th	4:10 pm Virgo	7th	1:22 pm Scorpio	7th	1:32 am Sagittarius
9th	7:28 am Virgo	8th	11:33 pm Libra	9th	2:45 pm Sagittarius	9th	1:08 am Capricorn
11th	3:01 pm Libra	11th	3:45 am Scorpio	11th	3:19 pm Capricorn	11th	0:57 am Aquarius
13th	8:18 pm Scorpio	13th	6:10 am Sagittarius	13th	4:51 pm Aquarius	13th	2:59 am Pisces
15th	11:58 pm Sagittarius	15th	8:13 am Capricorn	15th	8:30 pm Pisces	15th	8:05 am Aries
18th	2:47 am Capricorn	17th	11:03 am Aquarius	18th	2:32 am Aries	17th	4:20 pm Taurus
20th	5:27 am Aquarius	19th	3:06 pm Pisces	20th	10:39 am Taurus	20th	2:47 am Gemini
22nd	8:35 am Pisces	21st	8:36 pm Aries	22nd	8:35 pm Gemini	22nd	2:57 pm Cancer
24th	12:59 pm Aries	24th	3:52 am Taurus	25th	8:17 am Cancer	25th	3:35 am Leo
26th	7:35 pm Taurus	26th	1:20 pm Gemini	27th	9:09 pm Leo	27th	4:07 pm Virgo
29th	5:06 am Gemini	29th	0:59 am Cancer	30th	9:25 am Virgo	30th	2:41 am Libra
		31st	1:46 pm Leo				

January 1943		February 1943		March 1943		April 1943	
1st	9:32 am Scorpio	1st	11:14 pm Capricorn	1st	7:17 am Capricorn	1st	6:28 pm Pisces
3rd	12:28 pm Sagittarius	3rd	11:11 pm Aquarius	3rd	8:56 am Aquarius	3rd	9:18 pm Aries
5th	12:33 pm Capricorn	5th	11:09 pm Pisces	5th	9:56 am Pisces	6th	1:39 am Taurus
7th	11:45 am Aquarius	8th	1:01 am Aries	7th	11:46 am Aries	8th	8:46 am Gemini
9th	12:09 pm Pisces	10th	6:22 am Taurus	9th	3:58 pm Taurus	10th	7:04 pm Cancer
11th	3:27 pm Aries	12th	3:29 pm Gemini	11th	11:39 pm Gemini	13th	7:39 am Leo
13th	10:24 pm Taurus	15th	3:25 am Cancer	14th	10:53 am Cancer	15th	7:59 pm Virgo
16th	8:42 am Gemini	17th	4:18 pm Leo	16th	11:42 pm Leo	18th	5:39 am Libra
18th	8:54 pm Cancer	20th	4:19 am Virgo	19th	11:41 am Virgo	20th	12:01 pm Scorpio
21st	9:43 am Leo	22nd	2:28 pm Libra	21st	9:21 pm Libra	22nd	3:55 pm Sagittarius
23rd	10:02 pm Virgo	24th	10:24 pm Scorpio	24th	4:23 am Scorpio	24th	6:40 pm Capricorn
26th	8:44 am Libra	27th	3:58 am Sagittarius	26th	9:22 am Sagittarius	26th	9:22 pm Aquarius
28th	4:46 pm Scorpio			28th	1:04 pm Capricorn	29th	0:36 am Pisces
30th	9:32 pm Sagittarius			31st	3:57 pm Aquarius		

May 1943		June 1943		July 1943		August 1943	
1st	4:40 am Aries	2nd	0:31 am Gemini	1st	5:15 pm Cancer	3rd	0:44 am Virgo
3rd	9:60 am Taurus	4th	10:48 am Cancer	4th	5:40 am Leo	5th	12:48 pm Libra
5th	5:18 pm Gemini	6th	11:03 pm Leo	6th	6:43 pm Virgo	7th	10:39 pm Scorpio
8th	3:19 am Cancer	9th	12:01 pm Virgo	9th	6:41 am Libra	10th	5:04 am Sagittarius
10th	3:40 pm Leo	11th	11:21 pm Libra	11th	3:34 pm Scorpio	12th	8:05 am Capricorn
13th	4:20 am Virgo	14th	6:54 am Scorpio	13th	8:34 pm Sagittarius	14th	8:34 am Aquarius
15th	2:40 pm Libra	16th	10:32 am Sagittarius	15th	10:05 pm Capricorn	16th	8:07 am Pisces
17th	9:18 pm Scorpio	18th	11:29 am Capricorn	17th	9:46 pm Aquarius	18th	8:36 am Aries
20th	0:33 am Sagittarius	20th	11:36 am Aquarius	19th	9:32 pm Pisces	20th	11:46 am Taurus
22nd	2:01 am Capricorn	22nd	12:42 pm Pisces	21st	11:10 pm Aries	22nd	6:38 pm Gemini
24th	3:25 am Aquarius	24th	3:58 pm Aries	24th	3:56 am Taurus	25th	5:09 am Cancer
26th	6:01 am Pisces	26th	9:54 pm Taurus	26th	12:08 pm Gemini	27th	5:49 pm Leo
28th	10:20 am Aries	29th	6:30 am Gemini	28th	11:04 pm Cancer	30th	6:47 am Virgo
30th	4:26 pm Taurus			31st	11:44 am Leo		

September 1943		October 1943		November 1943		December 1943	
1st	6:31 pm Libra	1st	10:02 am Scorpio	2nd	3:36 am Capricorn	1st	1:01 pm Aquarius
4th	4:19 am Scorpio	3rd	5:01 pm Sagittarius	4th	7:09 am Aquarius	3rd	3:36 pm Pisces
6th	11:34 am Sagittarius	5th	10:10 pm Capricorn	6th	10:15 am Pisces	5th	7:01 pm Aries
8th	4:09 pm Capricorn	8th	1:39 am Aquarius	8th	1:11 pm Aries	7th	11:50 pm Taurus
10th	6:15 pm Aquarius	10th	3:43 am Pisces	10th	4:33 pm Taurus	10th	5:34 am Gemini
12th	6:45 pm Pisces	12th	5:12 am Aries	12th	9:31 pm Gemini	12th	1:49 pm Cancer
14th	7:09 pm Aries	14th	7:27 am Taurus	15th	5:24 am Cancer	15th	0:36 am Leo
16th	9:15 pm Taurus	16th	12:11 pm Gemini	17th	4:28 pm Leo	17th	1:20 pm Virgo
19th	2:43 am Gemini	18th	8:29 pm Cancer	20th	5:20 am Virgo	20th	1:54 am Libra
21st	12:13 pm Cancer	21st	8:13 am Leo	22nd	5:15 pm Libra	22nd	11:39 am Scorpio
24th	0:33 am Leo	23rd	9:08 pm Virgo	25th	2:07 am Scorpio	24th	5:39 pm Sagittarius
26th	1:29 pm Virgo	26th	8:33 am Libra	27th	7:31 am Sagittarius	26th	8:22 pm Capricorn
29th	0:56 am Libra	28th	5:11 pm Scorpio	29th	10:41 am Capricorn	28th	9:21 pm Aquarius
		30th	11:14 pm Sagittarius			30th	10:17 pm Pisces

Why Does He Say One Thing and Do Another?

January 1944
- 2nd 0:35 am Aries
- 4th 5:02 am Taurus
- 6th 11:48 am Gemini
- 8th 8:49 pm Cancer
- 11th 7:59 am Leo
- 13th 8:39 pm Virgo
- 16th 9:26 am Libra
- 18th 8:24 pm Scorpio
- 21st 3:49 am Sagittarius
- 23rd 7:22 am Capricorn
- 25th 8:07 am Aquarius
- 27th 7:49 am Pisces
- 29th 8:18 am Aries
- 31st 11:13 am Taurus

February 1944
- 2nd 5:22 pm Gemini
- 5th 2:42 am Cancer
- 7th 2:22 pm Leo
- 10th 3:07 am Virgo
- 12th 3:53 pm Libra
- 15th 3:21 am Scorpio
- 17th 12:08 pm Sagittarius
- 19th 5:28 pm Capricorn
- 21st 7:23 pm Aquarius
- 23rd 7:07 pm Pisces
- 25th 6:33 pm Aries
- 27th 7:40 pm Taurus

March 1944
- 1st 0:06 am Gemini
- 3rd 8:42 am Cancer
- 5th 8:20 pm Leo
- 8th 9:19 am Virgo
- 10th 9:55 pm Libra
- 13th 9:10 am Scorpio
- 15th 6:29 pm Sagittarius
- 18th 1:12 am Capricorn
- 20th 4:53 am Aquarius
- 22nd 5:56 am Pisces
- 24th 5:42 am Aries
- 26th 6:04 am Taurus
- 28th 9:04 am Gemini
- 30th 4:04 pm Cancer

April 1944
- 2nd 2:56 am Leo
- 4th 3:49 pm Virgo
- 7th 4:22 am Libra
- 9th 3:10 pm Scorpio
- 12th 0:04 am Sagittarius
- 14th 6:54 am Capricorn
- 16th 11:44 am Aquarius
- 18th 2:26 pm Pisces
- 20th 3:35 pm Aries
- 22nd 4:31 pm Taurus
- 24th 7:03 pm Gemini
- 27th 0:49 am Cancer
- 29th 10:40 am Leo

May 1944
- 1st 11:05 pm Virgo
- 4th 11:38 am Libra
- 6th 10:18 pm Scorpio
- 9th 6:26 am Sagittarius
- 11th 12:32 pm Capricorn
- 13th 5:08 pm Aquarius
- 15th 8:34 pm Pisces
- 17th 11:03 pm Aries
- 20th 1:16 am Taurus
- 22nd 4:30 am Gemini
- 24th 10:09 am Cancer
- 26th 7:07 pm Leo
- 29th 6:59 am Virgo
- 31st 7:37 pm Libra

June 1944
- 3rd 6:29 am Scorpio
- 5th 2:25 pm Sagittarius
- 7th 7:41 pm Capricorn
- 9th 11:12 pm Aquarius
- 12th 1:50 am Pisces
- 14th 4:42 am Aries
- 16th 7:54 am Taurus
- 18th 12:14 pm Gemini
- 20th 6:32 pm Cancer
- 23rd 3:27 am Leo
- 25th 2:59 pm Virgo
- 28th 3:39 am Libra
- 30th 3:07 pm Scorpio

July 1944
- 2nd 11:38 pm Sagittarius
- 5th 4:40 am Capricorn
- 7th 7:13 am Aquarius
- 9th 8:40 am Pisces
- 11th 10:22 am Aries
- 13th 1:21 pm Taurus
- 15th 6:14 pm Gemini
- 18th 1:23 am Cancer
- 20th 10:55 am Leo
- 22nd 10:24 pm Virgo
- 25th 11:06 am Libra
- 27th 11:16 pm Scorpio
- 30th 8:44 am Sagittarius

August 1944
- 1st 2:37 pm Capricorn
- 3rd 5:07 pm Aquarius
- 5th 5:34 pm Pisces
- 7th 5:45 pm Aries
- 9th 7:23 pm Taurus
- 11th 11:39 pm Gemini
- 14th 7:07 am Cancer
- 16th 5:11 pm Leo
- 19th 5:03 am Virgo
- 21st 5:45 pm Libra
- 24th 6:11 am Scorpio
- 26th 4:47 pm Sagittarius
- 29th 0:12 am Capricorn
- 31st 3:42 am Aquarius

September 1944
- 2nd 4:13 am Pisces
- 4th 3:27 am Aries
- 6th 3:30 am Taurus
- 8th 6:18 am Gemini
- 10th 12:52 pm Cancer
- 12th 10:51 pm Leo
- 15th 11:01 am Virgo
- 17th 11:48 pm Libra
- 20th 12:11 pm Scorpio
- 22nd 11:17 pm Sagittarius
- 25th 7:51 am Capricorn
- 27th 1:04 pm Aquarius
- 29th 2:53 pm Pisces

October 1944
- 1st 2:28 pm Aries
- 3rd 1:49 pm Taurus
- 5th 3:05 pm Gemini
- 7th 7:58 pm Cancer
- 10th 5:04 am Leo
- 12th 5:05 pm Virgo
- 15th 5:53 am Libra
- 17th 6:02 pm Scorpio
- 20th 4:49 am Sagittarius
- 22nd 1:45 pm Capricorn
- 24th 8:17 pm Aquarius
- 26th 11:53 pm Pisces
- 29th 0:53 am Aries
- 31st 0:45 am Taurus

November 1944
- 2nd 1:29 am Gemini
- 4th 5:07 am Cancer
- 6th 12:48 pm Leo
- 8th 11:58 pm Virgo
- 11th 12:42 pm Libra
- 14th 0:47 am Scorpio
- 16th 10:50 am Sagittarius
- 18th 7:18 pm Capricorn
- 21st 1:46 am Aquarius
- 23rd 6:16 am Pisces
- 25th 8:54 am Aries
- 27th 10:22 am Taurus
- 29th 11:57 am Gemini

December 1944
- 1st 3:21 pm Cancer
- 3rd 9:53 pm Leo
- 6th 8:06 am Virgo
- 8th 8:28 pm Libra
- 11th 8:40 am Scorpio
- 13th 6:48 pm Sagittarius
- 16th 2:20 am Capricorn
- 18th 7:41 am Aquarius
- 20th 11:38 am Pisces
- 22nd 2:42 pm Aries
- 24th 5:25 pm Taurus
- 26th 8:26 pm Gemini
- 29th 0:43 am Cancer
- 31st 7:22 am Leo

January 1945
- 2nd 4:50 pm Virgo
- 5th 4:43 am Libra
- 7th 5:09 pm Scorpio
- 10th 3:51 am Sagittarius
- 12th 11:22 am Capricorn
- 14th 3:53 pm Aquarius
- 16th 6:26 pm Pisces
- 18th 8:22 pm Aries
- 20th 10:49 pm Taurus
- 23rd 2:37 am Gemini
- 25th 8:08 am Cancer
- 27th 3:35 pm Leo
- 30th 1:09 am Virgo

February 1945
- 1st 12:46 pm Libra
- 4th 1:20 am Scorpio
- 6th 12:53 pm Sagittarius
- 8th 9:27 pm Capricorn
- 11th 2:09 am Aquarius
- 13th 3:51 am Pisces
- 15th 4:13 am Aries
- 17th 5:07 am Taurus
- 19th 8:05 am Gemini
- 21st 1:46 pm Cancer
- 23rd 10:00 pm Leo
- 26th 8:15 am Virgo
- 28th 7:57 pm Libra

March 1945
- 3rd 8:32 am Scorpio
- 5th 8:43 pm Sagittarius
- 8th 6:32 am Capricorn
- 10th 12:34 pm Aquarius
- 12th 2:44 pm Pisces
- 14th 2:30 pm Aries
- 16th 1:57 pm Taurus
- 18th 3:09 pm Gemini
- 20th 7:35 pm Cancer
- 23rd 3:34 am Leo
- 25th 2:13 pm Virgo
- 28th 2:15 am Libra
- 30th 2:51 pm Scorpio

April 1945
- 2nd 3:07 am Sagittarius
- 4th 1:48 pm Capricorn
- 6th 9:28 pm Aquarius
- 9th 1:10 am Pisces
- 11th 1:37 am Aries
- 13th 0:39 am Taurus
- 15th 0:31 am Gemini
- 17th 3:16 am Cancer
- 19th 9:56 am Leo
- 21st 8:05 pm Virgo
- 24th 8:16 am Libra
- 26th 8:52 pm Scorpio
- 29th 8:55 am Sagittarius

May 1945
- 1st 7:39 pm Capricorn
- 4th 4:03 am Aquarius
- 6th 9:16 am Pisces
- 8th 11:21 am Aries
- 10th 11:24 am Taurus
- 12th 11:16 am Gemini
- 14th 12:57 pm Cancer
- 16th 6:01 pm Leo
- 19th 2:57 am Virgo
- 21st 2:43 pm Libra
- 24th 3:21 am Scorpio
- 26th 3:09 pm Sagittarius
- 29th 1:23 am Capricorn
- 31st 9:32 am Aquarius

June 1945
- 2nd 3:22 pm Pisces
- 4th 6:48 pm Aries
- 6th 8:22 pm Taurus
- 8th 9:15 pm Gemini
- 10th 11:03 pm Cancer
- 13th 3:22 am Leo
- 15th 11:12 am Virgo
- 17th 10:06 pm Libra
- 20th 10:35 am Scorpio
- 22nd 10:27 pm Sagittarius
- 25th 8:13 am Capricorn
- 27th 3:34 pm Aquarius
- 29th 8:51 pm Pisces

July 1945
- 2nd 0:30 am Aries
- 4th 3:04 am Taurus
- 6th 5:21 am Gemini
- 8th 8:14 am Cancer
- 10th 12:48 pm Leo
- 12th 8:01 pm Virgo
- 15th 6:14 am Libra
- 17th 6:29 pm Scorpio
- 20th 6:33 am Sagittarius
- 22nd 4:25 pm Capricorn
- 24th 11:17 pm Aquarius
- 27th 3:26 am Pisces
- 29th 6:09 am Aries
- 31st 8:31 am Taurus

August 1945
- 2nd 11:27 am Gemini
- 4th 3:26 pm Cancer
- 6th 8:54 pm Leo
- 9th 4:26 am Virgo
- 11th 2:24 pm Libra
- 14th 2:24 am Scorpio
- 16th 2:54 pm Sagittarius
- 19th 1:30 am Capricorn
- 21st 8:26 am Aquarius
- 23rd 12:02 pm Pisces
- 25th 1:30 pm Aries
- 27th 1:26 pm Taurus
- 29th 1:30 pm Gemini
- 31st 9:02 pm Cancer

20

Moon Tables

September 1945
3rd 3:22 am Leo
5th 11:40 am Virgo
7th 9:51 pm Libra
10th 9:49 am Scorpio
12th 10:37 pm Sagittarius
15th 10:07 am Capricorn
17th 6:15 pm Aquarius
19th 10:17 pm Pisces
21st 11:10 pm Aries
23rd 10:53 pm Taurus
25th 11:31 pm Gemini
28th 2:40 am Cancer
30th 8:50 am Leo

October 1945
2nd 5:35 pm Virgo
5th 4:19 am Libra
7th 4:26 pm Scorpio
10th 5:18 am Sagittarius
12th 5:31 pm Capricorn
15th 3:05 am Aquarius
17th 8:27 am Pisces
19th 10:05 am Aries
21st 9:30 am Taurus
23rd 8:53 am Gemini
25th 10:15 am Cancer
27th 2:60 pm Leo
29th 11:12 pm Virgo

November 1945
1st 10:08 am Libra
3rd 10:29 pm Scorpio
6th 11:18 am Sagittarius
8th 11:36 pm Capricorn
11th 9:55 am Aquarius
13th 5:01 pm Pisces
15th 8:21 pm Aries
17th 8:46 pm Taurus
19th 8:04 pm Gemini
21st 8:15 pm Cancer
23rd 11:11 pm Leo
26th 6:02 am Virgo
28th 4:20 pm Libra

December 1945
1st 4:42 am Scorpio
3rd 5:28 pm Sagittarius
6th 5:22 am Capricorn
8th 3:31 pm Aquarius
10th 11:20 pm Pisces
13th 4:12 am Aries
15th 6:27 am Taurus
17th 7:02 am Gemini
19th 7:30 am Cancer
21st 9:35 am Leo
23rd 2:49 pm Virgo
25th 11:45 pm Libra
28th 11:43 am Scorpio
31st 0:32 am Sagittarius

January 1946
2nd 12:07 pm Capricorn
4th 9:36 pm Aquarius
7th 4:45 am Pisces
9th 9:53 am Aries
11th 1:23 pm Taurus
13th 3:42 pm Gemini
15th 5:33 pm Cancer
17th 8:05 pm Leo
20th 0:40 am Virgo
22nd 8:35 am Libra
24th 7:40 pm Scorpio
27th 8:24 am Sagittarius
29th 8:15 pm Capricorn

February 1946
1st 5:20 am Aquarius
3rd 11:28 am Pisces
5th 3:37 pm Aries
7th 6:46 pm Taurus
9th 9:46 pm Gemini
12th 1:00 am Cancer
14th 4:51 am Leo
16th 10:06 am Virgo
18th 5:38 pm Libra
21st 4:04 am Scorpio
23rd 4:39 pm Sagittarius
26th 4:58 am Capricorn
28th 2:28 pm Aquarius

March 1946
2nd 8:22 pm Pisces
4th 11:23 pm Aries
7th 1:08 am Taurus
9th 3:13 am Gemini
11th 6:31 am Cancer
13th 11:16 am Leo
15th 5:33 pm Virgo
18th 1:42 am Libra
20th 12:07 pm Scorpio
23rd 0:31 am Sagittarius
25th 1:15 pm Capricorn
27th 11:50 pm Aquarius
30th 6:20 am Pisces

April 1946
1st 9:12 am Aries
3rd 9:55 am Taurus
5th 10:27 am Gemini
7th 12:25 pm Cancer
9th 4:40 pm Leo
11th 11:19 pm Virgo
14th 8:15 am Libra
16th 7:04 pm Scorpio
19th 7:32 am Sagittarius
21st 8:27 pm Capricorn
24th 7:53 am Aquarius
26th 3:49 pm Pisces
28th 7:42 pm Aries
30th 8:29 pm Taurus

May 1946
2nd 8:04 pm Gemini
4th 8:23 pm Cancer
6th 10:05 pm Leo
9th 4:60 am Virgo
11th 1:55 pm Libra
14th 1:08 am Scorpio
16th 1:47 pm Sagittarius
19th 2:41 am Capricorn
21st 2:29 pm Aquarius
23rd 11:39 pm Pisces
26th 5:01 am Aries
28th 7:01 am Taurus
30th 6:54 am Gemini

June 1946
1st 6:31 am Cancer
3rd 7:44 am Leo
5th 12:02 pm Virgo
7th 7:59 pm Libra
10th 7:06 am Scorpio
12th 7:52 pm Sagittarius
15th 8:38 am Capricorn
17th 8:14 pm Aquarius
20th 5:40 am Pisces
22nd 12:15 pm Aries
24th 3:52 pm Taurus
26th 5:06 pm Gemini
28th 5:12 pm Cancer
30th 5:51 pm Leo

July 1946
2nd 8:48 pm Virgo
5th 3:24 am Libra
7th 1:45 pm Scorpio
10th 2:20 am Sagittarius
12th 3:04 pm Capricorn
15th 2:17 am Aquarius
17th 11:13 am Pisces
19th 5:57 pm Aries
21st 10:15 pm Taurus
24th 1:19 am Gemini
26th 2:45 am Cancer
28th 3:59 am Leo
30th 6:37 am Virgo

August 1946
1st 12:11 pm Libra
3rd 9:24 pm Scorpio
6th 9:37 am Sagittarius
8th 10:23 pm Capricorn
11th 9:20 am Aquarius
13th 5:39 pm Pisces
15th 11:39 pm Aries
18th 3:59 am Taurus
20th 7:23 am Gemini
22nd 10:07 am Cancer
24th 12:41 pm Leo
26th 3:57 pm Virgo
28th 9:17 pm Libra
31st 5:52 am Scorpio

September 1946
2nd 5:32 pm Sagittarius
5th 6:22 am Capricorn
7th 5:38 pm Aquarius
10th 1:44 am Pisces
12th 6:47 am Aries
14th 10:03 am Taurus
16th 12:47 pm Gemini
18th 3:44 pm Cancer
20th 7:15 pm Leo
22nd 11:39 pm Virgo
25th 5:44 am Libra
27th 2:17 pm Scorpio
30th 1:33 am Sagittarius

October 1946
2nd 2:29 pm Capricorn
5th 2:27 am Aquarius
7th 11:03 am Pisces
9th 4:01 pm Aries
11th 6:19 pm Taurus
13th 7:37 pm Gemini
15th 9:23 pm Cancer
18th 0:35 am Leo
20th 5:38 am Virgo
22nd 12:36 pm Libra
24th 9:43 pm Scorpio
27th 9:06 am Sagittarius
29th 9:50 pm Capricorn

November 1946
1st 10:35 am Aquarius
3rd 8:31 pm Pisces
6th 2:27 am Aries
8th 4:48 am Taurus
10th 5:08 am Gemini
12th 5:18 am Cancer
14th 6:55 am Leo
16th 11:09 am Virgo
18th 6:15 pm Libra
21st 3:59 am Scorpio
23rd 3:46 pm Sagittarius
26th 4:39 am Capricorn
28th 5:29 pm Aquarius

December 1946
1st 4:28 am Pisces
3rd 11:59 am Aries
5th 3:44 pm Taurus
7th 4:27 pm Gemini
9th 3:51 pm Cancer
11th 3:50 pm Leo
13th 6:12 pm Virgo
16th 0:08 am Libra
18th 9:46 am Scorpio
20th 9:49 pm Sagittarius
23rd 10:49 am Capricorn
25th 11:30 pm Aquarius
28th 10:41 am Pisces
30th 7:29 pm Aries

January 1947
2nd 1:05 am Taurus
4th 3:24 am Gemini
6th 3:27 am Cancer
8th 2:53 am Leo
10th 3:47 am Virgo
12th 7:59 am Libra
14th 4:19 pm Scorpio
17th 4:04 am Sagittarius
19th 5:09 pm Capricorn
22nd 5:35 am Aquarius
24th 4:21 pm Pisces
27th 1:10 am Aries
29th 7:42 am Taurus
31st 11:48 am Gemini

February 1947
2nd 1:36 pm Cancer
4th 2:01 pm Leo
6th 2:45 pm Virgo
8th 5:43 pm Libra
11th 0:27 am Scorpio
13th 11:17 am Sagittarius
16th 0:10 am Capricorn
18th 12:35 pm Aquarius
20th 10:57 pm Pisces
23rd 6:55 am Aries
25th 1:05 pm Taurus
27th 5:45 pm Gemini

March 1947
1st 8:59 pm Cancer
3rd 11:00 pm Leo
6th 0:47 am Virgo
8th 3:54 am Libra
10th 9:55 am Scorpio
12th 7:34 pm Sagittarius
15th 7:59 am Capricorn
17th 8:34 pm Aquarius
20th 6:53 am Pisces
22nd 2:18 pm Aries
24th 7:27 pm Taurus
26th 11:15 pm Gemini
29th 2:56 am Cancer
31st 5:23 am Leo

April 1947
2nd 8:32 am Virgo
4th 12:42 pm Libra
6th 6:59 pm Scorpio
9th 4:14 am Sagittarius
11th 4:09 pm Capricorn
14th 4:50 am Aquarius
16th 3:43 pm Pisces
18th 11:24 pm Aries
21st 3:53 am Taurus
23rd 6:26 am Gemini
25th 8:22 am Cancer
27th 10:45 am Leo
29th 2:17 pm Virgo

May 1947
1st 7:24 pm Libra
4th 2:37 am Scorpio
6th 12:12 pm Sagittarius
8th 11:54 pm Capricorn
11th 12:39 pm Aquarius
14th 0:19 am Pisces
16th 8:51 am Aries
18th 1:46 pm Taurus
20th 3:49 pm Gemini
22nd 4:26 pm Cancer
24th 5:10 pm Leo
26th 7:52 pm Virgo
29th 0:53 am Libra
31st 8:45 am Scorpio

June 1947
2nd 6:55 pm Sagittarius
5th 6:52 am Capricorn
7th 7:38 pm Aquarius
10th 7:44 am Pisces
12th 5:30 pm Aries
14th 11:46 pm Taurus
17th 2:20 am Gemini
19th 2:32 am Cancer
21st 2:07 am Leo
23rd 3:03 am Virgo
25th 6:55 am Libra
27th 2:21 pm Scorpio
30th 0:46 am Sagittarius

July 1947
2nd 1:03 pm Capricorn
5th 1:49 am Aquarius
7th 2:01 pm Pisces
10th 0:34 am Aries
12th 8:08 am Taurus
14th 12:12 pm Gemini
16th 1:12 pm Cancer
18th 12:35 pm Leo
20th 12:24 pm Virgo
22nd 2:19 pm Libra
24th 8:44 pm Scorpio
27th 6:42 am Sagittarius
29th 7:02 pm Capricorn

August 1947
1st 7:49 am Aquarius
3rd 7:48 pm Pisces
6th 6:18 am Aries
8th 2:40 pm Taurus
10th 8:16 pm Gemini
12th 10:49 pm Cancer
14th 11:06 pm Leo
16th 10:50 pm Virgo
19th 0:05 am Libra
21st 4:48 am Scorpio
23rd 1:39 pm Sagittarius
26th 1:31 am Capricorn
28th 2:16 pm Aquarius
31st 2:03 am Pisces

September 1947
2nd 12:01 pm Aries
4th 8:09 pm Taurus
7th 2:19 am Gemini
9th 6:11 am Cancer
11th 8:02 am Leo
13th 8:53 am Virgo
15th 10:21 am Libra
17th 2:17 pm Scorpio
19th 9:51 pm Sagittarius
22nd 8:60 am Capricorn
24th 9:36 pm Aquarius
27th 9:22 am Pisces
29th 6:36 pm Aries

October 1947
2nd 2:15 am Taurus
4th 7:42 am Gemini
6th 11:46 am Cancer
8th 2:41 pm Leo
10th 4:58 pm Virgo
12th 7:33 pm Libra
14th 11:48 pm Scorpio
17th 6:57 am Sagittarius
19th 5:17 pm Capricorn
22nd 5:39 am Aquarius
24th 5:44 pm Pisces
27th 3:30 am Aries
29th 10:13 am Taurus
31st 2:34 pm Gemini

November 1947
2nd 5:32 pm Cancer
4th 8:04 pm Leo
6th 10:55 pm Virgo
9th 2:44 am Libra
11th 8:07 am Scorpio
13th 3:38 pm Sagittarius
16th 1:39 am Capricorn
18th 1:47 pm Aquarius
21st 2:17 am Pisces
23rd 12:50 pm Aries
25th 8:04 pm Taurus
27th 11:55 pm Gemini
30th 1:31 am Cancer

December 1947
2nd 2:32 am Leo
4th 4:26 am Virgo
6th 8:17 am Libra
8th 2:27 pm Scorpio
10th 10:50 pm Sagittarius
13th 9:17 am Capricorn
15th 9:17 pm Aquarius
18th 9:59 am Pisces
20th 9:35 pm Aries
23rd 6:07 am Taurus
25th 10:42 am Gemini
27th 12:00 pm Cancer
29th 11:43 am Leo
31st 11:52 am Virgo

January 1948
2nd 2:15 pm Libra
4th 7:53 pm Scorpio
7th 4:42 am Sagittarius
9th 3:43 pm Capricorn
12th 3:55 am Aquarius
14th 4:35 pm Pisces
17th 4:42 am Aries
19th 2:38 pm Taurus
21st 8:50 pm Gemini
23rd 11:22 pm Cancer
25th 10:59 pm Leo
27th 9:58 pm Virgo
29th 10:31 pm Libra

February 1948
1st 2:29 am Scorpio
3rd 10:32 am Sagittarius
5th 9:30 pm Capricorn
8th 9:59 am Aquarius
10th 10:37 pm Pisces
13th 10:36 am Aries
15th 9:07 pm Taurus
18th 4:53 am Gemini
20th 9:04 am Cancer
22nd 10:03 am Leo
24th 9:23 am Virgo
26th 9:10 am Libra
28th 11:30 am Scorpio

March 1948
1st 5:45 pm Sagittarius
4th 3:52 am Capricorn
6th 4:14 pm Aquarius
9th 4:51 am Pisces
11th 4:31 pm Aries
14th 2:39 am Taurus
16th 10:41 am Gemini
18th 4:11 pm Cancer
20th 6:56 pm Leo
22nd 7:42 pm Virgo
24th 8:02 pm Libra
26th 9:50 pm Scorpio
29th 2:48 am Sagittarius
31st 11:37 am Capricorn

April 1948
2nd 11:18 pm Aquarius
5th 11:54 am Pisces
7th 11:27 pm Aries
10th 8:55 am Taurus
12th 4:17 pm Gemini
14th 9:39 pm Cancer
17th 1:14 am Leo
19th 3:29 am Virgo
21st 5:17 am Libra
23rd 7:53 am Scorpio
25th 12:36 pm Sagittarius
27th 8:23 pm Capricorn
30th 7:17 am Aquarius

May 1948
2nd 7:44 pm Pisces
5th 7:25 am Aries
7th 4:44 pm Taurus
9th 11:19 pm Gemini
12th 3:35 am Cancer
14th 6:37 am Leo
16th 9:14 am Virgo
18th 12:08 pm Libra
20th 3:58 pm Scorpio
22nd 9:25 pm Sagittarius
25th 5:10 am Capricorn
27th 3:33 pm Aquarius
30th 3:46 am Pisces

June 1948
1st 3:53 pm Aries
4th 1:42 am Taurus
6th 8:01 am Gemini
8th 11:24 am Cancer
10th 1:11 pm Leo
12th 2:49 pm Virgo
14th 5:35 pm Libra
16th 10:03 pm Scorpio
19th 4:29 am Sagittarius
21st 12:53 pm Capricorn
23rd 11:15 pm Aquarius
26th 11:24 am Pisces
28th 11:56 pm Aries

July 1948
1st 10:35 am Taurus
3rd 5:43 pm Gemini
5th 9:04 pm Cancer
7th 9:51 pm Leo
9th 10:04 pm Virgo
11th 11:30 pm Libra
14th 3:30 am Scorpio
16th 10:14 am Sagittarius
18th 7:15 pm Capricorn
21st 6:04 am Aquarius
23rd 6:13 pm Pisces
26th 6:55 am Aries
28th 6:31 pm Taurus
31st 2:59 am Gemini

August 1948
2nd 7:15 am Cancer
4th 8:11 am Leo
6th 7:33 am Virgo
8th 7:33 am Libra
10th 10:01 am Scorpio
12th 3:53 pm Sagittarius
15th 0:51 am Capricorn
17th 12:03 pm Aquarius
20th 0:22 am Pisces
22nd 1:04 pm Aries
25th 1:03 am Taurus
27th 10:34 am Gemini
29th 4:29 pm Cancer
31st 6:38 pm Leo

September 1948
2nd 6:20 pm Virgo
4th 5:38 pm Libra
6th 6:38 pm Scorpio
8th 10:52 pm Sagittarius
11th 6:59 am Capricorn
13th 5:59 pm Aquarius
16th 6:26 am Pisces
18th 7:02 pm Aries
21st 6:44 am Taurus
23rd 4:38 pm Gemini
25th 11:47 pm Cancer
28th 3:33 am Leo
30th 4:40 am Virgo

October 1948
2nd 4:32 am Libra
4th 5:02 am Scorpio
6th 7:6C am Sagittarius
8th 2:37 pm Capricorn
11th 0:42 am Aquarius
13th 1:04 pm Pisces
16th 1:36 am Aries
18th 12:52 pm Taurus
20th 10:14 pm Gemini
23rd 5:18 am Cancer
25th 10:07 am Leo
27th 12:51 pm Virgo
29th 2:16 pm Libra
31st 3:34 pm Scorpio

November 1948
2nd 6:15 pm Sagittarius
4th 11:42 pm Capricorn
7th 8:46 am Aquarius
9th 8:34 pm Pisces
12th 9:12 am Aries
14th 8:22 pm Taurus
17th 4:59 am Gemini
19th 11:08 am Cancer
21st 3:31 pm Leo
23rd 6:47 pm Virgo
25th 9:33 pm Libra
28th 0:19 am Scorpio
30th 3:55 am Sagittarius

December 1948
2nd 9:22 am Capricorn
4th 5:37 pm Aquarius
7th 4:48 am Pisces
9th 5:30 pm Aries
12th 5:07 am Taurus
14th 1:40 pm Gemini
16th 6:59 pm Cancer
18th 10:02 pm Leo
21st 0:19 am Virgo
23rd 2:60 am Libra
25th 6:40 am Scorpio
27th 11:31 am Sagittarius
29th 5:49 pm Capricorn

Moon Tables

<table>
<tr><td colspan="2">January 1949</td><td colspan="2">February 1949</td><td colspan="2">March 1949</td><td colspan="2">April 1949</td></tr>
</table>

January 1949
1st	2:10 am	Aquarius
3rd	1:02 pm	Pisces
6th	1:41 am	Aries
8th	2:01 pm	Taurus
10th	11:32 pm	Gemini
13th	4:54 am	Cancer
15th	7:07 am	Leo
17th	7:54 am	Virgo
19th	9:07 am	Libra
21st	12:03 pm	Scorpio
23rd	5:11 pm	Sagittarius
26th	0:23 am	Capricorn
28th	9:30 am	Aquarius
30th	8:27 pm	Pisces

February 1949
2nd	9:06 am	Aries
4th	9:57 pm	Taurus
7th	8:35 am	Gemini
9th	3:17 pm	Cancer
11th	5:58 pm	Leo
13th	6:05 pm	Virgo
15th	5:46 pm	Libra
17th	6:57 pm	Scorpio
19th	10:51 pm	Sagittarius
22nd	5:53 am	Capricorn
24th	3:27 pm	Aquarius
27th	2:55 am	Pisces

March 1949
1st	3:36 pm	Aries
4th	4:32 am	Taurus
6th	4:01 pm	Gemini
9th	0:21 am	Cancer
11th	4:30 am	Leo
13th	5:23 am	Virgo
15th	4:41 am	Libra
17th	4:28 am	Scorpio
19th	6:36 am	Sagittarius
21st	12:09 pm	Capricorn
23rd	9:11 pm	Aquarius
26th	8:50 am	Pisces
28th	9:42 pm	Aries
31st	10:27 am	Taurus

April 1949
2nd	10:02 pm	Gemini
5th	7:07 am	Cancer
7th	12:55 pm	Leo
9th	3:28 pm	Virgo
11th	3:47 pm	Libra
13th	3:29 pm	Scorpio
15th	4:28 pm	Sagittarius
17th	8:19 pm	Capricorn
20th	4:02 am	Aquarius
22nd	3:10 pm	Pisces
25th	3:60 am	Aries
27th	4:39 pm	Taurus
30th	3:45 am	Gemini

May 1949
2nd	12:40 pm	Cancer
4th	7:07 pm	Leo
6th	11:10 pm	Virgo
9th	1:07 am	Libra
11th	1:54 am	Scorpio
13th	2:59 am	Sagittarius
15th	6:02 am	Capricorn
17th	12:24 pm	Aquarius
19th	10:27 pm	Pisces
22nd	11:02 am	Aries
24th	11:42 pm	Taurus
27th	10:22 am	Gemini
29th	6:35 pm	Cancer

June 1949
1st	0:35 am	Leo
3rd	4:51 am	Virgo
5th	7:55 am	Libra
7th	10:12 am	Scorpio
9th	12:25 pm	Sagittarius
11th	3:43 pm	Capricorn
13th	9:28 pm	Aquarius
16th	6:42 am	Pisces
18th	6:46 pm	Aries
21st	7:28 am	Taurus
23rd	6:16 pm	Gemini
26th	1:60 am	Cancer
28th	6:58 am	Leo
30th	10:25 am	Virgo

July 1949
2nd	1:21 pm	Libra
4th	4:22 pm	Scorpio
6th	7:45 pm	Sagittarius
9th	0:02 am	Capricorn
11th	6:12 am	Aquarius
13th	3:04 pm	Pisces
16th	2:42 am	Aries
18th	3:34 pm	Taurus
21st	2:55 am	Gemini
23rd	10:46 am	Cancer
25th	3:16 pm	Leo
27th	5:35 pm	Virgo
29th	7:19 pm	Libra
31st	9:45 pm	Scorpio

August 1949
3rd	1:26 am	Sagittarius
5th	6:37 am	Capricorn
7th	1:37 pm	Aquarius
9th	10:47 pm	Pisces
12th	10:20 am	Aries
14th	11:17 pm	Taurus
17th	11:19 am	Gemini
19th	8:11 pm	Cancer
22nd	1:07 am	Leo
24th	2:55 am	Virgo
26th	3:24 am	Libra
28th	4:21 am	Scorpio
30th	7:03 am	Sagittarius

September 1949
1st	12:08 pm	Capricorn
3rd	7:39 pm	Aquarius
6th	5:27 am	Pisces
8th	5:13 pm	Aries
11th	6:11 am	Taurus
13th	6:44 pm	Gemini
16th	4:48 am	Cancer
18th	10:59 am	Leo
20th	1:30 pm	Virgo
22nd	1:41 pm	Libra
24th	1:23 pm	Scorpio
26th	2:25 pm	Sagittarius
28th	6:10 pm	Capricorn

October 1949
1st	1:14 am	Aquarius
3rd	11:21 am	Pisces
5th	11:28 pm	Aries
8th	12:25 pm	Taurus
11th	1:02 am	Gemini
13th	11:47 am	Cancer
15th	7:32 pm	Leo
17th	11:43 pm	Virgo
20th	0:48 am	Libra
22nd	0:19 am	Scorpio
24th	0:08 am	Sagittarius
26th	2:13 am	Capricorn
28th	7:56 am	Aquarius
30th	5:25 pm	Pisces

November 1949
2nd	5:36 am	Aries
4th	6:35 pm	Taurus
7th	6:53 am	Gemini
9th	5:33 pm	Cancer
12th	1:58 am	Leo
14th	7:38 am	Virgo
16th	10:32 am	Libra
18th	11:18 am	Scorpio
20th	11:18 am	Sagittarius
22nd	12:26 pm	Capricorn
24th	4:30 pm	Aquarius
27th	0:37 am	Pisces
29th	12:21 pm	Aries

December 1949
2nd	1:23 am	Taurus
4th	1:27 pm	Gemini
6th	11:31 pm	Cancer
9th	7:25 am	Leo
11th	1:27 pm	Virgo
13th	5:42 pm	Libra
15th	8:12 pm	Scorpio
17th	9:33 pm	Sagittarius
19th	11:02 pm	Capricorn
22nd	2:28 am	Aquarius
24th	9:26 am	Pisces
26th	8:08 pm	Aries
29th	8:58 am	Taurus
31st	9:13 pm	Gemini

January 1950
3rd	6:53 am	Cancer
5th	1:55 pm	Leo
7th	7:05 pm	Virgo
9th	11:08 pm	Libra
12th	2:28 am	Scorpio
14th	5:17 am	Sagittarius
16th	8:09 am	Capricorn
18th	12:12 pm	Aquarius
20th	6:46 pm	Pisces
23rd	4:41 am	Aries
25th	5:09 pm	Taurus
28th	5:42 am	Gemini
30th	3:47 pm	Cancer

February 1950
1st	10:34 pm	Leo
4th	2:36 am	Virgo
6th	5:20 am	Libra
8th	7:52 am	Scorpio
10th	10:53 am	Sagittarius
12th	2:47 pm	Capricorn
14th	7:60 pm	Aquarius
17th	3:14 am	Pisces
19th	1:04 pm	Aries
22nd	1:13 am	Taurus
24th	2:02 pm	Gemini
27th	1:02 am	Cancer

March 1950
1st	8:27 am	Leo
3rd	12:22 pm	Virgo
5th	2:00 pm	Libra
7th	2:57 pm	Scorpio
9th	4:41 pm	Sagittarius
11th	8:09 pm	Capricorn
14th	1:53 am	Aquarius
16th	10:02 am	Pisces
18th	8:21 pm	Aries
21st	8:33 am	Taurus
23rd	9:28 pm	Gemini
26th	9:13 am	Cancer
28th	6:02 pm	Leo
30th	11:01 pm	Virgo

April 1950
2nd	0:42 am	Libra
4th	0:37 am	Scorpio
6th	0:38 am	Sagittarius
8th	2:32 am	Capricorn
10th	7:28 am	Aquarius
12th	3:41 pm	Pisces
15th	2:32 am	Aries
17th	3:01 pm	Taurus
20th	3:54 am	Gemini
22nd	4:01 pm	Cancer
25th	1:55 am	Leo
27th	8:25 am	Virgo
29th	11:21 am	Libra

May 1950
1st	11:36 am	Scorpio
3rd	10:54 am	Sagittarius
5th	11:14 am	Capricorn
7th	2:28 pm	Aquarius
9th	9:37 pm	Pisces
12th	8:21 am	Aries
14th	8:59 pm	Taurus
17th	9:51 am	Gemini
19th	9:49 pm	Cancer
22nd	8:03 am	Leo
24th	3:46 pm	Virgo
26th	8:24 pm	Libra
28th	9:60 pm	Scorpio
30th	9:44 pm	Sagittarius

June 1950
1st	9:29 pm	Capricorn
3rd	11:19 pm	Aquarius
6th	5:02 am	Pisces
8th	2:48 pm	Aries
11th	3:13 am	Taurus
13th	4:04 pm	Gemini
16th	3:42 am	Cancer
18th	1:34 pm	Leo
20th	9:29 pm	Virgo
23rd	3:07 am	Libra
25th	6:15 am	Scorpio
27th	7:24 am	Sagittarius
29th	7:50 am	Capricorn

July 1950
1st	9:25 am	Aquarius
3rd	1:58 pm	Pisces
5th	10:26 pm	Aries
8th	10:16 am	Taurus
11th	11:01 pm	Gemini
13th	10:30 am	Cancer
15th	7:51 pm	Leo
18th	3:04 am	Virgo
20th	8:32 am	Libra
22nd	12:24 pm	Scorpio
24th	2:53 pm	Sagittarius
26th	4:39 pm	Capricorn
28th	6:57 pm	Aquarius
30th	11:19 pm	Pisces

August 1950
2nd	7:06 am	Aries
4th	6:08 pm	Taurus
7th	6:43 am	Gemini
9th	6:25 pm	Cancer
12th	3:34 am	Leo
14th	10:00 am	Virgo
16th	2:28 pm	Libra
18th	5:49 pm	Scorpio
20th	8:35 pm	Sagittarius
22nd	11:23 pm	Capricorn
25th	2:53 am	Aquarius
27th	8:05 am	Pisces
29th	3:48 pm	Aries

23

Why Does He Say One Thing and Do Another?

September 1950	October 1950	November 1950	December 1950
1st 2:18 am Taurus	3rd 10:57 am Cancer	2nd 5:35 am Leo	1st 9:51 am Virgo
3rd 2:45 pm Gemini	5th 9:39 pm Leo	4th 2:16 pm Virgo	4th 4:26 am Libra
6th 2:52 am Cancer	8th 4:50 am Virgo	6th 7:07 pm Libra	6th 7:15 am Scorpio
8th 12:29 pm Leo	10th 8:25 am Libra	8th 8:27 pm Scorpio	8th 7:16 am Sagittarius
10th 6:52 pm Virgo	12th 9:30 am Scorpio	10th 7:52 pm Sagittarius	10th 6:20 am Capricorn
12th 10:27 pm Libra	14th 9:47 am Sagittarius	12th 7:29 pm Capricorn	12th 6:40 am Aquarius
15th 0:26 am Scorpio	16th 10:60 am Capricorn	14th 9:17 pm Aquarius	14th 10:18 am Pisces
17th 2:12 am Sagittarius	18th 2:31 pm Aquarius	17th 2:40 am Pisces	16th 6:04 pm Aries
19th 4:50 am Capricorn	20th 8:55 pm Pisces	19th 11:43 am Aries	19th 5:12 am Taurus
21st 9:02 am Aquarius	23rd 5:60 am Aries	21st 11:08 pm Taurus	21st 5:49 pm Gemini
23rd 3:11 pm Pisces	25th 5:04 pm Taurus	24th 11:38 am Gemini	24th 6:17 am Cancer
25th 11:31 pm Aries	28th 5:22 am Gemini	27th 0:12 am Cancer	26th 5:43 pm Leo
28th 10:09 am Taurus	30th 6:03 pm Cancer	29th 11:59 am Leo	29th 3:39 am Virgo
30th 10:27 pm Gemini			31st 11:16 am Libra

January 1951	February 1951	March 1951	April 1951
2nd 3:53 pm Scorpio	1st 1:17 am Sagittarius	2nd 9:30 am Capricorn	2nd 10:46 pm Pisces
4th 5:35 pm Sagittarius	3rd 2:53 am Capricorn	4th 12:13 pm Aquarius	5th 5:18 am Aries
6th 5:32 pm Capricorn	5th 4:06 am Aquarius	6th 3:49 pm Pisces	7th 1:55 pm Taurus
8th 5:39 pm Aquarius	7th 6:33 am Pisces	8th 9:19 pm Aries	10th 0:42 am Gemini
10th 7:60 pm Pisces	9th 11:48 am Aries	11th 5:35 am Taurus	12th 1:05 pm Cancer
13th 2:09 am Aries	11th 8:37 pm Taurus	13th 4:38 pm Gemini	15th 1:18 am Leo
15th 12:15 pm Taurus	14th 8:19 am Gemini	16th 5:06 am Cancer	17th 11:03 am Virgo
18th 0:36 am Gemini	16th 8:51 pm Cancer	18th 4:43 pm Leo	19th 5:10 pm Libra
20th 1:06 pm Cancer	19th 7:60 am Leo	21st 1:40 am Virgo	21st 7:54 pm Scorpio
23rd 0:13 am Leo	21st 4:41 pm Virgo	23rd 7:19 am Libra	23rd 8:41 pm Sagittarius
25th 9:24 am Virgo	23rd 11:01 pm Libra	25th 10:35 am Scorpio	25th 9:22 pm Capricorn
27th 4:44 pm Libra	26th 3:32 am Scorpio	27th 12:42 pm Sagittarius	27th 11:33 pm Aquarius
29th 10:02 pm Scorpio	28th 6:50 am Sagittarius	29th 2:53 pm Capricorn	30th 4:15 am Pisces
		31st 6:05 pm Aquarius	

May 1951	June 1951	July 1951	August 1951
2nd 11:29 am Aries	1st 2:35 am Taurus	3rd 8:28 am Cancer	2nd 3:07 am Leo
4th 8:47 pm Taurus	3rd 2:04 pm Gemini	5th 8:59 pm Leo	4th 2:16 pm Virgo
7th 7:51 am Gemini	6th 2:32 am Cancer	8th 8:32 am Virgo	6th 11:35 pm Libra
9th 8:13 pm Cancer	8th 3:10 pm Leo	10th 6:01 pm Libra	9th 6:21 am Scorpio
12th 8:48 am Leo	11th 2:44 am Virgo	13th 0:17 am Scorpio	11th 10:26 am Sagittarius
14th 7:42 pm Virgo	13th 11:25 am Libra	15th 3:00 am Sagittarius	13th 12:15 pm Capricorn
17th 3:04 am Libra	15th 4:11 pm Scorpio	17th 3:13 am Capricorn	15th 12:53 pm Aquarius
19th 6:21 am Scorpio	17th 5:23 pm Sagittarius	19th 2:44 am Aquarius	17th 1:55 pm Pisces
21st 6:43 am Sagittarius	19th 4:39 pm Capricorn	21st 3:31 am Pisces	19th 5:02 pm Aries
23rd 6:10 am Capricorn	21st 4:09 pm Aquarius	23rd 7:28 am Aries	21st 11:27 pm Taurus
25th 6:47 am Aquarius	23rd 5:54 pm Pisces	25th 3:12 pm Taurus	24th 9:30 am Gemini
27th 10:12 am Pisces	25th 11:15 pm Aries	28th 2:09 am Gemini	26th 9:44 pm Cancer
29th 4:57 pm Aries	28th 8:21 am Taurus	30th 2:43 pm Cancer	29th 10:08 am Leo
	30th 7:53 pm Gemini		31st 8:50 pm Virgo

September 1951	October 1951	November 1951	December 1951
3rd 5:31 am Libra	2nd 6:21 pm Scorpio	1st 5:19 am Sagittarius	2nd 3:48 pm Aquarius
5th 11:47 am Scorpio	4th 9:47 pm Sagittarius	3rd 6:41 am Capricorn	4th 6:12 pm Pisces
7th 4:10 pm Sagittarius	7th 0:30 am Capricorn	5th 8:46 am Aquarius	6th 11:19 pm Aries
9th 7:05 pm Capricorn	9th 3:20 am Aquarius	7th 12:26 pm Pisces	9th 7:07 am Taurus
11th 9:12 pm Aquarius	11th 6:48 am Pisces	9th 5:54 pm Aries	11th 4:56 pm Gemini
13th 11:21 pm Pisces	13th 11:21 am Aries	12th 1:08 am Taurus	14th 4:23 am Cancer
16th 2:48 am Aries	15th 5:39 pm Taurus	14th 10:17 am Gemini	16th 5:05 pm Leo
18th 8:45 am Taurus	18th 2:22 am Gemini	16th 9:28 pm Cancer	19th 5:50 am Virgo
20th 5:49 pm Gemini	20th 1:45 pm Cancer	19th 10:11 am Leo	21st 4:36 pm Libra
23rd 5:35 am Cancer	23rd 2:25 am Leo	21st 10:34 pm Virgo	23rd 11:39 pm Scorpio
25th 6:07 pm Leo	25th 1:58 pm Virgo	24th 8:04 am Libra	26th 2:26 am Sagittarius
28th 5:03 am Virgo	27th 10:24 pm Libra	26th 1:27 pm Scorpio	28th 2:24 am Capricorn
30th 1:05 pm Libra	30th 3:08 am Scorpio	28th 3:17 pm Sagittarius	30th 1:37 am Aquarius
		30th 3:23 pm Capricorn	

January 1952	February 1952	March 1952	April 1952
1st 2:13 am Pisces	1st 7:55 pm Taurus	2nd 12:42 pm Gemini	1st 7:42 am Cancer
3rd 5:47 am Aries	4th 4:59 am Gemini	4th 11:40 pm Cancer	3rd 8:10 pm Leo
5th 12:49 pm Taurus	6th 4:46 pm Cancer	7th 12:31 pm Leo	6th 8:40 am Virgo
7th 10:44 pm Gemini	9th 5:37 am Leo	10th 0:53 am Virgo	8th 6:55 pm Libra
10th 10:36 am Cancer	11th 6:02 pm Virgo	12th 11:15 am Libra	11th 2:14 am Scorpio
12th 11:19 pm Leo	14th 4:58 am Libra	14th 7:20 pm Scorpio	13th 7:07 am Sagittarius
15th 11:59 am Virgo	16th 1:42 pm Scorpio	17th 1:15 am Sagittarius	15th 10:42 am Capricorn
17th 11:19 pm Libra	18th 7:41 pm Sagittarius	19th 5:18 am Capricorn	17th 1:44 pm Aquarius
20th 7:39 am Scorpio	20th 10:49 pm Capricorn	21st 7:54 am Aquarius	19th 4:41 pm Pisces
22nd 12:39 pm Sagittarius	22nd 11:49 pm Aquarius	23rd 9:40 am Pisces	21st 7:58 pm Aries
24th 1:36 pm Capricorn	25th 0:02 am Pisces	25th 11:37 am Aries	24th 0:16 am Taurus
26th 1:07 pm Aquarius	27th 1:13 am Aries	27th 3:10 pm Taurus	26th 6:44 am Gemini
28th 12:50 pm Pisces	29th 5:05 am Taurus	29th 9:37 pm Gemini	28th 4:10 pm Cancer
30th 2:39 pm Aries			

Moon Tables

May 1952
1st 4:14 am Leo
3rd 4:56 pm Virgo
6th 3:38 am Libra
8th 10:45 am Scorpio
10th 2:49 pm Sagittarius
12th 5:10 pm Capricorn
14th 7:15 am Aquarius
16th 10:07 pm Pisces
19th 2:09 am Aries
21st 7:32 am Taurus
23rd 2:41 pm Gemini
26th 0:06 am Cancer
28th 12:01 pm Leo
31st 0:58 am Virgo

June 1952
2nd 12:21 pm Libra
4th 8:17 pm Scorpio
7th 0:22 am Sagittarius
9th 1:47 am Capricorn
11th 2:29 am Aquarius
13th 4:04 am Pisces
15th 7:34 am Aries
17th 1:14 pm Taurus
19th 9:05 pm Gemini
22nd 7:07 am Cancer
24th 7:03 pm Leo
27th 8:05 am Virgo
29th 8:16 pm Libra

July 1952
4th 5:20 am Scorpio
4th 10:21 am Sagittarius
6th 12:00 pm Capricorn
8th 11:55 am Aquarius
10th 12:04 pm Pisces
12th 2:03 pm Aries
14th 6:50 pm Taurus
17th 2:40 am Gemini
19th 1:08 pm Cancer
22nd 1:21 am Leo
24th 2:24 pm Virgo
27th 2:52 am Libra
29th 12:58 pm Scorpio
31st 7:33 pm Sagittarius

August 1952
2nd 10:25 pm Capricorn
4th 10:40 pm Aquarius
6th 10:06 pm Pisces
8th 10:35 pm Aries
11th 1:47 am Taurus
13th 8:42 am Gemini
15th 6:55 pm Cancer
18th 7:21 am Leo
20th 8:23 pm Virgo
23rd 8:40 am Libra
25th 7:09 pm Scorpio
28th 2:51 am Sagittarius
30th 7:19 am Capricorn

September 1952
1st 8:60 am Aquarius
3rd 8:60 am Pisces
5th 9:01 am Aries
7th 10:35 am Taurus
9th 4:10 pm Gemini
12th 1:25 am Cancer
14th 1:40 pm Leo
17th 2:42 am Virgo
19th 2:40 pm Libra
22nd 0:43 am Scorpio
24th 8:31 am Sagittarius
26th 2:03 pm Capricorn
28th 5:21 pm Aquarius
30th 6:51 pm Pisces

October 1952
2nd 7:34 pm Aries
4th 9:06 pm Taurus
7th 1:15 am Gemini
9th 9:20 am Cancer
11th 8:50 pm Leo
14th 9:49 am Virgo
16th 9:44 pm Libra
19th 7:07 am Scorpio
21st 2:10 pm Sagittarius
23rd 7:27 pm Capricorn
25th 11:27 pm Aquarius
28th 2:22 am Pisces
30th 4:34 am Aries

November 1952
1st 6:50 am Taurus
3rd 11:07 am Gemini
5th 6:15 pm Cancer
8th 4:58 am Leo
10th 5:47 pm Virgo
13th 5:54 am Libra
15th 3:15 pm Scorpio
17th 9:32 pm Sagittarius
20th 1:39 am Capricorn
22nd 4:51 am Aquarius
24th 7:55 am Pisces
26th 11:10 am Aries
28th 2:56 pm Taurus
30th 7:55 pm Gemini

December 1952
3rd 3:10 am Cancer
5th 1:24 pm Leo
8th 1:58 am Virgo
10th 2:32 pm Libra
13th 0:39 am Scorpio
15th 6:55 am Sagittarius
17th 10:15 am Capricorn
19th 12:02 pm Aquarius
21st 1:48 pm Pisces
23rd 4:33 pm Aries
25th 8:48 pm Taurus
28th 2:50 am Gemini
30th 10:57 am Cancer

January 1953
1st 9:18 pm Leo
4th 9:42 am Virgo
6th 10:35 pm Libra
9th 9:39 am Scorpio
11th 5:09 pm Sagittarius
13th 8:53 pm Capricorn
15th 9:57 pm Aquarius
17th 10:08 pm Pisces
19th 11:11 pm Aries
22nd 2:23 am Taurus
24th 8:26 am Gemini
26th 5:10 pm Cancer
29th 4:08 am Leo
31st 4:36 pm Virgo

February 1953
3rd 5:31 am Libra
5th 5:18 pm Scorpio
8th 2:18 am Sagittarius
10th 7:27 am Capricorn
12th 9:12 am Aquarius
14th 8:58 am Pisces
16th 8:34 am Aries
18th 9:56 am Taurus
20th 2:33 pm Gemini
22nd 10:49 pm Cancer
25th 10:09 am Leo
27th 10:53 pm Virgo

March 1953
2nd 11:41 am Libra
4th 11:32 pm Scorpio
7th 9:16 am Sagittarius
9th 4:07 pm Capricorn
11th 7:35 pm Aquarius
13th 8:16 pm Pisces
15th 7:40 pm Aries
17th 7:48 pm Taurus
19th 10:37 pm Gemini
22nd 5:33 am Cancer
24th 4:18 pm Leo
27th 5:06 am Virgo
29th 5:51 pm Libra

April 1953
1st 5:19 am Scorpio
3rd 2:57 pm Sagittarius
5th 10:29 pm Capricorn
8th 3:26 am Aquarius
10th 5:48 am Pisces
12th 6:19 am Aries
14th 6:35 am Taurus
16th 8:33 am Gemini
18th 2:00 pm Cancer
20th 11:29 pm Leo
23rd 11:54 am Virgo
26th 0:42 am Libra
28th 11:50 am Scorpio
30th 8:52 pm Sagittarius

May 1953
3rd 3:55 am Capricorn
5th 9:11 am Aquarius
7th 12:45 pm Pisces
9th 2:48 pm Aries
11th 4:14 pm Taurus
13th 6:31 pm Gemini
15th 11:17 pm Cancer
18th 7:51 am Leo
20th 7:33 pm Virgo
23rd 8:16 am Libra
25th 7:31 pm Scorpio
28th 4:07 am Sagittarius
30th 10:16 am Capricorn

June 1953
1st 2:44 pm Aquarius
3rd 6:12 pm Pisces
5th 9:03 pm Aries
7th 11:41 pm Taurus
10th 3:05 am Gemini
12th 8:23 am Cancer
14th 4:31 pm Leo
17th 3:38 am Virgo
19th 4:17 pm Libra
22nd 3:56 am Scorpio
24th 12:44 pm Sagittarius
26th 6:27 pm Capricorn
28th 9:53 pm Aquarius

July 1953
1st 0:10 am Pisces
3rd 2:25 am Aries
5th 5:26 am Taurus
7th 9:46 am Gemini
9th 3:59 pm Cancer
12th 0:29 am Leo
14th 11:31 am Virgo
17th 0:04 am Libra
19th 12:14 pm Scorpio
21st 9:57 pm Sagittarius
24th 4:04 am Capricorn
26th 7:01 am Aquarius
28th 8:07 am Pisces
30th 8:59 am Aries

August 1953
1st 11:02 am Taurus
3rd 3:16 pm Gemini
5th 10:03 pm Cancer
8th 7:20 am Leo
10th 6:36 pm Virgo
13th 7:09 am Libra
15th 7:43 pm Scorpio
18th 6:27 am Sagittarius
20th 1:47 pm Capricorn
22nd 5:25 pm Aquarius
24th 6:10 pm Pisces
26th 5:47 pm Aries
28th 6:14 pm Taurus
30th 9:10 pm Gemini

September 1953
2nd 3:33 am Cancer
4th 1:09 pm Leo
7th 0:48 am Virgo
9th 1:28 pm Libra
12th 2:06 am Scorpio
14th 1:30 pm Sagittarius
16th 10:20 pm Capricorn
19th 3:28 am Aquarius
21st 5:04 am Pisces
23rd 4:31 am Aries
25th 3:47 am Taurus
27th 5:05 am Gemini
29th 10:01 am Cancer

October 1953
1st 6:57 pm Leo
4th 6:42 am Virgo
7th 7:28 am Libra
9th 7:56 am Scorpio
12th 7:19 am Sagittarius
14th 4:49 am Capricorn
16th 11:29 am Aquarius
18th 2:51 pm Pisces
20th 3:24 am Aries
22nd 2:48 pm Taurus
24th 3:09 am Gemini
26th 6:27 pm Cancer
29th 1:56 am Leo
31st 1:06 pm Virgo

November 1953
3rd 1:51 am Libra
5th 2:10 pm Scorpio
8th 1:07 am Sagittarius
10th 10:16 am Capricorn
12th 5:29 pm Aquarius
14th 10:16 pm Pisces
17th 0:34 am Aries
19th 1:14 am Taurus
21st 1:56 am Gemini
23rd 4:34 am Leo
25th 10:45 am Leo
27th 8:43 pm Virgo
30th 9:06 am Libra

December 1953
2nd 9:30 pm Scorpio
5th 8:06 am Sagittarius
7th 4:30 pm Capricorn
9th 10:59 pm Aquarius
12th 3:44 am Pisces
14th 7:05 am Aries
16th 9:22 am Taurus
18th 11:30 am Gemini
20th 2:44 pm Cancer
22nd 8:25 pm Leo
25th 5:26 am Virgo
27th 5:11 pm Libra
30th 5:41 am Scorpio

25

Why Does He Say One Thing and Do Another?

January 1954
1st 4:37 pm Sagittarius
4th 0:45 am Capricorn
6th 6:07 am Aquarius
8th 9:42 am Pisces
10th 12:28 pm Aries
12th 3:12 pm Taurus
14th 6:31 pm Gemini
16th 11:02 pm Cancer
19th 5:27 am Leo
21st 2:16 pm Virgo
24th 1:31 am Libra
26th 2:01 pm Scorpio
29th 1:40 am Sagittarius
31st 10:21 am Capricorn

February 1954
2nd 3:34 pm Aquarius
4th 6:02 pm Pisces
6th 7:15 pm Aries
8th 8:49 pm Taurus
10th 11:55 pm Gemini
13th 5:13 am Cancer
15th 12:39 pm Leo
17th 10:02 pm Virgo
20th 9:17 am Libra
22nd 9:44 pm Scorpio
25th 9:57 am Sagittarius
27th 7:54 pm Capricorn

March 1954
2nd 2:05 am Aquarius
4th 4:29 am Pisces
6th 4:40 am Aries
8th 4:35 am Taurus
10th 6:11 am Gemini
12th 10:42 am Cancer
14th 6:20 pm Leo
17th 4:22 am Virgo
19th 3:59 pm Libra
22nd 4:27 am Scorpio
24th 4:55 pm Sagittarius
27th 3:52 am Capricorn
29th 11:32 am Aquarius
31st 3:12 pm Pisces

April 1954
2nd 3:37 pm Aries
4th 2:44 pm Taurus
6th 2:45 pm Gemini
8th 5:33 pm Cancer
11th 0:06 am Leo
13th 10:06 am Virgo
15th 9:59 pm Libra
18th 10:34 am Scorpio
20th 10:56 pm Sagittarius
23rd 10:09 am Capricorn
25th 6:50 pm Aquarius
28th 0:22 am Pisces
30th 2:08 am Aries

May 1954
2nd 1:44 am Taurus
4th 1:08 am Gemini
6th 2:33 am Cancer
8th 7:34 am Leo
10th 4:27 pm Virgo
13th 4:04 am Libra
15th 4:43 pm Scorpio
18th 4:54 am Sagittarius
20th 3:48 pm Capricorn
23rd 0:48 am Aquarius
25th 7:06 am Pisces
27th 10:28 am Aries
29th 11:33 am Taurus
31st 10:21 am Gemini

June 1954
2nd 12:51 pm Cancer
4th 4:40 pm Leo
7th 0:08 am Virgo
9th 11:01 am Libra
11th 11:30 pm Scorpio
14th 11:37 am Sagittarius
16th 10:04 pm Capricorn
19th 6:25 am Aquarius
21st 12:35 pm Pisces
23rd 4:42 pm Aries
25th 7:09 pm Taurus
27th 8:44 pm Gemini
29th 10:38 pm Cancer

July 1954
2nd 2:19 am Leo
4th 9:01 am Virgo
6th 7:19 pm Libra
9th 7:04 am Scorpio
11th 7:19 pm Sagittarius
14th 5:38 am Capricorn
16th 1:16 pm Aquarius
18th 6:33 pm Pisces
20th 10:09 pm Aries
23rd 0:54 am Taurus
25th 3:52 am Gemini
27th 6:45 am Cancer
29th 11:15 am Leo
31st 5:54 pm Virgo

August 1954
3rd 3:17 am Libra
5th 3:04 pm Scorpio
8th 3:31 am Sagittarius
10th 2:16 pm Capricorn
12th 9:53 pm Aquarius
15th 2:17 am Pisces
17th 4:39 am Aries
19th 6:29 am Taurus
21st 8:50 am Gemini
23rd 12:54 pm Cancer
25th 6:26 pm Leo
28th 1:46 am Virgo
30th 11:16 am Libra

September 1954
1st 10:50 pm Scorpio
4th 11:32 am Sagittarius
6th 11:09 pm Capricorn
9th 7:26 am Aquarius
11th 11:51 am Pisces
13th 1:21 pm Aries
15th 1:47 pm Taurus
17th 2:59 pm Gemini
19th 6:17 pm Cancer
22nd 0:06 am Leo
24th 8:14 am Virgo
26th 6:14 pm Libra
29th 5:55 am Scorpio

October 1954
1st 6:43 pm Sagittarius
4th 7:02 am Capricorn
6th 4:41 pm Aquarius
8th 10:16 pm Pisces
10th 11:58 pm Aries
12th 11:33 pm Taurus
14th 11:10 pm Gemini
17th 0:50 am Cancer
19th 5:44 am Leo
21st 1:48 pm Virgo
24th 0:12 am Libra
26th 12:12 pm Scorpio
29th 1:01 am Sagittarius
31st 1:35 pm Capricorn

November 1954
3rd 0:23 am Aquarius
5th 7:30 am Pisces
7th 10:37 am Aries
9th 10:47 am Taurus
11th 9:53 am Gemini
13th 10:05 am Cancer
15th 1:09 pm Leo
17th 7:55 pm Virgo
20th 6:03 am Libra
22nd 6:14 pm Scorpio
25th 7:01 am Sagittarius
27th 7:24 pm Capricorn
30th 6:18 am Aquarius

December 1954
2nd 2:35 pm Pisces
4th 7:33 pm Aries
6th 9:22 pm Taurus
8th 9:16 pm Gemini
10th 9:08 pm Cancer
12th 10:49 pm Leo
15th 3:57 am Virgo
17th 12:56 pm Libra
20th 0:43 am Scorpio
22nd 1:34 pm Sagittarius
25th 1:40 am Capricorn
27th 11:58 am Aquarius
29th 8:08 pm Pisces

January 1955
1st 1:55 am Aries
3rd 5:25 am Taurus
5th 7:03 am Gemini
7th 8:02 am Cancer
9th 9:45 am Leo
11th 1:48 pm Virgo
13th 9:17 pm Libra
16th 8:15 am Scorpio
18th 9:01 pm Sagittarius
21st 9:06 am Capricorn
23rd 6:55 pm Aquarius
26th 2:11 am Pisces
28th 7:19 am Aries
30th 11:05 am Taurus

February 1955
1st 2:03 pm Gemini
3rd 4:37 pm Cancer
5th 7:30 pm Leo
7th 11:42 pm Virgo
10th 6:37 am Libra
12th 4:41 pm Scorpio
15th 5:06 am Sagittarius
17th 5:52 pm Capricorn
20th 3:30 am Aquarius
22nd 10:04 am Pisces
24th 2:04 pm Aries
26th 4:46 pm Taurus
28th 7:26 pm Gemini

March 1955
2nd 10:41 pm Cancer
5th 2:51 am Leo
7th 8:12 am Virgo
9th 3:24 pm Libra
12th 1:05 am Scorpio
14th 1:14 pm Sagittarius
17th 1:50 am Capricorn
19th 12:41 pm Aquarius
21st 7:41 pm Pisces
23rd 11:08 pm Aries
26th 0:31 am Taurus
28th 1:42 am Gemini
30th 4:07 am Cancer

April 1955
1st 8:23 am Leo
3rd 2:33 pm Virgo
5th 10:35 pm Libra
8th 8:41 am Scorpio
10th 8:44 pm Sagittarius
13th 9:40 am Capricorn
15th 9:20 pm Aquarius
18th 5:24 am Pisces
20th 9:25 am Aries
22nd 10:27 am Taurus
24th 10:25 am Gemini
26th 11:12 am Cancer
28th 2:12 pm Leo
30th 7:59 pm Virgo

May 1955
3rd 4:28 am Libra
5th 3:06 pm Scorpio
8th 3:19 am Sagittarius
10th 4:19 pm Capricorn
13th 4:28 am Aquarius
15th 1:48 pm Pisces
17th 7:18 pm Aries
19th 9:10 pm Taurus
21st 8:57 pm Gemini
23rd 8:34 pm Cancer
25th 9:55 pm Leo
28th 2:17 am Virgo
30th 10:12 am Libra

June 1955
1st 8:55 pm Scorpio
4th 9:25 am Sagittarius
6th 10:21 pm Capricorn
9th 10:28 am Aquarius
11th 8:51 pm Pisces
14th 3:21 am Aries
16th 6:47 am Taurus
18th 7:36 am Gemini
20th 7:18 am Cancer
22nd 7:41 am Leo
24th 10:32 am Virgo
26th 5:01 pm Libra
29th 3:06 am Scorpio

July 1955
1st 3:36 pm Sagittarius
4th 4:30 am Capricorn
6th 4:17 pm Aquarius
9th 2:09 am Pisces
11th 9:31 am Aries
13th 2:17 pm Taurus
15th 4:42 pm Gemini
17th 5:31 pm Cancer
19th 6:07 pm Leo
21st 8:09 pm Virgo
24th 1:18 am Libra
26th 10:23 am Scorpio
28th 10:25 pm Sagittarius
31st 11:18 am Capricorn

August 1955
2nd 10:51 pm Aquarius
5th 8:02 am Pisces
7th 2:59 pm Aries
9th 8:04 pm Taurus
11th 11:34 pm Gemini
14th 1:53 am Cancer
16th 3:36 am Leo
18th 6:02 am Virgo
20th 10:40 am Libra
22nd 6:42 pm Scorpio
25th 6:05 am Sagittarius
27th 6:56 pm Capricorn
30th 6:33 am Aquarius

26

Moon Tables

September 1955
1st 3:20 pm Pisces
3rd 9:24 am Aries
6th 1:38 am Taurus
8th 4:50 am Gemini
10th 8:03 am Cancer
12th 11:05 am Leo
14th 2:37 pm Virgo
16th 7:40 pm Libra
19th 3:22 am Scorpio
21st 2:15 pm Sagittarius
24th 3:02 am Capricorn
26th 3:05 pm Aquarius
29th 0:13 am Pisces

October 1955
1st 5:45 am Aries
3rd 8:51 am Taurus
5th 10:50 am Gemini
7th 1:25 pm Cancer
9th 4:44 pm Leo
11th 9:13 pm Virgo
14th 3:16 am Libra
16th 11:29 am Scorpio
18th 10:09 pm Sagittarius
21st 10:54 am Capricorn
23rd 11:34 pm Aquarius
26th 9:33 am Pisces
28th 3:43 pm Aries
30th 6:28 pm Taurus

November 1955
1st 7:23 pm Gemini
3rd 8:13 pm Cancer
5th 10:20 pm Leo
8th 2:38 am Virgo
10th 9:19 am Libra
12th 6:15 pm Scorpio
15th 5:19 am Sagittarius
17th 6:02 pm Capricorn
20th 6:58 am Aquarius
22nd 6:08 pm Pisces
25th 1:47 am Aries
27th 5:24 am Taurus
29th 6:11 am Gemini

December 1955
1st 5:49 am Cancer
3rd 6:11 am Leo
5th 8:55 am Virgo
7th 2:53 pm Libra
9th 12:00 pm Scorpio
12th 11:36 am Sagittarius
15th 0:24 am Capricorn
17th 1:20 pm Aquarius
20th 1:02 am Pisces
22nd 10:01 am Aries
24th 3:28 pm Taurus
26th 5:31 pm Gemini
28th 5:17 pm Cancer
30th 4:39 pm Leo

January 1956
1st 5:35 pm Virgo
3rd 9:46 pm Libra
6th 6:03 am Scorpio
8th 5:35 pm Sagittarius
11th 6:33 am Capricorn
13th 7:18 pm Aquarius
16th 6:47 am Pisces
18th 4:15 pm Aries
20th 11:11 pm Taurus
23rd 3:05 am Gemini
25th 4:19 am Cancer
27th 4:07 am Leo
29th 4:21 am Virgo
31st 7:01 am Libra

February 1956
2nd 1:38 pm Scorpio
5th 0:12 am Sagittarius
7th 1:07 pm Capricorn
10th 1:51 am Aquarius
12th 12:49 pm Pisces
14th 9:49 pm Aries
17th 4:47 am Taurus
19th 9:48 am Gemini
21st 12:48 pm Cancer
23rd 2:10 pm Leo
25th 3:07 pm Virgo
27th 5:25 pm Libra
29th 10:45 pm Scorpio

March 1956
3rd 8:13 am Sagittarius
5th 8:33 pm Capricorn
8th 9:16 am Aquarius
10th 8:08 pm Pisces
13th 4:25 am Aries
15th 10:30 am Taurus
17th 3:10 pm Gemini
19th 6:47 pm Cancer
21st 9:32 pm Leo
23rd 11:53 pm Virgo
26th 3:02 am Libra
28th 8:23 am Scorpio
30th 4:50 pm Sagittarius

April 1956
2nd 4:38 am Capricorn
4th 5:23 pm Aquarius
7th 4:33 am Pisces
9th 12:42 pm Aries
11th 6:00 pm Taurus
13th 9:30 pm Gemini
16th 0:14 am Cancer
18th 3:00 am Leo
20th 6:18 am Virgo
22nd 10:39 am Libra
24th 4:48 pm Scorpio
27th 1:26 am Sagittarius
29th 12:46 pm Capricorn

May 1956
2nd 1:29 am Aquarius
4th 1:11 pm Pisces
6th 10:05 pm Aries
9th 3:22 am Taurus
11th 5:59 am Gemini
13th 7:20 am Cancer
15th 8:53 am Leo
17th 11:43 am Virgo
19th 4:27 pm Libra
21st 11:27 pm Scorpio
24th 8:49 am Sagittarius
26th 8:12 pm Capricorn
29th 8:53 am Aquarius
31st 9:09 pm Pisces

June 1956
3rd 7:01 am Aries
5th 1:16 pm Taurus
7th 4:06 pm Gemini
9th 4:41 pm Cancer
11th 4:47 pm Leo
13th 6:07 pm Virgo
15th 10:00 pm Libra
18th 5:05 am Scorpio
20th 2:59 pm Sagittarius
23rd 2:44 am Capricorn
25th 3:26 pm Aquarius
28th 3:54 am Pisces
30th 2:39 pm Aries

July 1956
2nd 10:25 pm Taurus
5th 2:24 am Gemini
7th 3:20 am Cancer
9th 2:43 am Leo
11th 2:36 am Virgo
13th 4:58 am Libra
15th 11:02 am Scorpio
17th 8:40 pm Sagittarius
20th 8:42 am Capricorn
22nd 9:28 pm Aquarius
25th 9:50 am Pisces
27th 8:53 pm Aries
30th 5:37 am Taurus

August 1956
1st 11:12 am Gemini
3rd 1:29 pm Cancer
5th 1:27 pm Leo
7th 12:53 pm Virgo
9th 1:57 pm Libra
11th 6:25 pm Scorpio
14th 3:01 am Sagittarius
16th 2:49 pm Capricorn
19th 3:38 am Aquarius
21st 3:45 pm Pisces
24th 2:30 am Aries
26th 11:21 am Taurus
28th 5:57 pm Gemini
30th 9:51 pm Cancer

September 1956
1st 11:14 pm Leo
3rd 11:22 pm Virgo
6th 0:05 am Libra
8th 3:30 am Scorpio
10th 10:51 am Sagittarius
12th 9:46 pm Capricorn
15th 10:27 am Aquarius
17th 10:33 pm Pisces
20th 8:46 am Aries
22nd 5:00 pm Taurus
24th 11:26 pm Gemini
27th 3:50 am Cancer
29th 6:48 am Leo

October 1956
1st 8:25 am Virgo
3rd 10:06 am Libra
5th 1:25 pm Scorpio
7th 7:51 pm Sagittarius
10th 5:51 am Capricorn
12th 6:10 pm Aquarius
15th 6:23 am Pisces
17th 4:33 pm Aries
20th 0:07 am Taurus
22nd 5:28 am Gemini
24th 9:22 am Cancer
26th 12:27 pm Leo
28th 3:11 pm Virgo
30th 6:12 pm Libra

November 1956
1st 10:27 pm Scorpio
4th 5:00 am Sagittarius
6th 2:30 pm Capricorn
9th 2:22 am Aquarius
11th 2:51 pm Pisces
14th 1:36 am Aries
16th 9:09 am Taurus
18th 1:43 pm Gemini
20th 4:16 pm Cancer
22nd 6:11 pm Leo
24th 8:34 pm Virgo
27th 0:11 am Libra
29th 5:37 am Scorpio

December 1956
1st 1:03 pm Sagittarius
3rd 10:38 pm Capricorn
6th 10:19 am Aquarius
8th 10:59 pm Pisces
11th 10:34 am Aries
13th 7:13 pm Taurus
16th 0:07 am Gemini
18th 1:52 am Cancer
20th 2:12 am Leo
22nd 2:58 am Virgo
24th 5:43 am Libra
26th 11:12 am Scorpio
29th 7:22 pm Sagittarius
31st 5:40 am Capricorn

January 1957
2nd 5:26 pm Aquarius
5th 6:06 am Pisces
7th 6:21 pm Aries
10th 4:24 am Taurus
12th 10:39 am Gemini
14th 1:01 pm Cancer
16th 12:50 pm Leo
18th 12:08 pm Virgo
20th 1:02 pm Libra
22nd 5:07 pm Scorpio
25th 0:54 am Sagittarius
27th 11:34 am Capricorn
29th 11:42 pm Aquarius

February 1957
1st 12:21 pm Pisces
4th 0:44 am Aries
6th 11:34 am Taurus
8th 7:32 pm Gemini
10th 11:40 pm Cancer
13th 0:19 am Leo
14th 11:18 pm Virgo
16th 10:51 pm Libra
19th 1:07 am Scorpio
21st 7:28 am Sagittarius
23rd 5:29 pm Capricorn
26th 5:42 am Aquarius
28th 6:25 pm Pisces

March 1957
3rd 6:30 am Aries
5th 5:19 pm Taurus
8th 2:02 am Gemini
10th 7:42 am Cancer
12th 10:08 am Leo
14th 10:19 am Virgo
16th 10:03 am Libra
18th 11:20 am Scorpio
20th 3:59 pm Sagittarius
23rd 0:35 am Capricorn
25th 12:18 pm Aquarius
28th 0:58 am Pisces
30th 12:52 pm Aries

April 1957
1st 11:28 pm Taurus
4th 7:28 am Gemini
6th 1:35 pm Cancer
8th 5:21 pm Leo
10th 7:12 pm Virgo
12th 8:09 pm Libra
14th 9:46 pm Scorpio
17th 1:45 am Sagittarius
19th 9:13 am Capricorn
21st 7:55 pm Aquarius
24th 8:22 am Pisces
26th 8:20 pm Aries
29th 6:15 am Taurus

Why Does He Say One Thing and Do Another?

May 1957		June 1957		July 1957		August 1957	
1st	1:43 pm Gemini	2nd	4:45 am Leo	1st	1:25 pm Virgo	2nd	1:02 am Scorpio
3rd	7:06 pm Cancer	4th	6:59 am Virgo	3rd	3:18 pm Libra	4th	6:51 am Sagittarius
5th	10:53 pm Leo	6th	9:47 am Libra	5th	7:12 pm Scorpio	6th	3:25 pm Capricorn
8th	1:36 am Virgo	8th	1:43 pm Scorpio	8th	1:22 am Sagittarius	9th	2:01 am Aquarius
10th	3:57 am Libra	10th	7:11 pm Sagittarius	10th	9:37 am Capricorn	11th	2:03 pm Pisces
12th	6:50 am Scorpio	13th	2:38 am Capricorn	12th	7:43 pm Aquarius	14th	2:46 am Aries
14th	11:17 am Sagittarius	15th	12:27 pm Aquarius	15th	7:34 am Pisces	16th	2:59 pm Taurus
16th	6:17 pm Capricorn	18th	0:16 am Pisces	17th	8:13 pm Aries	19th	0:51 am Gemini
19th	4:14 am Aquarius	20th	12:45 pm Aries	20th	7:34 am Taurus	21st	6:45 am Cancer
21st	4:22 pm Pisces	22nd	11:39 pm Taurus	22nd	4:29 pm Gemini	23rd	8:47 am Leo
24th	4:32 am Aries	25th	7:02 am Gemini	24th	9:02 pm Cancer	25th	8:27 am Virgo
26th	2:39 pm Taurus	27th	10:56 am Cancer	26th	10:15 pm Leo	27th	7:46 am Libra
28th	9:45 pm Gemini	29th	12:30 pm Leo	28th	9:59 pm Virgo	29th	8:51 am Scorpio
31st	2:04 am Cancer			30th	10:21 pm Libra	31st	1:12 pm Sagittarius

September 1957		October 1957		November 1957		December 1957	
2nd	9:07 pm Capricorn	2nd	2:07 pm Aquarius	1st	9:20 am Pisces	1st	5:57 am Aries
5th	7:51 am Aquarius	5th	2:18 am Pisces	3rd	10:01 pm Aries	3rd	5:47 pm Taurus
7th	8:04 pm Pisces	7th	2:56 pm Aries	6th	9:36 am Taurus	6th	2:58 am Gemini
10th	8:45 am Aries	10th	2:47 am Taurus	8th	7:07 pm Gemini	8th	9:13 am Cancer
12th	8:57 pm Taurus	12th	12:58 pm Gemini	11th	2:23 am Cancer	10th	1:22 pm Leo
15th	7:23 am Gemini	14th	8:53 pm Cancer	13th	7:34 am Leo	12th	4:28 pm Virgo
17th	2:45 pm Cancer	17th	1:59 am Leo	15th	11:05 am Virgo	14th	7:23 pm Libra
19th	6:28 pm Leo	19th	4:23 am Virgo	17th	1:25 pm Libra	16th	10:36 pm Scorpio
21st	7:11 pm Virgo	21st	5:04 am Libra	19th	3:20 pm Scorpio	19th	2:33 am Sagittarius
23rd	6:35 pm Libra	23rd	5:35 am Scorpio	21st	5:55 pm Sagittarius	21st	7:52 am Capricorn
25th	6:44 pm Scorpio	25th	7:38 am Sagittarius	23rd	10:33 pm Capricorn	23rd	3:23 pm Aquarius
27th	9:30 pm Sagittarius	27th	12:48 pm Capricorn	26th	6:22 am Aquarius	26th	1:44 am Pisces
30th	4:03 am Capricorn	29th	9:35 pm Aquarius	28th	5:20 pm Pisces	28th	2:14 pm Aries
						31st	2:37 am Taurus

January 1958		February 1958		March 1958		April 1958	
2nd	12:18 pm Gemini	1st	4:38 am Cancer	2nd	6:24 am Leo	1st	5:59 am Virgo
4th	6:19 pm Cancer	3rd	7:35 am Leo	4th	7:14 pm Virgo	3rd	5:54 am Libra
6th	9:21 pm Leo	5th	8:12 am Virgo	6th	6:37 pm Libra	5th	5:19 am Scorpio
8th	10:59 pm Virgo	7th	8:28 am Libra	8th	6:38 pm Scorpio	7th	6:11 am Sagittarius
11th	0:52 am Libra	9th	10:08 am Scorpio	10th	8:59 pm Sagittarius	9th	10:07 am Capricorn
13th	4:04 am Scorpio	11th	2:16 pm Sagittarius	13th	2:38 am Capricorn	11th	5:45 pm Aquarius
15th	8:53 am Sagittarius	13th	8:57 pm Capricorn	15th	11:31 am Aquarius	14th	4:40 am Pisces
17th	3:16 pm Capricorn	16th	5:53 am Aquarius	17th	10:42 pm Pisces	16th	5:23 pm Aries
19th	11:24 pm Aquarius	18th	4:42 pm Pisces	20th	11:17 am Aries	19th	6:15 am Taurus
22nd	9:45 am Pisces	21st	5:03 am Aries	23rd	0:16 am Taurus	21st	6:01 pm Gemini
24th	10:04 pm Aries	23rd	6:05 pm Taurus	25th	12:17 pm Gemini	24th	3:44 am Cancer
27th	10:55 am Taurus	26th	5:50 am Gemini	27th	9:52 pm Cancer	26th	10:39 am Leo
29th	9:47 pm Gemini	28th	2:12 pm Cancer	30th	3:44 am Leo	28th	2:37 pm Virgo
						30th	4:05 pm Libra

May 1958		June 1958		July 1958		August 1958	
2nd	4:14 pm Scorpio	1st	2:55 am Sagittarius	2nd	7:47 pm Aquarius	1st	12:14 pm Pisces
4th	4:46 pm Sagittarius	3rd	5:26 am Capricorn	5th	3:39 am Pisces	3rd	11:14 pm Aries
6th	7:24 pm Capricorn	5th	10:40 am Aquarius	7th	3:20 pm Aries	6th	12:04 pm Taurus
9th	1:31 am Aquarius	7th	7:27 pm Pisces	10th	4:08 am Taurus	9th	0:16 am Gemini
11th	11:30 am Pisces	10th	7:22 am Aries	12th	3:43 pm Gemini	11th	9:19 am Cancer
13th	11:58 pm Aries	12th	8:12 pm Taurus	15th	0:14 am Cancer	13th	2:39 pm Leo
16th	12:48 pm Taurus	15th	7:28 am Gemini	17th	5:28 am Leo	15th	5:05 pm Virgo
19th	0:13 am Gemini	17th	3:50 pm Cancer	19th	8:41 am Virgo	17th	6:16 pm Libra
21st	9:19 am Cancer	19th	10:03 pm Leo	21st	11:12 am Libra	19th	7:50 pm Scorpio
23rd	4:11 pm Leo	22nd	2:21 am Virgo	23rd	1:58 pm Scorpio	21st	10:48 pm Sagittarius
25th	8:58 pm Virgo	24th	5:41 am Libra	25th	5:26 pm Sagittarius	24th	3:40 am Capricorn
27th	11:55 pm Libra	26th	8:30 am Scorpio	27th	9:53 pm Capricorn	26th	10:30 am Aquarius
30th	1:34 am Scorpio	28th	11:12 am Sagittarius	30th	3:54 am Aquarius	28th	7:27 pm Pisces
		30th	2:35 pm Capricorn			31st	6:36 am Aries

September 1958		October 1958		November 1958		December 1958	
2nd	7:23 pm Taurus	2nd	2:48 pm Gemini	1st	8:06 am Cancer	3rd	5:13 am Virgo
5th	8:04 am Gemini	5th	1:50 am Cancer	3rd	4:59 pm Leo	5th	9:27 am Libra
7th	6:19 pm Cancer	7th	9:46 am Leo	5th	10:44 pm Virgo	7th	11:26 am Scorpio
10th	0:41 am Leo	9th	1:46 pm Virgo	8th	1:16 am Libra	9th	12:02 pm Sagittarius
12th	3:19 am Virgo	11th	2:42 pm Libra	10th	1:30 am Scorpio	11th	12:51 pm Capricorn
14th	3:45 am Libra	13th	2:13 pm Scorpio	12th	1:04 am Sagittarius	13th	3:45 pm Aquarius
16th	3:51 am Scorpio	15th	2:13 pm Sagittarius	14th	1:57 am Capricorn	15th	10:16 pm Pisces
18th	5:19 am Sagittarius	17th	4:28 pm Capricorn	16th	5:59 am Aquarius	18th	8:50 am Aries
20th	9:17 am Capricorn	19th	10:07 pm Aquarius	18th	2:02 pm Pisces	20th	9:39 pm Taurus
22nd	4:06 pm Aquarius	22nd	7:22 am Pisces	21st	1:29 am Aries	23rd	10:07 am Gemini
25th	1:34 am Pisces	24th	7:12 pm Aries	23rd	2:31 pm Taurus	25th	8:31 pm Cancer
27th	1:08 pm Aries	27th	8:07 am Taurus	26th	2:59 am Gemini	28th	4:32 am Leo
30th	1:58 am Taurus	29th	8:49 pm Gemini	28th	1:48 pm Cancer	30th	10:38 am Virgo
				30th	10:39 pm Leo		

Moon Tables

January 1959
1st 3:19 pm Libra
3rd 6:41 pm Scorpio
5th 8:57 pm Sagittarius
7th 10:52 pm Capricorn
10th 1:54 am Aquarius
12th 7:46 am Pisces
14th 5:13 pm Aries
17th 5:34 am Taurus
19th 6:15 pm Gemini
22nd 4:45 am Cancer
24th 12:12 pm Leo
26th 5:12 pm Virgo
28th 8:55 pm Libra
31st 0:07 am Scorpio

February 1959
2nd 3:13 am Sagittarius
4th 6:31 am Capricorn
6th 10:44 am Aquarius
8th 4:55 pm Pisces
11th 1:56 am Aries
13th 1:48 pm Taurus
16th 2:40 am Gemini
18th 1:48 pm Cancer
20th 9:38 pm Leo
23rd 2:07 am Virgo
25th 4:29 am Libra
27th 6:16 am Scorpio

March 1959
1st 8:36 am Sagittarius
3rd 12:09 pm Capricorn
5th 5:19 pm Aquarius
8th 0:26 am Pisces
10th 9:57 am Aries
12th 9:37 pm Taurus
15th 10:31 am Gemini
17th 10:27 pm Cancer
20th 7:19 am Leo
22nd 12:25 pm Virgo
24th 2:25 pm Libra
26th 2:55 pm Scorpio
28th 3:35 pm Sagittarius
30th 5:53 pm Capricorn

April 1959
1st 10:43 pm Aquarius
4th 6:25 am Pisces
6th 4:37 pm Aries
9th 4:31 am Taurus
11th 5:25 pm Gemini
14th 5:46 am Cancer
16th 3:51 pm Leo
18th 10:27 pm Virgo
21st 1:20 am Libra
23rd 1:35 am Scorpio
25th 1:01 am Sagittarius
27th 1:36 am Capricorn
29th 5:01 am Aquarius

May 1959
1st 12:04 pm Pisces
3rd 10:19 pm Aries
6th 10:39 am Taurus
8th 11:34 pm Gemini
11th 11:55 am Cancer
13th 10:39 pm Leo
16th 6:34 am Virgo
18th 11:02 am Libra
20th 12:21 pm Scorpio
22nd 11:52 am Sagittarius
24th 11:29 am Capricorn
26th 1:17 pm Aquarius
28th 6:47 pm Pisces
31st 4:21 am Aries

June 1959
2nd 4:38 pm Taurus
5th 5:35 am Gemini
7th 5:43 pm Cancer
10th 4:16 am Leo
12th 12:45 pm Virgo
14th 6:38 pm Libra
16th 9:37 pm Scorpio
18th 10:14 pm Sagittarius
20th 10:02 pm Capricorn
22nd 11:02 pm Aquarius
25th 3:12 am Pisces
27th 11:34 am Aries
29th 11:12 pm Taurus

July 1959
2nd 12:04 pm Gemini
5th 0:04 am Cancer
7th 10:05 am Leo
9th 6:13 pm Virgo
12th 0:26 am Libra
14th 4:31 am Scorpio
16th 6:39 am Sagittarius
18th 7:42 am Capricorn
20th 9:09 am Aquarius
22nd 12:46 pm Pisces
24th 7:57 pm Aries
27th 6:44 am Taurus
29th 7:23 pm Gemini

August 1959
1st 7:21 am Cancer
3rd 5:06 pm Leo
6th 0:29 am Virgo
8th 5:55 am Libra
10th 9:58 am Scorpio
12th 12:57 pm Sagittarius
14th 3:19 pm Capricorn
16th 5:55 pm Aquarius
18th 10:00 pm Pisces
21st 4:54 am Aries
23rd 3:01 pm Taurus
26th 3:18 am Gemini
28th 3:30 pm Cancer
31st 1:33 am Leo

September 1959
2nd 8:27 am Virgo
4th 12:54 pm Libra
6th 3:53 pm Scorpio
8th 6:20 pm Sagittarius
10th 9:05 pm Capricorn
13th 0:44 am Aquarius
15th 5:56 am Pisces
17th 1:19 pm Aries
19th 11:11 pm Taurus
22nd 11:16 am Gemini
24th 11:50 pm Cancer
27th 10:32 am Leo
29th 6:01 pm Virgo

October 1959
1st 10:07 pm Libra
3rd 11:33 pm Scorpio
6th 0:54 am Sagittarius
8th 2:39 am Capricorn
10th 6:14 am Aquarius
12th 12:09 pm Pisces
14th 8:21 pm Aries
17th 6:40 am Taurus
19th 6:39 pm Gemini
22nd 7:21 am Cancer
24th 7:02 pm Leo
27th 3:46 am Virgo
29th 8:37 am Libra
31st 10:11 am Scorpio

November 1959
2nd 10:03 am Sagittarius
4th 10:10 am Capricorn
6th 12:19 pm Aquarius
8th 5:39 pm Pisces
11th 2:10 am Aries
13th 1:06 pm Taurus
16th 1:15 am Gemini
18th 1:55 pm Cancer
21st 2:02 am Leo
23rd 12:03 pm Virgo
25th 6:37 pm Libra
27th 9:20 pm Scorpio
29th 9:11 pm Sagittarius

December 1959
1st 8:14 pm Capricorn
3rd 8:38 pm Aquarius
6th 0:16 am Pisces
8th 8:04 am Aries
10th 6:57 pm Taurus
13th 7:25 am Gemini
15th 8:00 pm Cancer
18th 7:56 am Leo
20th 6:27 pm Virgo
23rd 2:27 am Libra
25th 6:57 am Scorpio
27th 8:13 am Sagittarius
29th 7:39 am Capricorn
31st 7:20 am Aquarius

January 1960
2nd 9:26 am Pisces
4th 3:28 pm Aries
7th 1:24 am Taurus
9th 1:46 pm Gemini
12th 2:24 am Cancer
14th 1:59 pm Leo
17th 0:04 am Virgo
19th 8:10 am Libra
21st 1:55 pm Scorpio
23rd 4:50 pm Sagittarius
25th 5:58 pm Capricorn
27th 6:21 pm Aquarius
29th 7:59 pm Pisces

February 1960
1st 0:41 am Aries
3rd 9:21 am Taurus
5th 9:01 pm Gemini
8th 9:36 am Cancer
10th 9:09 pm Leo
13th 6:33 am Virgo
15th 1:53 pm Libra
17th 7:23 pm Scorpio
19th 11:12 pm Sagittarius
22nd 1:40 am Capricorn
24th 3:34 am Aquarius
26th 6:06 am Pisces
28th 10:42 am Aries

March 1960
1st 6:22 pm Taurus
4th 5:09 am Gemini
6th 5:36 pm Cancer
9th 5:23 am Leo
11th 2:45 pm Virgo
13th 9:19 pm Libra
16th 1:37 am Scorpio
18th 4:39 am Sagittarius
20th 7:16 am Capricorn
22nd 10:12 am Aquarius
24th 2:05 pm Pisces
26th 7:31 pm Aries
29th 3:15 am Taurus
31st 1:34 pm Gemini

April 1960
3rd 1:47 am Cancer
5th 1:59 pm Leo
8th 0:04 am Virgo
10th 6:34 am Libra
12th 9:59 am Scorpio
14th 11:38 am Sagittarius
16th 1:04 pm Capricorn
18th 3:34 pm Aquarius
20th 7:57 pm Pisces
23rd 2:23 am Aries
25th 10:53 am Taurus
27th 9:16 pm Gemini
30th 9:24 am Cancer

May 1960
2nd 9:59 pm Leo
5th 8:55 am Virgo
7th 4:26 pm Libra
9th 8:05 pm Scorpio
11th 8:55 pm Sagittarius
13th 8:53 pm Capricorn
15th 9:54 pm Aquarius
18th 1:26 am Pisces
20th 7:59 am Aries
22nd 5:02 pm Taurus
25th 3:55 am Gemini
27th 4:07 pm Cancer
30th 4:50 am Leo

June 1960
1st 4:35 pm Virgo
4th 1:30 am Libra
6th 6:16 am Scorpio
8th 7:29 am Sagittarius
10th 6:50 am Capricorn
12th 6:28 am Aquarius
14th 8:24 am Pisces
16th 1:48 pm Aries
18th 10:35 pm Taurus
21st 9:48 am Gemini
23rd 10:11 pm Cancer
26th 10:50 am Leo
28th 10:52 pm Virgo

July 1960
1st 8:41 am Libra
3rd 3:02 pm Scorpio
5th 5:37 pm Sagittarius
7th 5:32 pm Capricorn
9th 4:45 pm Aquarius
11th 5:24 pm Pisces
13th 9:10 pm Aries
16th 4:51 am Taurus
18th 3:43 pm Cancer
21st 4:09 am Cancer
23rd 4:46 pm Leo
26th 4:30 am Virgo
28th 2:30 pm Libra
30th 9:53 pm Scorpio

August 1960
2nd 2:02 am Sagittarius
4th 3:24 am Capricorn
6th 3:21 am Aquarius
8th 3:43 am Pisces
10th 6:25 am Aries
12th 12:41 pm Taurus
14th 10:30 pm Gemini
17th 10:43 am Cancer
19th 11:18 pm Leo
22nd 10:39 am Virgo
24th 8:08 pm Libra
27th 3:22 am Scorpio
29th 8:16 am Sagittarius
31st 11:06 am Capricorn

29

Why Does He Say One Thing and Do Another?

September 1960	October 1960	November 1960	December 1960
2nd 12:34 pm Aquarius	1st 10:15 pm Pisces	2nd 3:28 pm Taurus	2nd 7:02 am Gemini
4th 1:53 pm Pisces	4th 1:47 am Aries	4th 11:43 pm Gemini	4th 5:53 pm Cancer
6th 4:29 pm Aries	6th 7:11 am Taurus	7th 10:27 am Cancer	7th 6:20 am Leo
8th 9:46 pm Taurus	8th 3:19 pm Gemini	9th 10:59 pm Leo	9th 7:12 pm Virgo
11th 6:33 am Gemini	11th 2:19 am Cancer	12th 11:20 am Virgo	12th 6:05 am Libra
13th 6:12 pm Cancer	13th 2:54 pm Leo	14th 9:05 pm Libra	14th 1:07 pm Scorpio
16th 6:45 am Leo	16th 2:39 am Virgo	17th 2:51 am Scorpio	16th 4:02 pm Sagittarius
18th 6:05 pm Virgo	18th 11:27 am Libra	19th 5:15 am Sagittarius	18th 4:15 pm Capricorn
21st 2:57 am Libra	20th 5:03 pm Scorpio	21st 6:03 am Capricorn	20th 3:52 pm Aquarius
23rd 9:16 am Scorpio	22nd 8:15 pm Sagittarius	23rd 7:07 am Aquarius	22nd 4:52 pm Pisces
25th 1:41 pm Sagittarius	24th 10:28 pm Capricorn	25th 9:53 am Pisces	24th 8:37 pm Aries
27th 4:53 pm Capricorn	27th 0:58 am Aquarius	27th 2:54 pm Aries	27th 3:34 am Taurus
29th 7:32 pm Aquarius	29th 4:27 am Pisces	29th 10:01 pm Taurus	29th 1:04 pm Gemini
	31st 9:13 am Aries		

January 1961	February 1961	March 1961	April 1961
1st 0:22 am Cancer	2nd 7:48 am Virgo	1st 2:11 pm Virgo	2nd 4:35 pm Scorpio
3rd 12:55 pm Leo	4th 7:25 pm Libra	4th 1:21 am Libra	4th 10:35 pm Sagittarius
6th 1:47 am Virgo	7th 4:48 am Scorpio	6th 10:21 am Scorpio	7th 2:52 am Capricorn
8th 1:26 pm Libra	9th 10:56 am Sagittarius	8th 5:01 pm Sagittarius	9th 6:02 am Aquarius
10th 10:06 pm Scorpio	11th 1:46 pm Capricorn	10th 9:18 pm Capricorn	11th 8:32 am Pisces
13th 2:38 am Sagittarius	13th 2:13 pm Aquarius	12th 11:30 pm Aquarius	13th 10:57 am Aries
15th 3:39 am Capricorn	15th 1:55 pm Pisces	15th 0:26 am Pisces	15th 2:20 pm Taurus
17th 2:56 am Aquarius	17th 2:45 pm Aries	17th 1:34 am Aries	17th 7:58 pm Gemini
19th 2:33 am Pisces	19th 6:26 pm Taurus	19th 4:28 am Taurus	20th 4:53 am Cancer
21st 4:31 am Aries	22nd 1:54 am Gemini	21st 10:38 am Gemini	22nd 4:45 pm Leo
23rd 9:57 am Taurus	24th 12:52 pm Cancer	23rd 8:24 pm Cancer	25th 5:30 am Virgo
25th 6:54 pm Gemini	27th 1:35 am Leo	26th 8:49 am Leo	27th 4:33 pm Libra
28th 6:25 am Cancer		28th 9:31 pm Virgo	30th 0:29 am Scorpio
30th 7:06 pm Leo		31st 8:19 am Libra	

May 1961	June 1961	July 1961	August 1961
2nd 5:24 am Sagittarius	2nd 5:47 am Aquarius	2nd 2:55 am Pisces	2nd 4:25 am Taurus
4th 8:40 am Capricorn	4th 7:52 pm Pisces	4th 5:16 am Aries	4th 11:06 pm Gemini
6th 11:25 am Aquarius	6th 11:25 pm Aries	6th 10:06 am Taurus	7th 8:59 am Cancer
8th 2:24 pm Pisces	9th 4:39 am Taurus	8th 5:31 pm Gemini	9th 9:01 pm Leo
10th 5:57 pm Aries	11th 11:44 am Gemini	11th 3:15 am Cancer	12th 10:01 am Virgo
12th 10:25 pm Taurus	13th 8:51 pm Cancer	13th 2:58 pm Leo	14th 10:43 pm Libra
15th 4:36 am Gemini	16th 8:17 am Leo	16th 3:54 am Virgo	17th 9:41 am Scorpio
17th 1:21 pm Cancer	18th 9:11 pm Virgo	18th 4:35 pm Libra	19th 5:40 pm Sagittarius
20th 0:45 am Leo	21st 9:29 am Libra	21st 3:01 am Scorpio	21st 10:05 pm Capricorn
22nd 1:38 pm Virgo	23rd 6:47 pm Scorpio	23rd 9:35 am Sagittarius	23rd 11:24 pm Aquarius
25th 1:17 am Libra	26th 0:05 am Sagittarius	25th 12:24 pm Capricorn	25th 11:02 pm Pisces
27th 9:30 am Scorpio	28th 1:50 am Capricorn	27th 12:40 pm Aquarius	27th 10:49 pm Aries
29th 2:08 pm Sagittarius	30th 2:18 am Aquarius	29th 12:15 pm Pisces	30th 0:37 am Taurus
31st 4:20 pm Capricorn		31st 1:01 pm Aries	

September 1961	October 1961	November 1961	December 1961
1st 5:56 am Gemini	3rd 9:44 am Leo	2nd 6:16 am Virgo	2nd 3:06 am Libra
3rd 3:04 pm Cancer	5th 10:45 pm Virgo	4th 6:40 pm Libra	4th 1:24 pm Scorpio
6th 3:01 am Leo	8th 11:01 am Libra	7th 4:37 am Scorpio	6th 8:21 pm Sagittarius
8th 4:05 pm Virgo	10th 9:19 pm Scorpio	9th 11:47 am Sagittarius	9th 0:31 am Capricorn
11th 4:32 am Libra	13th 5:19 am Sagittarius	11th 4:58 pm Capricorn	11th 3:12 am Aquarius
13th 3:21 pm Scorpio	15th 11:21 am Capricorn	13th 8:59 pm Aquarius	13th 5:42 am Pisces
15th 11:54 pm Sagittarius	17th 3:34 pm Aquarius	16th 0:19 am Pisces	15th 8:45 am Aries
18th 5:38 am Capricorn	19th 6:08 pm Pisces	18th 3:10 am Aries	17th 12:40 pm Taurus
20th 8:40 am Aquarius	21st 7:34 pm Aries	20th 6:03 am Taurus	19th 5:49 pm Gemini
22nd 9:34 am Pisces	23rd 9:07 pm Taurus	22nd 10:01 am Gemini	22nd 0:49 am Cancer
24th 9:41 am Aries	26th 0:23 am Gemini	24th 4:24 pm Cancer	24th 10:28 am Leo
26th 10:46 am Taurus	28th 7:06 am Cancer	27th 2:01 am Leo	26th 10:29 pm Virgo
28th 2:36 pm Gemini	30th 5:32 pm Leo	29th 2:24 pm Virgo	29th 11:24 am Libra
30th 10:19 pm Cancer			31st 10:40 pm Scorpio

January 1962	February 1962	March 1962	April 1962
3rd 6:19 am Sagittarius	1st 9:07 am Capricorn	1st 6:33 am Capricorn	1st 8:42 pm Pisces
5th 10:19 am Capricorn	3rd 10:56 pm Aquarius	3rd 9:47 am Aquarius	3rd 8:40 pm Aries
7th 11:58 am Aquarius	5th 10:52 pm Pisces	5th 10:14 am Pisces	5th 8:27 pm Taurus
9th 12:55 pm Pisces	7th 10:51 pm Aries	7th 9:34 am Aries	7th 10:02 pm Gemini
11th 2:37 pm Aries	10th 0:36 am Taurus	9th 9:45 am Taurus	10th 3:14 am Cancer
13th 6:05 pm Taurus	12th 5:22 am Gemini	11th 12:41 pm Gemini	12th 12:39 pm Leo
15th 11:42 pm Gemini	14th 1:24 pm Cancer	13th 7:30 pm Cancer	15th 0:57 am Virgo
18th 7:42 am Cancer	17th 0:04 am Leo	16th 5:58 am Leo	17th 1:54 pm Libra
20th 5:52 pm Leo	19th 12:28 pm Virgo	18th 6:35 pm Virgo	20th 1:37 am Scorpio
23rd 5:54 am Virgo	22nd 1:21 am Libra	21st 7:28 am Libra	22nd 11:26 am Sagittarius
25th 6:51 pm Libra	24th 1:34 pm Scorpio	23rd 7:28 pm Scorpio	24th 7:19 pm Capricorn
28th 6:50 am Scorpio	26th 11:45 pm Sagittarius	26th 5:48 am Sagittarius	27th 1:08 am Aquarius
30th 5:08 pm Sagittarius		28th 1:41 pm Capricorn	29th 4:39 am Pisces
		30th 6:41 pm Aquarius	

30

Moon Tables

May 1962
1st 6:12 am Aries
3rd 6:50 am Taurus
5th 8:21 am Gemini
7th 12:34 pm Cancer
9th 8:39 pm Leo
12th 8:12 am Virgo
14th 9:04 pm Libra
17th 8:42 am Scorpio
19th 6:01 pm Sagittarius
22nd 1:08 am Capricorn
24th 6:30 am Aquarius
26th 10:28 am Pisces
28th 1:15 pm Aries
30th 3:17 pm Taurus

June 1962
1st 5:43 pm Gemini
3rd 9:50 pm Cancer
6th 5:26 am Leo
8th 4:14 pm Virgo
11th 4:51 am Libra
13th 4:43 pm Scorpio
16th 2:03 am Sagittarius
18th 8:28 am Capricorn
20th 12:47 pm Aquarius
22nd 3:59 pm Pisces
24th 6:44 pm Aries
26th 9:35 pm Taurus
29th 1:10 am Gemini

July 1962
1st 6:23 am Cancer
3rd 2:00 pm Leo
6th 0:22 am Virgo
8th 12:48 pm Libra
11th 1:05 am Scorpio
13th 10:55 am Sagittarius
15th 5:28 pm Capricorn
17th 9:07 pm Aquarius
19th 11:00 pm Pisces
22nd 0:35 am Aries
24th 2:50 am Taurus
26th 7:00 am Gemini
28th 1:05 pm Cancer
30th 9:24 pm Leo

August 1962
2nd 7:50 am Virgo
4th 8:18 pm Libra
7th 8:54 am Scorpio
9th 7:46 pm Sagittarius
12th 3:14 am Capricorn
14th 7:03 am Aquarius
16th 8:16 am Pisces
18th 8:27 am Aries
20th 9:24 am Taurus
22nd 12:33 pm Gemini
24th 6:38 pm Cancer
27th 3:32 am Leo
29th 2:38 pm Virgo

September 1962
1st 3:02 am Libra
3rd 3:46 pm Scorpio
6th 3:25 am Sagittarius
8th 12:15 pm Capricorn
10th 5:21 pm Aquarius
12th 6:59 pm Pisces
14th 6:33 pm Aries
16th 6:04 pm Taurus
18th 7:32 pm Gemini
21st 0:26 am Cancer
23rd 9:11 am Leo
25th 8:32 pm Virgo
28th 9:09 am Libra
30th 9:49 pm Scorpio

October 1962
3rd 9:38 am Sagittarius
5th 7:32 pm Capricorn
8th 2:19 am Aquarius
10th 5:25 am Pisces
12th 5:38 am Aries
14th 4:45 am Taurus
16th 4:54 am Gemini
18th 8:10 am Cancer
20th 3:35 pm Leo
23rd 2:31 am Virgo
25th 3:13 pm Libra
28th 3:48 am Scorpio
30th 3:18 pm Sagittarius

November 1962
1st 1:17 am Capricorn
4th 8:58 am Aquarius
6th 1:47 pm Pisces
8th 3:42 pm Aries
10th 3:44 pm Taurus
12th 3:47 pm Gemini
14th 5:52 pm Cancer
16th 11:40 pm Leo
19th 9:56 am Virgo
21st 9:58 pm Libra
24th 10:30 am Scorpio
26th 9:41 pm Sagittarius
28th 6:58 am Capricorn

December 1962
1st 2:23 pm Aquarius
3rd 7:52 pm Pisces
5th 11:16 pm Aries
8th 0:59 am Taurus
10th 2:07 am Gemini
12th 4:24 am Cancer
14th 9:24 am Leo
16th 6:02 pm Virgo
19th 5:41 am Libra
21st 6:16 pm Scorpio
24th 5:29 am Sagittarius
26th 2:14 pm Capricorn
28th 8:41 pm Aquarius
31st 1:19 am Pisces

January 1963
2nd 4:47 am Aries
4th 7:34 am Taurus
6th 10:16 am Gemini
8th 1:44 pm Cancer
10th 7:03 pm Leo
13th 3:08 am Virgo
15th 2:06 pm Libra
18th 2:33 am Scorpio
20th 2:16 pm Sagittarius
22nd 11:23 pm Capricorn
25th 5:11 am Aquarius
27th 8:33 am Pisces
29th 10:43 am Aries
31st 12:56 pm Taurus

February 1963
2nd 4:06 pm Gemini
4th 8:42 pm Cancer
7th 3:08 am Leo
9th 11:39 am Virgo
11th 10:19 pm Libra
14th 10:37 am Scorpio
16th 10:54 pm Sagittarius
19th 8:54 am Capricorn
21st 3:18 pm Aquarius
23rd 6:13 pm Pisces
25th 7:04 pm Aries
27th 7:40 pm Taurus

March 1963
1st 9:40 pm Gemini
4th 2:09 am Cancer
6th 9:18 am Leo
8th 6:35 pm Virgo
11th 5:36 am Libra
13th 5:52 pm Scorpio
16th 6:26 am Sagittarius
18th 5:31 pm Capricorn
21st 1:19 am Aquarius
23rd 4:60 am Pisces
25th 5:35 am Aries
27th 4:58 am Taurus
29th 5:16 am Gemini
31st 8:18 am Cancer

April 1963
2nd 2:49 pm Leo
5th 0:22 am Virgo
7th 11:51 am Libra
10th 0:14 am Scorpio
12th 12:48 pm Sagittarius
15th 0:27 am Capricorn
17th 9:30 am Aquarius
19th 2:48 pm Pisces
21st 4:25 pm Aries
23rd 3:50 pm Taurus
25th 3:09 pm Gemini
27th 4:32 pm Cancer
29th 9:26 pm Leo

May 1963
2nd 6:16 am Virgo
4th 5:43 pm Libra
7th 6:16 am Scorpio
9th 6:43 pm Sagittarius
12th 6:13 am Capricorn
14th 3:48 pm Aquarius
16th 10:32 pm Pisces
19th 1:46 am Aries
21st 2:21 am Taurus
23rd 1:55 am Gemini
25th 2:31 am Cancer
27th 6:03 am Leo
29th 1:27 pm Virgo

June 1963
1st 0:10 am Libra
3rd 12:38 pm Scorpio
6th 1:02 am Sagittarius
8th 12:05 pm Capricorn
10th 9:22 pm Aquarius
13th 4:20 am Pisces
15th 8:44 am Aries
17th 10:53 am Taurus
19th 11:45 am Gemini
21st 12:51 pm Cancer
23rd 3:50 pm Leo
25th 9:58 pm Virgo
28th 7:43 am Libra
30th 7:48 pm Scorpio

July 1963
3rd 8:10 am Sagittarius
5th 7:02 pm Capricorn
8th 3:35 am Aquarius
10th 9:51 am Pisces
12th 2:15 pm Aries
14th 5:15 pm Taurus
16th 7:28 pm Gemini
18th 9:47 pm Cancer
21st 1:16 am Leo
23rd 7:11 am Virgo
25th 4:06 pm Libra
28th 3:38 am Scorpio
30th 4:06 pm Sagittarius

August 1963
2nd 3:11 am Capricorn
4th 11:22 am Aquarius
6th 4:44 pm Pisces
8th 8:07 pm Aries
10th 10:39 pm Taurus
13th 1:17 am Gemini
15th 4:41 am Cancer
17th 9:20 am Leo
19th 3:44 pm Virgo
22nd 0:27 am Libra
24th 11:41 am Scorpio
27th 0:14 am Sagittarius
29th 11:53 am Capricorn
31st 8:35 pm Aquarius

September 1963
3rd 1:37 am Pisces
5th 3:52 am Aries
7th 5:04 am Taurus
9th 6:49 am Gemini
11th 10:12 am Cancer
13th 3:33 pm Leo
15th 10:49 pm Virgo
18th 8:03 am Libra
20th 7:12 pm Scorpio
23rd 7:51 am Sagittarius
25th 8:15 pm Capricorn
28th 5:58 am Aquarius
30th 11:40 am Pisces

October 1963
2nd 1:44 pm Aries
4th 1:50 pm Taurus
6th 2:01 pm Gemini
8th 4:04 pm Cancer
10th 8:55 pm Leo
13th 4:36 am Virgo
15th 2:27 pm Libra
18th 1:53 am Scorpio
20th 2:33 pm Sagittarius
23rd 3:20 am Capricorn
25th 2:15 pm Aquarius
27th 9:35 pm Pisces
30th 9:39 am Aries

November 1963
1st 0:42 am Taurus
2nd 11:49 pm Gemini
5th 0:08 am Cancer
7th 3:26 am Leo
9th 10:17 am Virgo
11th 8:09 pm Libra
14th 7:57 am Scorpio
16th 8:41 am Sagittarius
19th 9:22 am Capricorn
21st 8:50 pm Aquarius
24th 5:28 am Pisces
26th 10:19 am Aries
28th 11:46 am Taurus
30th 11:15 am Gemini

December 1963
2nd 10:48 am Cancer
4th 12:26 pm Leo
6th 5:30 pm Virgo
9th 2:23 am Libra
11th 2:05 pm Scorpio
14th 2:52 am Sagittarius
16th 3:20 pm Capricorn
19th 2:28 am Aquarius
21st 11:25 am Pisces
23rd 5:37 pm Aries
25th 8:55 pm Taurus
27th 9:57 pm Gemini
29th 10:08 pm Cancer
31st 11:09 pm Leo

Why Does He Say One Thing and Do Another?

January 1964

3rd	2:49 am	Virgo
5th	10:14 am	Libra
7th	9:04 pm	Scorpio
10th	9:47 am	Sagittarius
12th	10:12 pm	Capricorn
15th	8:44 am	Aquarius
17th	5:01 pm	Pisces
19th	11:10 pm	Aries
22nd	3:23 am	Taurus
24th	6:03 am	Gemini
26th	7:52 am	Cancer
28th	9:47 am	Leo
30th	1:13 pm	Virgo

February 1964

1st	7:28 pm	Libra
4th	5:14 am	Scorpio
6th	5:34 pm	Sagittarius
9th	6:07 am	Capricorn
11th	4:35 pm	Aquarius
14th	0:07 am	Pisces
16th	5:08 am	Aries
18th	8:44 am	Taurus
20th	11:48 am	Gemini
22nd	2:50 pm	Cancer
24th	6:12 pm	Leo
26th	10:30 pm	Virgo
29th	4:49 am	Libra

March 1964

2nd	1:57 pm	Scorpio
5th	1:46 am	Sagittarius
7th	2:32 pm	Capricorn
10th	1:33 am	Aquarius
12th	9:00 am	Pisces
14th	1:11 pm	Aries
16th	3:30 pm	Taurus
18th	5:27 pm	Gemini
20th	8:13 pm	Cancer
23rd	0:16 am	Leo
25th	5:43 am	Virgo
27th	12:50 pm	Libra
29th	10:04 pm	Scorpio

April 1964

1st	9:42 am	Sagittarius
3rd	10:37 pm	Capricorn
6th	10:19 am	Aquarius
8th	6:42 pm	Pisces
10th	11:07 pm	Aries
13th	0:36 am	Taurus
15th	1:05 am	Gemini
17th	2:23 am	Cancer
19th	5:42 am	Leo
21st	11:20 am	Virgo
23rd	7:09 pm	Libra
26th	5:03 am	Scorpio
28th	4:47 pm	Sagittarius

May 1964

1st	5:42 am	Capricorn
3rd	6:04 pm	Aquarius
6th	3:40 am	Pisces
8th	9:11 am	Aries
10th	11:05 am	Taurus
12th	11:01 am	Gemini
14th	10:56 am	Cancer
16th	12:36 pm	Leo
18th	5:06 pm	Virgo
21st	0:40 am	Libra
23rd	11:01 am	Scorpio
25th	11:04 pm	Sagittarius
28th	12:00 pm	Capricorn
31st	0:32 am	Aquarius

June 1964

2nd	10:57 am	Pisces
4th	5:50 pm	Aries
6th	9:18 pm	Taurus
8th	9:49 pm	Gemini
10th	9:17 pm	Cancer
12th	9:37 pm	Leo
15th	0:27 am	Virgo
17th	6:57 am	Libra
19th	4:52 pm	Scorpio
22nd	5:05 am	Sagittarius
24th	6:01 pm	Capricorn
27th	6:20 am	Aquarius
29th	4:54 pm	Pisces

July 1964

2nd	0:52 am	Aries
4th	5:40 am	Taurus
6th	7:41 am	Gemini
8th	7:57 am	Cancer
10th	8:04 am	Leo
12th	9:49 am	Virgo
14th	2:47 pm	Libra
16th	11:33 pm	Scorpio
19th	11:30 am	Sagittarius
22nd	0:28 am	Capricorn
24th	12:28 pm	Aquarius
26th	10:36 pm	Pisces
29th	6:23 am	Aries
31st	11:57 am	Taurus

August 1964

2nd	3:27 pm	Gemini
4th	5:13 pm	Cancer
6th	6:12 pm	Leo
8th	7:52 pm	Virgo
10th	11:53 pm	Libra
13th	7:36 am	Scorpio
15th	6:45 pm	Sagittarius
18th	7:38 am	Capricorn
20th	7:37 pm	Aquarius
23rd	5:11 am	Pisces
25th	12:15 pm	Aries
27th	5:22 pm	Taurus
29th	9:17 pm	Gemini

September 1964

1st	0:15 am	Cancer
3rd	2:38 am	Leo
5th	5:15 am	Virgo
7th	9:24 am	Libra
9th	4:24 pm	Scorpio
12th	2:49 am	Sagittarius
14th	3:29 pm	Capricorn
17th	3:45 am	Aquarius
19th	1:18 pm	Pisces
21st	7:42 pm	Aries
23rd	11:46 pm	Taurus
26th	2:46 am	Gemini
28th	5:40 am	Cancer
30th	8:54 am	Leo

October 1964

2nd	12:45 pm	Virgo
4th	5:47 pm	Libra
7th	0:59 am	Scorpio
9th	11:06 am	Sagittarius
11th	11:34 pm	Capricorn
14th	12:15 pm	Aquarius
16th	10:32 pm	Pisces
19th	5:02 am	Aries
21st	8:22 am	Taurus
23rd	10:04 am	Gemini
25th	11:39 am	Cancer
27th	2:17 pm	Leo
29th	6:27 pm	Virgo

November 1964

1st	0:24 am	Libra
3rd	8:28 am	Scorpio
5th	6:46 pm	Sagittarius
8th	7:08 am	Capricorn
10th	8:09 pm	Aquarius
13th	7:26 am	Pisces
15th	3:05 pm	Aries
17th	6:55 pm	Taurus
19th	7:58 pm	Gemini
21st	8:04 pm	Cancer
23rd	9:00 pm	Leo
26th	0:02 am	Virgo
28th	5:57 am	Libra
30th	2:34 pm	Scorpio

December 1964

3rd	1:24 am	Sagittarius
5th	1:55 pm	Capricorn
8th	2:58 am	Aquarius
10th	2:57 pm	Pisces
13th	0:13 am	Aries
15th	5:29 am	Taurus
17th	7:18 am	Gemini
19th	7:02 am	Cancer
21st	6:34 am	Leo
23rd	7:46 am	Virgo
25th	12:10 pm	Libra
27th	8:12 pm	Scorpio
30th	7:22 am	Sagittarius

January 1965

1st	8:06 pm	Capricorn
4th	9:03 am	Aquarius
6th	9:05 pm	Pisces
9th	7:05 am	Aries
11th	2:05 pm	Taurus
13th	5:44 pm	Gemini
15th	6:32 pm	Cancer
17th	5:58 pm	Leo
19th	5:58 pm	Virgo
21st	8:31 pm	Libra
24th	3:03 am	Scorpio
26th	1:34 pm	Sagittarius
29th	2:21 am	Capricorn
31st	3:16 pm	Aquarius

February 1965

3rd	2:55 am	Pisces
5th	12:41 pm	Aries
7th	8:22 pm	Taurus
10th	1:36 am	Gemini
12th	4:12 am	Cancer
14th	4:53 am	Leo
16th	5:08 am	Virgo
18th	6:50 am	Libra
20th	11:51 am	Scorpio
22nd	8:58 pm	Sagittarius
25th	9:16 am	Capricorn
27th	10:13 pm	Aquarius

March 1965

2nd	9:34 am	Pisces
4th	6:43 pm	Aries
7th	1:50 am	Taurus
9th	7:12 am	Gemini
11th	11:01 am	Cancer
13th	1:22 pm	Leo
15th	2:57 pm	Virgo
17th	5:07 pm	Libra
19th	9:34 pm	Scorpio
22nd	5:39 am	Sagittarius
24th	5:09 pm	Capricorn
27th	5:56 am	Aquarius
29th	5:28 pm	Pisces

April 1965

1st	2:17 am	Aries
3rd	8:25 am	Taurus
5th	12:53 pm	Gemini
7th	4:22 pm	Cancer
9th	7:24 pm	Leo
11th	10:15 pm	Virgo
14th	1:39 am	Libra
16th	6:45 am	Scorpio
18th	2:35 pm	Sagittarius
21st	1:25 am	Capricorn
23rd	2:03 pm	Aquarius
26th	2:00 am	Pisces
28th	11:06 am	Aries
30th	4:59 pm	Taurus

May 1965

2nd	8:25 pm	Gemini
4th	10:38 pm	Cancer
7th	0:49 am	Leo
9th	3:48 am	Virgo
11th	8:05 am	Libra
13th	2:12 pm	Scorpio
15th	10:32 pm	Sagittarius
18th	9:21 am	Capricorn
20th	9:50 pm	Aquarius
23rd	10:12 am	Pisces
25th	8:16 pm	Aries
28th	2:47 am	Taurus
30th	5:56 am	Gemini

June 1965

1st	7:04 am	Cancer
3rd	7:48 am	Leo
5th	9:36 am	Virgo
7th	1:33 pm	Libra
9th	8:05 pm	Scorpio
12th	5:12 am	Sagittarius
14th	4:21 pm	Capricorn
17th	4:52 am	Aquarius
19th	5:28 pm	Pisces
22nd	4:27 am	Aries
24th	12:11 pm	Taurus
26th	4:13 pm	Gemini
28th	5:17 pm	Cancer
30th	4:50 pm	Leo

July 1965

2nd	5:14 pm	Virgo
4th	7:45 pm	Libra
7th	1:40 am	Scorpio
9th	10:56 am	Sagittarius
11th	10:30 pm	Capricorn
14th	11:07 am	Aquarius
16th	11:44 pm	Pisces
19th	11:09 am	Aries
21st	8:11 pm	Taurus
24th	1:47 am	Gemini
26th	3:52 am	Cancer
28th	3:37 am	Leo
30th	2:57 am	Virgo

August 1965

1st	3:57 am	Libra
3rd	8:26 am	Scorpio
5th	4:53 pm	Sagittarius
8th	4:23 am	Capricorn
10th	5:08 pm	Aquarius
13th	5:37 am	Pisces
15th	4:55 pm	Aries
18th	2:27 am	Taurus
20th	9:17 am	Gemini
22nd	1:00 pm	Cancer
24th	1:59 pm	Leo
26th	1:38 pm	Virgo
28th	1:57 pm	Libra
30th	4:50 pm	Scorpio

Moon Tables

September 1965
1st 11:60 pm Sagittarius
4th 10:54 am Capricorn
6th 11:34 am Aquarius
9th 11:35 am Pisces
11th 10:50 pm Aries
14th 7:54 am Taurus
16th 3:03 pm Gemini
18th 8:00 pm Cancer
20th 10:35 pm Leo
22nd 11:31 pm Virgo
25th 0:17 am Libra
27th 2:50 am Scorpio
29th 8:47 am Sagittarius

October 1965
1st 6:31 pm Capricorn
4th 6:49 am Aquarius
6th 7:12 pm Pisces
9th 5:51 am Aries
11th 2:15 pm Taurus
13th 8:39 pm Gemini
16th 1:26 am Cancer
18th 4:50 am Leo
20th 7:14 am Virgo
22nd 9:24 am Libra
24th 12:37 pm Scorpio
26th 6:14 pm Sagittarius
29th 3:09 am Capricorn
31st 2:51 pm Aquarius

November 1965
3rd 3:23 am Pisces
5th 2:19 pm Aries
7th 10:30 pm Taurus
10th 3:52 am Gemini
12th 7:28 am Cancer
14th 10:14 am Leo
16th 12:55 pm Virgo
18th 4:11 pm Libra
20th 8:39 pm Scorpio
23rd 2:59 am Sagittarius
25th 11:49 am Capricorn
27th 11:06 pm Aquarius
30th 11:40 am Pisces

December 1965
2nd 11:23 pm Aries
5th 8:07 am Taurus
7th 1:24 pm Gemini
9th 3:55 pm Cancer
11th 5:08 pm Leo
13th 6:37 pm Virgo
15th 9:34 pm Libra
18th 2:42 am Scorpio
20th 10:04 am Sagittarius
22nd 7:29 pm Capricorn
25th 6:46 am Aquarius
27th 7:18 pm Pisces
30th 7:38 am Aries

January 1966
1st 5:42 pm Taurus
4th 0:07 am Gemini
6th 2:39 am Cancer
8th 2:50 am Leo
10th 2:37 am Virgo
12th 5:57 am Libra
14th 8:13 am Scorpio
16th 3:42 pm Sagittarius
19th 1:45 am Capricorn
21st 1:27 pm Aquarius
24th 1:59 am Pisces
26th 2:32 pm Aries
29th 1:41 am Taurus
31st 9:38 am Gemini

February 1966
2nd 1:35 pm Cancer
4th 2:11 pm Leo
6th 1:13 pm Virgo
8th 12:56 pm Libra
10th 3:20 pm Scorpio
12th 9:35 pm Sagittarius
15th 7:27 am Capricorn
17th 7:26 pm Aquarius
20th 8:05 am Pisces
22nd 8:29 pm Aries
25th 7:51 am Taurus
27th 4:59 pm Gemini

March 1966
1st 10:48 pm Cancer
4th 0:56 am Leo
6th 0:36 am Virgo
7th 11:49 pm Libra
10th 0:48 am Scorpio
12th 5:22 am Sagittarius
14th 1:50 pm Capricorn
17th 1:33 am Aquarius
19th 2:18 pm Pisces
22nd 2:33 am Aries
24th 1:29 pm Taurus
26th 10:41 pm Gemini
29th 5:21 am Cancer
31st 9:08 am Leo

April 1966
2nd 10:29 am Virgo
4th 10:41 am Libra
6th 11:35 am Scorpio
8th 2:59 pm Sagittarius
10th 10:03 pm Capricorn
13th 8:44 am Aquarius
15th 9:12 pm Pisces
18th 9:25 am Aries
20th 7:57 pm Taurus
23rd 4:24 am Gemini
25th 10:45 am Cancer
27th 3:06 pm Leo
29th 5:47 pm Virgo

May 1966
1st 7:31 pm Libra
3rd 9:24 pm Scorpio
6th 0:53 am Sagittarius
8th 7:17 am Capricorn
10th 4:54 pm Aquarius
13th 4:55 am Pisces
15th 5:13 pm Aries
18th 3:45 am Taurus
20th 11:35 am Gemini
22nd 4:57 pm Cancer
24th 8:35 pm Leo
26th 11:21 pm Virgo
29th 1:59 am Libra
31st 5:12 am Scorpio

June 1966
2nd 9:41 am Sagittarius
4th 4:13 pm Capricorn
7th 1:23 am Aquarius
9th 12:58 pm Pisces
12th 1:26 am Aries
14th 12:26 pm Taurus
16th 8:23 pm Gemini
19th 1:03 am Cancer
21st 3:27 am Leo
23rd 5:08 am Virgo
25th 7:24 am Libra
27th 11:06 am Scorpio
29th 4:33 pm Sagittarius

July 1966
1st 11:51 pm Capricorn
4th 9:16 am Aquarius
6th 8:40 pm Pisces
9th 9:15 am Aries
11th 9:01 pm Taurus'
14th 5:46 am Gemini
16th 10:38 am Cancer
18th 12:24 pm Leo
20th 12:47 pm Virgo
22nd 1:41 pm Libra
24th 4:35 pm Scorpio
26th 10:06 pm Sagittarius
29th 6:06 am Capricorn
31st 4:03 pm Aquarius

August 1966
3rd 3:35 am Pisces
5th 4:14 pm Aries
8th 4:36 am Taurus
10th 2:33 pm Gemini
12th 8:38 pm Cancer
14th 10:49 pm Leo
16th 10:35 pm Virgo
18th 10:05 pm Libra
20th 11:23 pm Scorpio
23rd 3:53 am Sagittarius
25th 11:40 am Capricorn
27th 9:56 pm Aquarius
30th 9:48 am Pisces

September 1966
1st 10:27 pm Aries
4th 10:57 am Taurus
6th 9:50 pm Gemini
9th 5:23 am Cancer
11th 8:57 am Leo
13th 9:24 am Virgo
15th 8:36 am Libra
17th 8:38 am Scorpio
19th 11:27 am Sagittarius
21st 5:56 pm Capricorn
24th 3:48 am Aquarius
26th 3:48 pm Pisces
29th 4:29 am Aries

October 1966
1st 4:45 pm Taurus
4th 3:42 am Gemini
6th 12:08 pm Cancer
8th 5:21 pm Leo
10th 7:25 pm Virgo
12th 7:30 pm Libra
14th 7:24 pm Scorpio
16th 9:01 pm Sagittarius
19th 1:58 am Capricorn
21st 10:46 am Aquarius
23rd 10:21 pm Pisces
26th 11:02 am Aries
28th 11:04 pm Taurus
31st 9:25 am Gemini

November 1966
2nd 5:40 pm Cancer
4th 11:35 pm Leo
7th 3:08 am Virgo
9th 4:54 am Libra
11th 5:56 am Scorpio
13th 7:41 am Sagittarius
15th 11:43 am Capricorn
17th 7:08 pm Aquarius
20th 5:55 am Pisces
22nd 6:32 pm Aries
25th 6:35 am Taurus
27th 4:28 pm Gemini
29th 11:49 pm Cancer

December 1966
2nd 4:59 am Leo
4th 8:46 am Virgo
6th 11:42 am Libra
8th 2:18 pm Scorpio
10th 5:15 pm Sagittarius
12th 9:34 pm Capricorn
15th 4:23 am Aquarius
17th 2:22 pm Pisces
20th 2:40 am Aries
22nd 3:06 pm Taurus
25th 1:14 am Gemini
27th 7:55 am Cancer
29th 11:55 am Leo
31st 2:33 pm Virgo

January 1967
2nd 5:04 pm Libra
4th 8:17 pm Scorpio
7th 0:28 am Sagittarius
9th 5:55 am Capricorn
11th 1:10 pm Aquarius
13th 10:46 pm Pisces
16th 10:49 am Aries
18th 11:40 pm Taurus
21st 10:34 am Gemini
23rd 5:48 pm Cancer
25th 9:20 pm Leo
27th 10:37 pm Virgo
29th 11:34 pm Libra

February 1967
1st 1:45 am Scorpio
3rd 5:58 am Sagittarius
5th 12:14 pm Capricorn
7th 8:19 pm Aquarius
10th 6:21 am Pisces
12th 6:19 pm Aries
15th 7:18 am Taurus
17th 7:13 pm Gemini
20th 3:46 am Cancer
22nd 8:01 am Leo
24th 9:03 am Virgo
26th 8:47 am Libra
28th 9:14 am Scorpio

March 1967
2nd 11:58 am Sagittarius
4th 5:38 pm Capricorn
7th 2:04 am Aquarius
9th 12:44 pm Pisces
12th 0:53 am Aries
14th 1:54 pm Taurus
17th 2:18 am Gemini
19th 12:06 pm Cancer
21st 6:01 pm Leo
23rd 8:06 pm Virgo
25th 7:49 pm Libra
27th 7:13 pm Scorpio
29th 8:11 pm Sagittarius

April 1967
1st 0:11 am Capricorn
3rd 7:52 am Aquarius
5th 6:30 pm Pisces
8th 6:56 am Aries
10th 7:54 pm Taurus
13th 8:12 am Gemini
15th 6:33 pm Cancer
18th 1:53 am Leo
20th 5:39 am Virgo
22nd 6:39 am Libra
24th 6:20 am Scorpio
26th 6:31 am Sagittarius
28th 8:59 am Capricorn
30th 3:02 pm Aquarius

Why Does He Say One Thing and Do Another?

May 1967
3rd   0:48 am Pisces
5th   1:10 pm Aries
8th   2:09 am Taurus
10th 2:03 pm Gemini
13th 0:09 am Cancer
15th 7:46 am Leo
17th 12:48 pm Virgo
19th 3:27 pm Libra
21st 4:29 pm Scorpio
23rd 5:08 pm Sagittarius
25th 7:01 pm Capricorn
27th 11:46 pm Aquarius
30th 8:22 am Pisces

June 1967
1st   8:08 pm Aries
4th   9:03 am Taurus
6th   8:49 pm Gemini
9th   6:14 am Cancer
11th 1:16 pm Leo
13th 6:21 pm Virgo
15th 9:57 pm Libra
18th 0:25 am Scorpio
20th 2:20 am Sagittarius
22nd 4:48 am Capricorn
24th 9:15 am Aquarius
26th 4:53 pm Pisces
29th 3:54 am Aries

July 1967
1st   4:42 pm Taurus
4th   4:36 am Gemini
6th   1:42 pm Cancer
8th   7:56 pm Leo
11th 0:07 am Virgo
13th 3:19 am Libra
15th 6:17 am Scorpio
17th 9:23 am Sagittarius
19th 12:50 pm Capricorn
21st 6:01 pm Aquarius
24th 1:28 am Pisces
26th 12:02 pm Aries
29th 0:41 am Taurus
31st 12:56 pm Gemini

August 1967
2nd   10:30 pm Cancer
5th   4:23 am Leo
7th   7:34 am Virgo
9th   9:34 am Libra
11th 11:45 am Scorpio
13th 2:54 pm Sagittarius
15th 7:19 pm Capricorn
18th 1:17 am Aquarius
20th 9:20 am Pisces
22nd 7:48 pm Aries
25th 8:21 am Taurus
27th 9:07 pm Gemini
30th 7:30 am Cancer

September 1967
1st   2:02 pm Leo
3rd   5:04 pm Virgo
5th   6:02 pm Libra
7th   6:45 pm Scorpio
9th   8:41 pm Sagittarius
12th 0:43 am Capricorn
14th 7:10 am Aquarius
16th 3:55 pm Pisces
19th 2:46 am Aries
21st 3:19 pm Taurus
24th 4:19 am Gemini
26th 3:42 pm Cancer
28th 11:42 pm Leo .

October 1967
1st• 3:37 am Virgo
3rd   4:34 am Libra
5th   4:15 am Scorpio
7th   4:34 am Sagittarius
9th   7:08 am Capricorn
11th 12:49 pm Aquarius
13th 9:39 pm Pisces
16th 8:58 am Aries
18th 9:40 pm Taurus
21st 10:36 am Gemini
23rd 10:27 pm Cancer
26th 7:36 am Leo
28th 1:14 pm Virgo
30th 3:27 pm Libra

November 1967
1st   3:26 pm Scorpio
3rd   2:54 pm Sagittarius
5th   3:50 pm Capricorn
7th   7:49 pm Aquarius
10th 3:45 am Pisces
12th 3:01 pm Aries
15th 3:52 am Taurus
17th 4:39 pm Gemini
20th 4:11 am Cancer
22nd 1:43 pm Leo
24th 8:44 pm Virgo
27th 0:48 am Libra
29th 2:13 am Scorpio

December 1967
1st   2:11 am Sagittarius
3rd   2:27 am Capricorn
5th   5:03 am Aquarius
7th   11:26 am Pisces
9th   9:45 pm Aries
12th 10:32 am Taurus
14th 11:18 pm Gemini
17th 10:20 am Cancer
19th 7:19 pm Leo
22nd 2:00 am Virgo
24th 7:21 am Libra
26th 10:34 am Scorpio
28th 12:08 pm Sagittarius
30th 1:14 pm Capricorn

January 1968
1st   3:29 pm Aquarius
3rd   8:40 pm Pisces
6th   5:50 am Aries
8th   6:05 pm Taurus
11th 6:54 am Gemini
13th 5:51 pm Cancer
16th 2:09 am Leo
18th 8:10 am Virgo
20th 12:46 pm Libra
22nd 4:27 pm Scorpio
24th 7:25 pm Sagittarius
26th 9:57 pm Capricorn
29th 1:08 am Aquarius
31st 6:21 am Pisces

February 1968
2nd   2:44 pm Aries
5th   2:16 am Taurus
7th   3:08 pm Gemini
10th 2:33 am Cancer
12th 10:47 am Leo
14th 4:01 pm Virgo
16th 7:22 pm Libra
18th 10:00 pm Scorpio
21st 0:49 am Sagittarius
23rd 4:13 am Capricorn
25th 8:40 am Aquarius
27th 2:46 pm Pisces
29th 11:16 pm Aries

March 1968
3rd   10:29 am Taurus
5th   11:17 pm Gemini
8th   11:18 am Cancer
10th 8:26 pm Leo
13th 1:51 am Virgo
15th 4:23 am Libra
17th 5:34 am Scorpio
19th 6:57 am Sagittarius
21st 9:39 am Capricorn
23rd 2:20 pm Aquarius
25th 9:16 pm Pisces
28th 6:34 am Aries
30th 5:55 pm Taurus

April 1968
2nd   6:41 am Gemini
4th   7:12 pm Cancer
7th   5:25 am Leo
9th   12:00 pm Virgo
11th 2:58 pm Libra
13th 3:32 pm Scorpio
15th 3:26 pm Sagittarius
17th 4:28 pm Capricorn
19th 7:50 pm Aquarius
22nd 2:47 am Pisces
24th 12:34 pm Aries
27th 0:22 am Taurus
29th 1:10 pm Gemini

May 1968
2nd   1:50 am Cancer
4th   12:50 pm Leo
6th   8:57 pm Virgo
9th   1:20 am Libra
11th 2:29 am Scorpio
13th 1:54 am Sagittarius
15th 1:33 am Capricorn
17th 3:27 am Aquarius
19th 8:59 am Pisces
21st 6:18 pm Aries
24th 6:17 am Taurus
26th 7:12 pm Gemini
29th 7:41 am Cancer
31st 6:52 pm Leo

June 1968
3rd   3:50 am Virgo
5th   9:44 am Libra
7th   12:25 pm Scorpio
9th   12:40 pm Sagittarius
11th 12:09 pm Capricorn
13th 12:53 pm Aquarius
15th 4:49 pm Pisces
18th 0:51 am Aries
20th 12:27 pm Taurus
23rd 1:23 am Gemini
25th 1:41 pm Cancer
28th 0:31 am Leo
30th 9:22 am Virgo

July 1968
2nd   4:06 pm Libra
4th   8:18 pm Scorpio
6th   10:04 pm Sagittarius
8th   10:24 pm Capricorn
10th 11:04 pm Aquarius
13th 2:05 am Pisces
15th 8:57 am Aries
17th 7:33 pm Taurus
20th 8:13 am Gemini
22nd 8:31 pm Cancer
25th 6:53 am Leo
27th 3:07 pm Virgo
29th 9:31 pm Libra

August 1968
1st   2:10 am Scorpio
3rd   5:09 am Sagittarius
5th   6:57 am Capricorn
7th   8:39 am Aquarius
9th   11:50 am Pisces
11th 5:57 pm Aries
14th 3:37 am Taurus
16th 3:52 pm Gemini
19th 4:13 am Cancer
21st 2:36 pm Leo
23rd 10:19 pm Virgo
26th 3:43 am Libra
28th 7:37 am Scorpio
30th 10:40 am Sagittarius

September 1968
1st   1:22 pm Capricorn
3rd   4:30 pm Aquarius
5th   8:29 pm Pisces
8th   2:51 am Aries
10th 12:08 pm Taurus
12th 11:54 pm Gemini
15th 12:27 pm Cancer
17th 11:25 pm Leo
20th 7:11 am Virgo
22nd 11:57 am Libra
24th 2:37 pm Scorpio
26th 4:31 pm Sagittarius
28th 6:46 pm Capricorn
30th 10:11 pm Aquarius

October 1968
3rd   3:22 am Pisces
5th   10:37 am Aries
7th   8:07 pm Taurus
10th 7:44 am Gemini
12th 8:24 pm Cancer
15th 8:05 am Leo
17th 4:54 pm Virgo
19th 10:04 pm Libra
22nd 0:06 am Scorpio
24th 0:32 am Sagittarius
26th 1:15 am Capricorn
28th 3:45 am Aquarius
30th 8:58 am Pisces

November 1968
1st   4:53 pm Aries
4th   3:02 am Taurus
6th   2:48 pm Gemini
9th   3:26 am Cancer
11th 3:43 pm Leo
14th 1:53 am Virgo
16th 8:21 am Libra
18th 11:01 am Scorpio
20th 11:03 am Sagittarius
22nd 10:24 am Capricorn
24th 11:08 am Aquarius
26th 2:58 pm Pisces
28th 10:27 pm Aries

December 1968
1st   9:00 am Taurus
3rd   9:05 pm Gemini
6th   9:42 am Cancer
8th   10:02 pm Leo
11th 8:54 am Virgo
13th 5:04 pm Libra
15th 9:30 pm Scorpio
17th 10:27 pm Sagittarius
19th 9:33 pm Capricorn
21st 9:03 pm Aquarius
23rd 11:02 pm Pisces
26th 5:08 am Aries
28th 3:01 pm Taurus
31st 3:12 am Gemini

Moon Tables

January 1969
2nd 3:52 pm Cancer
5th 3:53 am Leo
7th 2:39 pm Virgo
9th 11:32 pm Libra
12th 5:29 am Scorpio
14th 8:15 am Sagittarius
16th 8:38 am Capricorn
18th 8:20 am Aquarius
20th 9:27 am Pisces
22nd 1:50 pm Aries
24th 10:16 pm Taurus
27th 9:56 am Gemini
29th 10:37 pm Cancer

February 1969
1st 10:28 am Leo
3rd 8:41 pm Virgo
6th 4:59 am Libra
8th 11:16 am Scorpio
10th 3:20 pm Sagittarius
12th 5:27 pm Capricorn
14th 6:32 pm Aquarius
16th 8:05 pm Pisces
18th 11:49 pm Aries
21st 7:06 am Taurus
23rd 5:44 pm Gemini
26th 6:12 am Cancer
28th 6:12 pm Leo

March 1969
3rd 4:06 am Virgo
5th 11:32 am Libra
7th 4:55 pm Scorpio
9th 8:48 pm Sagittarius
11th 11:41 pm Capricorn
14th 2:10 am Aquarius
16th 5:07 am Pisces
18th 9:32 am Aries
20th 4:24 pm Taurus
23rd 2:13 am Gemini
25th 2:18 pm Cancer
28th 2:36 am Leo
30th 12:51 pm Virgo

April 1969
1st 8:02 pm Libra
4th 0:24 am Scorpio
6th 2:59 am Sagittarius
8th 5:05 am Capricorn
10th 7:49 am Aquarius
12th 11:44 am Pisces
14th 5:15 pm Aries
17th 0:44 am Taurus
19th 10:31 am Gemini
21st 10:17 pm Cancer
24th 10:50 am Leo
26th 9:56 pm Virgo
29th 5:42 am Libra

May 1969
1st 9:46 am Scorpio
3rd 11:18 am Sagittarius
5th 11:00 am Capricorn
7th 1:32 pm Aquarius
9th 5:08 pm Pisces
11th 11:09 pm Aries
14th 7:30 am Taurus
16th 5:43 pm Gemini
19th 5:31 am Cancer
21st 6:12 pm Leo
24th 6:04 am Virgo
26th 3:02 pm Libra
28th 8:03 pm Scorpio
30th 9:29 pm Sagittarius

June 1969
1st 9:08 pm Capricorn
3rd 9:07 pm Aquarius
5th 11:16 pm Pisces
8th 4:41 am Aries
10th 1:10 pm Taurus
12th 11:48 pm Gemini
15th 11:54 am Cancer
18th 0:34 am Leo
20th 12:51 pm Virgo
22nd 11:03 pm Libra
25th 5:27 am Scorpio
27th 7:55 am Sagittarius
29th 7:44 am Capricorn

July 1969
1st 6:53 am Aquarius
3rd 7:33 am Pisces
5th 11:23 am Aries
7th 6:58 pm Taurus
10th 5:33 am Gemini
12th 5:48 pm Cancer
15th 6:29 am Leo
17th 6:41 pm Virgo
20th 5:16 am Libra
22nd 12:58 pm Scorpio
24th 5:05 pm Sagittarius
26th 6:06 pm Capricorn
28th 5:35 pm Aquarius
30th 5:34 pm Pisces

August 1969
1st 7:58 pm Aries
4th 2:05 am Taurus
6th 11:53 am Gemini
8th 11:58 pm Cancer
11th 12:38 pm Leo
14th 0:33 am Virgo
16th 10:48 am Libra
18th 6:52 pm Scorpio
21st 0:12 am Sagittarius
23rd 2:47 am Capricorn
25th 3:36 am Aquarius
27th 4:04 am Pisces
29th 6:01 am Aries
31st 10:55 am Taurus

September 1969
2nd 7:26 pm Gemini
5th 6:57 am Cancer
7th 7:35 pm Leo
10th 7:18 am Virgo
12th 4:50 pm Libra
15th 0:25 am Scorpio
17th 5:40 am Sagittarius
19th 9:12 am Capricorn
21st 11:30 am Aquarius
23rd 1:23 pm Pisces
25th 3:57 pm Aries
27th 8:30 pm Taurus
30th 4:08 am Gemini

October 1969
2nd 2:55 pm Cancer
5th 3:24 am Leo
7th 3:19 pm Virgo
10th 0:48 am Libra
12th 7:16 am Scorpio
14th 11:32 am Sagittarius
16th 2:35 pm Capricorn
18th 5:22 pm Aquarius
20th 8:26 pm Pisces
23rd 0:18 am Aries
25th 5:34 am Taurus
27th 1:03 pm Gemini
29th 11:13 pm Cancer

November 1969
1st 11:35 am Leo
3rd 12:00 pm Virgo
6th 9:54 am Libra
8th 4:13 pm Scorpio
10th 7:28 pm Sagittarius
12th 9:09 pm Capricorn
14th 10:53 pm Aquarius
17th 1:53 am Pisces
19th 6:34 am Aries
21st 12:54 pm Taurus
23rd 9:00 pm Gemini
26th 7:12 am Cancer
28th 7:23 pm Leo

December 1969
1st 8:11 am Virgo
3rd 7:13 pm Libra
6th 2:28 am Scorpio
8th 5:40 am Sagittarius
10th 6:21 am Capricorn
12th 6:30 am Aquarius
14th 8:00 am Pisces
16th 12:01 pm Aries
18th 6:38 pm Taurus
21st 3:29 am Gemini
23rd 2:11 pm Cancer
26th 2:22 am Leo
28th 3:19 pm Virgo
31st 3:16 am Libra

January 1970
2nd 11:56 am Scorpio
4th 4:28 pm Sagittarius
6th 5:27 pm Capricorn
8th 4:49 pm Aquarius
10th 4:42 pm Pisces
12th 6:52 pm Aries
15th 0:22 am Taurus
17th 9:11 am Gemini
19th 8:15 pm Cancer
22nd 8:41 am Leo
24th 9:32 pm Virgo
27th 9:40 am Libra
29th 7:32 pm Scorpio

February 1970
1st 1:48 am Sagittarius
3rd 4:19 am Capricorn
5th 4:18 am Aquarius
7th 3:39 am Pisces
9th 4:21 am Aries
11th 8:05 am Taurus
13th 3:34 pm Gemini
16th 2:19 am Cancer
18th 2:56 pm Leo
21st 3:43 am Virgo
23rd 3:28 pm Libra
26th 1:22 am Scorpio
28th 8:35 am Sagittarius

March 1970
2nd 12:50 pm Capricorn
4th 2:32 pm Aquarius
6th 2:49 pm Pisces
8th 3:20 pm Aries
10th 5:48 pm Taurus
12th 11:38 pm Gemini
15th 9:23 am Cancer
17th 9:40 pm Leo
20th 10:29 am Virgo
22nd 9:57 pm Libra
25th 7:08 am Scorpio
27th 2:05 pm Sagittarius
29th 6:59 pm Capricorn
31st 10:08 pm Aquarius

April 1970
3rd 0:02 am Pisces
5th 1:33 am Aries
7th 4:04 am Taurus
9th 9:07 am Gemini
11th 5:37 pm Cancer
14th 5:16 am Leo
16th 6:08 pm Virgo
19th 5:33 am Libra
21st 2:13 pm Scorpio
23rd 8:15 pm Sagittarius
26th 0:27 am Capricorn
28th 3:43 am Aquarius
30th 6:38 am Pisces

May 1970
2nd 9:34 am Aries
4th 1:08 pm Taurus
6th 6:21 pm Gemini
9th 2:20 am Cancer
11th 1:25 pm Leo
14th 2:11 am Virgo
16th 2:00 pm Libra
18th 10:49 pm Scorpio
21st 4:10 am Sagittarius
23rd 7:13 am Capricorn
25th 9:28 am Aquarius
27th 12:02 pm Pisces
29th 3:29 am Aries
31st 8:05 pm Taurus

June 1970
3rd 2:11 am Gemini
5th 10:30 am Cancer
7th 9:19 pm Leo
10th 10:02 am Virgo
12th 10:28 pm Libra
15th 7:58 am Scorpio
17th 1:35 pm Sagittarius
19th 4:03 pm Capricorn
21st 5:02 pm Aquarius
23rd 6:14 pm Pisces
25th 8:55 pm Aries
28th 1:37 am Taurus
30th 8:28 am Gemini

July 1970
2nd 5:25 pm Cancer
5th 4:27 am Leo
7th 5:11 pm Virgo
10th 6:01 am Libra
12th 4:36 pm Scorpio
14th 11:24 pm Sagittarius
17th 2:19 am Capricorn
19th 2:45 am Aquarius
21st 2:39 am Pisces
23rd 3:46 am Aries
25th 7:24 am Taurus
27th 1:58 pm Gemini
29th 11:15 pm Cancer

August 1970
1st 10:48 am Leo
3rd 11:36 pm Virgo
6th 12:30 pm Libra
8th 11:56 pm Scorpio
11th 8:02 am Sagittarius
13th 12:19 pm Capricorn
15th 1:28 pm Aquarius
17th 1:02 pm Pisces
19th 12:54 pm Aries
21st 2:51 pm Taurus
23rd 8:07 pm Gemini
26th 5:00 am Cancer
28th 4:40 pm Leo
31st 5:38 am Virgo

Why Does He Say One Thing and Do Another?

September 1970
2nd 6:25 pm Libra
5th 5:53 am Scorpio
7th 2:54 pm Sagittarius
9th 8:48 pm Capricorn
11th 11:33 pm Aquarius
13th 11:57 pm Pisces
15th 11:35 pm Aries
18th 0:20 am Taurus
20th 4:06 am Gemini
22nd 11:46 am Cancer
24th 10:54 pm Leo
27th 11:54 am Virgo
30th 0:34 am Libra

October 1970
2nd 11:34 am Scorpio
4th 8:31 pm Sagittarius
7th 3:09 am Capricorn
9th 7:23 am Aquarius
11th 9:28 am Pisces
13th 10:12 am Aries
15th 11:02 am Taurus
17th 1:48 pm Gemini
19th 8:02 pm Cancer
22nd 6:15 am Leo
24th 6:57 pm Virgo
27th 7:35 am Libra
29th 6:12 pm Scorpio

November 1970
1st 2:24 am Sagittarius
3rd 8:31 am Capricorn
5th 1:08 pm Aquarius
7th 4:31 pm Pisces
9th 6:51 pm Aries
11th 8:50 pm Taurus
13th 11:48 pm Gemini
16th 5:26 am Cancer
18th 2:39 pm Leo
21st 2:51 am Virgo
23rd 3:38 pm Libra
26th 2:23 am Scorpio
28th 9:58 am Sagittarius
30th 3:04 pm Capricorn

December 1970
2nd 6:43 pm Aquarius
4th 9:56 pm Pisces
7th 1:03 am Aries
9th 4:26 am Taurus
11th 8:36 am Gemini
13th 2:36 pm Cancer
15th 11:21 pm Leo
18th 11:06 am Virgo
21st 0:02 am Libra
23rd 11:22 am Scorpio
25th 7:23 pm Sagittarius
28th 0:02 am Capricorn
30th 2:24 am Aquarius

January 1971
1st 4:08 am Pisces
3rd 6:29 am Aries
5th 10:04 am Taurus
7th 3:11 pm Gemini
9th 10:11 pm Cancer
12th 7:27 am Leo
14th 6:58 pm Virgo
17th 7:51 am Libra
19th 8:01 pm Scorpio
22nd 5:10 am Sagittarius
24th 10:27 am Capricorn
26th 12:33 pm Aquarius
28th 1:02 pm Pisces
30th 1:39 pm Aries

February 1971
1st 3:54 pm Taurus
3rd 8:38 pm Gemini
6th 4:10 am Cancer
8th 2:10 pm Leo
11th 1:59 am Virgo
13th 2:51 pm Libra
16th 3:20 am Scorpio
18th 1:40 pm Sagittarius
20th 8:33 pm Capricorn
22nd 11:43 pm Aquarius
25th 0:05 am Pisces
26th 11:30 pm Aries
28th 11:55 pm Taurus

March 1971
3rd 3:05 am Gemini
5th 9:52 am Cancer
7th 7:48 pm Leo
10th 8:13 am Virgo
12th 9:07 pm Libra
15th 9:30 am Scorpio
17th 8:23 pm Sagittarius
20th 4:34 am Capricorn
22nd 9:24 am Aquarius
24th 11:04 am Pisces
26th 10:45 am Aries
28th 10:19 am Taurus
30th 11:50 am Gemini

April 1971
1st 4:56 pm Cancer
4th 2:07 am Leo
6th 2:19 pm Virgo
9th 3:18 am Libra
11th 3:28 pm Scorpio
14th 2:04 am Sagittarius
16th 10:35 am Capricorn
18th 4:44 pm Aquarius
20th 8:06 pm Pisces
22nd 9:09 pm Aries
24th 9:07 pm Taurus
26th 10:01 pm Gemini
29th 1:45 am Cancer

May 1971
1st 9:40 am Leo
3rd 9:05 pm Virgo
6th 9:59 am Libra
8th 10:05 pm Scorpio
11th 8:07 am Sagittarius
13th 4:09 pm Capricorn
15th 10:20 pm Aquarius
18th 2:40 am Pisces
20th 5:11 am Aries
22nd 6:32 am Taurus
24th 8:05 am Gemini
26th 11:33 am Cancer
28th 6:20 pm Leo
31st 4:51 am Virgo

June 1971
2nd 5:27 pm Libra
5th 5:35 am Scorpio
7th 3:26 pm Sagittarius
9th 10:45 pm Capricorn
12th 4:03 am Aquarius
14th 8:02 am Pisces
16th 11:06 am Aries
18th 1:40 pm Taurus
20th 4:27 am Gemini
22nd 8:34 pm Cancer
25th 3:15 am Leo
27th 1:10 pm Virgo
30th 1:23 am Libra

July 1971
2nd 1:43 pm Scorpio
4th 11:60 pm Sagittarius
7th 7:01 am Capricorn
9th 11:25 am Aquarius
11th 2:15 pm Pisces
13th 4:35 pm Aries
15th 7:13 pm Taurus
17th 10:49 pm Gemini
20th 3:50 am Cancer
22nd 11:21 am Leo
24th 9:12 pm Virgo
27th 9:13 am Libra
29th 9:49 pm Scorpio

August 1971
1st 8:45 am Sagittarius
3rd 4:28 pm Capricorn
5th 8:45 pm Aquarius
7th 10:35 pm Pisces
9th 11:27 pm Aries
12th 0:57 am Taurus
14th 4:15 am Gemini
16th 9:54 am Cancer
18th 6:02 pm Leo
21st 4:22 am Virgo
23rd 4:24 pm Libra
26th 5:09 am Scorpio
28th 4:24 pm Sagittarius
31st 1:52 am Capricorn

September 1971
2nd 6:59 am Aquarius
4th 8:48 am Pisces
6th 8:44 am Aries
8th 8:41 am Taurus
10th 10:31 am Gemini
12th 3:26 pm Cancer
14th 11:39 pm Leo
17th 10:32 am Virgo
19th 10:49 pm Libra
22nd 11:34 am Scorpio
24th 11:44 pm Sagittarius
27th 9:49 am Capricorn
29th 4:34 pm Aquarius

October 1971
1st 7:33 pm Pisces
3rd 7:39 pm Aries
5th 6:44 pm Taurus
7th 6:56 pm Gemini
9th 10:12 pm Cancer
12th 5:34 am Leo
14th 4:18 pm Virgo
17th 4:48 am Libra
19th 5:31 pm Scorpio
22nd 5:32 am Sagittarius
24th 4:03 pm Capricorn
27th 0:11 am Aquarius
29th 4:53 am Pisces
31st 6:24 am Aries

November 1971
2nd 5:56 am Taurus
4th 5:31 am Gemini
6th 7:20 am Cancer
8th 1:02 pm Leo
10th 10:45 pm Virgo
13th 11:05 am Libra
15th 11:50 pm Scorpio
18th 11:28 am Sagittarius
20th 9:36 pm Capricorn
23rd 5:30 am Aquarius
25th 11:44 am Pisces
27th 2:50 pm Aries
29th 4:06 pm Taurus

December 1971
1st 4:26 pm Gemini
3rd 5:55 pm Cancer
5th 10:18 pm Leo
8th 6:44 am Virgo
10th 6:21 pm Libra
13th 7:00 am Scorpio
15th 6:35 pm Sagittarius
18th 4:05 am Capricorn
20th 11:30 am Aquarius
22nd 5:09 pm Pisces
24th 9:08 pm Aries
26th 11:45 pm Taurus
29th 1:58 am Gemini
31st 4:03 am Cancer

January 1972
2nd 8:26 am Leo
4th 3:54 pm Virgo
7th 2:34 am Libra
9th 3:03 pm Scorpio
12th 2:55 am Sagittarius
14th 12:51 pm Capricorn
16th 7:01 pm Aquarius
18th 11:27 pm Pisces
21st 2:36 am Aries
23rd 5:18 am Taurus
25th 8:16 am Gemini
27th 12:05 pm Cancer
29th 5:25 pm Leo

February 1972
1st 0:56 am Virgo
3rd 11:09 am Libra
5th 11:18 pm Scorpio
8th 11:33 am Sagittarius
10th 9:48 pm Capricorn
13th 4:33 am Aquarius
15th 8:07 am Pisces
17th 9:51 am Aries
19th 11:14 am Taurus
21st 1:39 pm Gemini
23rd 5:56 pm Cancer
26th 0:17 am Leo
28th 8:43 am Virgo

March 1972
1st 7:03 pm Libra
4th 7:02 am Scorpio
7th 7:36 pm Sagittarius
9th 6:46 am Capricorn
11th 2:37 pm Aquarius
13th 6:36 pm Pisces
15th 7:35 pm Aries
17th 7:29 pm Taurus
19th 8:15 pm Gemini
21st 11:27 pm Cancer
24th 5:50 am Leo
26th 2:51 pm Virgo
29th 1:44 am Libra
31st 1:52 pm Scorpio

April 1972
3rd 2:29 am Sagittarius
5th 2:18 pm Capricorn
7th 11:37 pm Aquarius
10th 4:54 am Pisces
12th 6:30 am Aries
14th 5:55 am Taurus
16th 5:20 am Gemini
18th 6:50 am Cancer
20th 11:53 am Leo
22nd 8:26 pm Virgo
25th 7:36 am Libra
27th 7:58 pm Scorpio
30th 8:32 am Sagittarius

Moon Tables

May 1972
- 2nd 8:29 pm Capricorn
- 5th 6:32 am Aquarius
- 7th 1:23 pm Pisces
- 9th 4:31 pm Aries
- 11th 4:46 pm Taurus
- 13th 3:59 pm Gemini
- 15th 4:21 pm Cancer
- 17th 7:42 pm Leo
- 20th 2:59 am Virgo
- 22nd 1:40 pm Libra
- 25th 2:01 am Scorpio
- 27th 2:34 pm Sagittarius
- 30th 2:13 am Capricorn

June 1972
- 1st 12:13 pm Aquarius
- 3rd 7:51 pm Pisces
- 6th 0:29 am Aries
- 8th 2:14 am Taurus
- 10th 2:26 am Gemini
- 12th 2:48 am Cancer
- 14th 5:15 am Leo
- 16th 11:09 am Virgo
- 18th 8:40 pm Libra
- 21st 8:44 am Scorpio
- 23rd 9:15 pm Sagittarius
- 26th 8:35 am Capricorn
- 28th 6:01 pm Aquarius

July 1972
- 1st 1:19 am Pisces
- 3rd 6:21 am Aries
- 5th 9:24 am Taurus
- 7th 11:06 am Gemini
- 9th 12:33 pm Cancer
- 11th 3:11 pm Leo
- 13th 8:19 pm Virgo
- 16th 4:53 am Libra
- 18th 4:16 pm Scorpio
- 21st 4:46 am Sagittarius
- 23rd 4:08 pm Capricorn
- 26th 1:08 am Aquarius
- 28th 7:28 am Pisces
- 30th 11:51 am Aries

August 1972
- 1st 2:59 pm Taurus
- 3rd 5:36 pm Gemini
- 5th 8:21 pm Cancer
- 7th 11:58 pm Leo
- 10th 5:27 am Virgo
- 12th 1:32 pm Libra
- 15th 0:20 am Scorpio
- 17th 12:48 pm Sagittarius
- 20th 0:39 am Capricorn
- 22nd 9:38 am Aquarius
- 24th 3:26 pm Pisces
- 26th 6:40 pm Aries
- 28th 8:45 pm Taurus
- 30th 10:58 pm Gemini

September 1972
- 2nd 2:14 am Cancer
- 4th 6:57 am Leo
- 6th 1:19 pm Virgo
- 8th 9:39 pm Libra
- 11th 8:19 am Scorpio
- 13th 8:44 pm Sagittarius
- 16th 9:05 am Capricorn
- 18th 7:02 pm Aquarius
- 21st 1:09 am Pisces
- 23rd 3:44 am Aries
- 25th 4:28 am Taurus
- 27th 5:17 am Gemini
- 29th 7:42 am Cancer

October 1972
- 1st 12:30 pm Leo
- 3rd 7:34 pm Virgo
- 6th 4:38 am Libra
- 8th 3:31 pm Scorpio
- 11th 3:54 am Sagittarius
- 13th 4:44 pm Capricorn
- 16th 3:49 am Aquarius
- 18th 11:07 am Pisces
- 20th 2:18 pm Aries
- 22nd 2:36 pm Taurus
- 24th 2:06 pm Gemini
- 26th 2:49 pm Cancer
- 28th 6:17 pm Leo
- 31st 1:01 am Virgo

November 1972
- 2nd 10:29 am Libra
- 4th 9:48 pm Scorpio
- 7th 10:19 am Sagittarius
- 9th 11:11 pm Capricorn
- 12th 11:00 am Aquarius
- 14th 7:54 pm Pisces
- 17th 0:43 am Aries
- 19th 1:52 am Taurus
- 21st 1:06 am Gemini
- 23rd 0:33 am Cancer
- 25th 2:14 am Leo
- 27th 7:29 am Virgo
- 29th 4:19 pm Libra

December 1972
- 2nd 3:44 am Scorpio
- 4th 4:24 pm Sagittarius
- 7th 5:06 am Capricorn
- 9th 4:53 pm Aquarius
- 12th 2:32 am Pisces
- 14th 8:55 am Aries
- 16th 11:54 am Taurus
- 18th 12:05 pm Gemini
- 20th 11:59 am Cancer
- 22nd 12:40 pm Leo
- 24th 4:08 pm Virgo
- 26th 11:22 pm Libra
- 29th 10:13 am Scorpio
- 31st 10:51 pm Sagittarius

January 1973
- 3rd 11:29 am Capricorn
- 5th 10:48 pm Aquarius
- 8th 8:01 am Pisces
- 10th 2:55 pm Aries
- 12th 7:23 pm Taurus
- 14th 9:41 pm Gemini
- 16th 10:39 pm Cancer
- 18th 11:40 pm Leo
- 21st 2:26 am Virgo
- 23rd 8:21 pm Libra
- 25th 5:55 pm Scorpio
- 28th 6:10 am Sagittarius
- 30th 6:52 pm Capricorn

February 1973
- 2nd 5:52 am Aquarius
- 4th 2:19 pm Pisces
- 6th 8:28 pm Aries
- 9th 0:53 am Taurus
- 11th 4:10 am Gemini
- 13th 6:45 am Cancer
- 15th 9:14 am Leo
- 17th 12:35 pm Virgo
- 19th 6:02 pm Libra
- 22nd 2:37 am Scorpio
- 24th 2:14 pm Sagittarius
- 27th 3:03 am Capricorn

March 1973
- 1st 2:18 pm Aquarius
- 3rd 10:30 pm Pisces
- 6th 3:35 am Aries
- 8th 6:51 am Taurus
- 10th 9:32 am Gemini
- 12th 12:31 pm Cancer
- 14th 4:09 pm Leo
- 16th 8:44 pm Virgo
- 19th 2:50 am Libra
- 21st 11:19 am Scorpio
- 23rd 10:26 pm Sagittarius
- 26th 11:15 am Capricorn
- 28th 11:13 pm Aquarius
- 31st 7:50 am Pisces

April 1973
- 2nd 12:43 pm Aries
- 4th 2:56 pm Taurus
- 6th 4:12 pm Gemini
- 8th 6:06 pm Cancer
- 10th 9:33 pm Leo
- 13th 2:47 am Virgo
- 15th 9:53 am Libra
- 17th 6:53 pm Scorpio
- 20th 6:04 am Sagittarius
- 22nd 6:50 pm Capricorn
- 25th 7:19 am Aquarius
- 27th 5:06 pm Pisces
- 29th 10:52 pm Aries

May 1973
- 2nd 1:01 am Taurus
- 4th 1:15 am Gemini
- 6th 1:35 am Cancer
- 8th 3:49 am Leo
- 10th 8:16 am Virgo
- 12th 3:34 pm Libra
- 15th 1:11 am Scorpio
- 17th 12:44 pm Sagittarius
- 20th 1:30 am Capricorn
- 22nd 2:16 pm Aquarius
- 25th 1:06 am Pisces
- 27th 8:09 am Aries
- 29th 11:24 am Taurus
- 31st 11:51 am Gemini

June 1973
- 2nd 11:23 am Cancer
- 4th 11:53 am Leo
- 6th 2:57 pm Virgo
- 8th 9:19 pm Libra
- 11th 6:54 am Scorpio
- 13th 6:45 pm Sagittarius
- 16th 7:37 am Capricorn
- 18th 8:19 pm Aquarius
- 21st 7:26 am Pisces
- 23rd 3:45 pm Aries
- 25th 8:35 pm Taurus
- 27th 10:17 pm Gemini
- 29th 10:09 pm Cancer

July 1973
- 1st 9:57 pm Leo
- 3rd 11:32 pm Virgo
- 6th 4:27 am Libra
- 8th 1:10 pm Scorpio
- 11th 0:49 am Sagittarius
- 13th 1:47 pm Capricorn
- 16th 2:15 am Aquarius
- 18th 1:06 pm Pisces
- 20th 9:44 pm Aries
- 23rd 3:39 am Taurus
- 25th 6:57 am Gemini
- 27th 8:11 am Cancer
- 29th 8:32 am Leo
- 31st 9:40 am Virgo

August 1973
- 2nd 1:19 pm Libra
- 4th 8:39 pm Scorpio
- 7th 7:39 am Sagittarius
- 9th 8:31 pm Capricorn
- 12th 8:51 am Aquarius
- 14th 7:13 pm Pisces
- 17th 3:17 am Aries
- 19th 9:13 am Taurus
- 21st 1:26 pm Gemini
- 23rd 4:08 pm Cancer
- 25th 5:51 pm Leo
- 27th 7:36 pm Virgo
- 29th 10:54 pm Libra

September 1973
- 1st 5:22 am Scorpio
- 3rd 3:28 pm Sagittarius
- 6th 4:02 am Capricorn
- 8th 4:28 pm Aquarius
- 11th 2:39 am Pisces
- 13th 9:53 am Aries
- 15th 2:59 pm Taurus
- 17th 6:49 pm Gemini
- 19th 10:02 pm Cancer
- 22nd 0:58 am Leo
- 24th 4:01 am Virgo
- 26th 8:05 am Libra
- 28th 2:25 pm Scorpio
- 30th 11:48 pm Sagittarius

October 1973
- 3rd 12:04 pm Capricorn
- 6th 0:50 am Aquarius
- 8th 11:19 am Pisces
- 10th 6:26 pm Aries
- 12th 10:36 pm Taurus
- 15th 1:09 am Gemini
- 17th 3:29 am Cancer
- 19th 6:26 am Leo
- 21st 10:21 am Virgo
- 23rd 3:32 pm Libra
- 25th 10:31 pm Scorpio
- 28th 8:02 am Sagittarius
- 30th 7:50 pm Capricorn

November 1973
- 2nd 8:59 am Aquarius
- 4th 8:26 pm Pisces
- 7th 4:18 am Aries
- 9th 8:22 am Taurus
- 11th 9:59 am Gemini
- 13th 10:48 am Cancer
- 15th 12:23 pm Leo
- 17th 3:45 pm Virgo
- 19th 9:17 pm Libra
- 22nd 5:09 am Scorpio
- 24th 3:15 pm Sagittarius
- 27th 3:15 am Capricorn
- 29th 4:18 pm Aquarius

December 1973
- 2nd 4:32 am Pisces
- 4th 1:46 pm Aries
- 7th 7:06 pm Taurus
- 8th 8:57 pm Gemini
- 10th 8:53 pm Cancer
- 12th 8:47 pm Leo
- 14th 10:23 pm Virgo
- 17th 2:33 am Libra
- 19th 10:48 am Scorpio
- 21st 9:22 pm Sagittarius
- 24th 9:43 am Capricorn
- 26th 10:45 pm Aquarius
- 29th 11:08 am Pisces
- 31st 9:33 pm Aries

Why Does He Say One Thing and Do Another?

January 1974
3rd 4:35 am Taurus
5th 7:57 am Gemini
7th 8:26 am Cancer
9th 7:44 am Leo
11th 7:47 am Virgo
13th 10:28 am Libra
15th 4:59 pm Scorpio
18th 3:14 am Sagittarius
20th 3:48 pm Capricorn
23rd 4:49 am Aquarius
25th 4:59 pm Pisces
28th 3:31 am Aries
30th 11:37 am Taurus

February 1974
1st 4:51 pm Gemini
3rd 7:04 pm Cancer
5th 7:11 pm Leo
7th 6:53 pm Virgo
9th 8:14 pm Libra
12th 0:59 am Scorpio
14th 10:05 am Sagittarius
16th 10:16 pm Capricorn
19th 11:20 am Aquarius
21st 11:15 pm Pisces
24th 9:11 am Aries
26th 5:10 pm Taurus
28th 11:10 pm Gemini

March 1974
3rd 2:50 am Cancer
5th 4:49 am Leo
7th 5:35 am Virgo
9th 6:56 am Libra
11th 10:46 am Scorpio
13th 6:24 pm Sagittarius
16th 5:42 am Capricorn
18th 6:37 pm Aquarius
21st 6:30 am Pisces
23rd 3:59 pm Aries
25th 11:09 pm Taurus
28th 4:32 am Gemini
30th 8:38 am Cancer

April 1974
1st 11:40 am Leo
3rd 1:57 pm Virgo
5th 4:25 pm Libra
7th 8:28 pm Scorpio
10th 3:30 am Sagittarius
12th 1:00 pm Capricorn
15th 2:34 am Aquarius
17th 2:41 pm Pisces
20th 0:20 am Aries
22nd 6:50 am Taurus
24th 11:08 am Gemini
26th 2:17 pm Cancer
28th 5:04 pm Leo
30th 7:50 pm Virgo

May 1974
2nd 11:39 pm Libra
5th 4:45 am Scorpio
7th 12:09 pm Sagittarius
9th 10:16 pm Capricorn
12th 10:36 am Aquarius
14th 11:04 pm Pisces
17th 9:15 am Aries
19th 4:07 pm Taurus
21st 7:52 pm Gemini
23rd 9:45 pm Cancer
25th 11:12 pm Leo
28th 1:26 am Virgo
30th 5:17 am Libra

June 1974
1st 11:13 am Scorpio
3rd 7:24 pm Sagittarius
6th 5:50 am Capricorn
8th 6:04 pm Aquarius
11th 6:43 am Pisces
13th 5:50 pm Aries
16th 1:45 am Taurus
18th 5:55 am Gemini
20th 7:19 am Cancer
22nd 7:30 am Leo
24th 8:15 am Virgo
26th 11:02 am Libra
28th 4:43 pm Scorpio

July 1974
1st 1:22 am Sagittarius
3rd 12:22 pm Capricorn
6th 0:41 am Aquarius
8th 1:25 pm Pisces
11th 1:10 am Aries
13th 10:17 am Taurus
15th 3:50 pm Gemini
17th 5:53 pm Cancer
19th 5:43 pm Leo
21st 5:12 pm Virgo
23rd 6:23 pm Libra
25th 10:47 pm Scorpio
28th 7:03 am Sagittarius
30th 6:12 pm Capricorn

August 1974
2nd 6:47 am Aquarius
4th 7:26 pm Pisces
7th 7:14 am Aries
9th 5:10 pm Taurus
12th 0:16 am Gemini
14th 3:47 am Cancer
16th 4:26 am Leo
18th 3:45 am Virgo
20th 3:48 am Libra
22nd 6:43 am Scorpio
24th 1:40 pm Sagittarius
27th 0:16 am Capricorn
29th 12:53 pm Aquarius

September 1974
1st 1:30 am Pisces
3rd 12:56 pm Aries
5th 10:51 pm Taurus
8th 6:34 am Gemini
10th 11:37 am Cancer
12th 1:52 pm Leo
14th 2:13 pm Virgo
16th 2:22 pm Libra
18th 4:20 pm Scorpio
20th 9:48 pm Sagittarius
23rd 7:26 am Capricorn
25th 7:39 pm Aquarius
28th 8:13 am Pisces
30th 7:25 pm Aries

October 1974
3rd 4:38 am Taurus
5th 11:59 am Gemini
7th 5:28 pm Cancer
9th 9:02 pm Leo
11th 10:57 pm Virgo
14th 0:12 am Libra
16th 2:27 am Scorpio
18th 7:21 am Sagittarius
20th 3:50 pm Capricorn
23rd 3:22 am Aquarius
25th 3:57 pm Pisces
28th 5:12 am Aries
30th 11:57 am Taurus

November 1974
1st 6:22 pm Gemini
3rd 11:01 pm Cancer
6th 2:30 am Leo
8th 5:19 am Virgo
10th 8:01 am Libra
12th 11:28 am Scorpio
14th 4:44 pm Sagittarius
17th 0:45 am Capricorn
19th 11:43 am Aquarius
22nd 0:14 am Pisces
24th 11:57 am Aries
26th 9:04 pm Taurus
29th 2:57 am Gemini

December 1974
1st 6:21 am Cancer
3rd 8:32 am Leo
5th 10:42 am Virgo
7th 1:45 pm Libra
9th 6:16 pm Scorpio
12th 0:35 am Sagittarius
14th 9:09 am Capricorn
16th 7:52 pm Aquarius
19th 8:14 am Pisces
21st 8:36 pm Aries
24th 6:42 am Taurus
26th 1:12 pm Gemini
28th 4:13 pm Cancer
30th 5:05 pm Leo

January 1975
1st 5:35 pm Virgo
3rd 7:25 pm Libra
5th 11:39 pm Scorpio
8th 6:43 am Sagittarius
10th 4:01 pm Capricorn
13th 3:04 am Aquarius
15th 3:26 pm Pisces
18th 4:04 am Aries
20th 3:17 pm Taurus
22nd 11:23 pm Gemini
25th 3:20 am Cancer
27th 3:50 am Leo
29th 3:16 am Virgo
31st 3:17 am Libra

February 1975
2nd 5:58 am Scorpio
4th 12:16 pm Sagittarius
6th 9:44 pm Capricorn
9th 9:18 am Aquarius
11th 9:47 pm Pisces
14th 10:22 am Aries
16th 10:09 pm Taurus
19th 7:31 am Gemini
21st 1:14 pm Cancer
23rd 3:09 pm Leo
25th 2:36 pm Virgo
27th 1:43 pm Libra

March 1975
1st 2:40 am Scorpio
3rd 7:10 pm Sagittarius
6th 3:41 am Capricorn
8th 3:11 pm Aquarius
11th 3:49 am Pisces
13th 4:18 pm Aries
16th 3:53 am Taurus
18th 1:40 pm Gemini
20th 8:47 pm Cancer
23rd 0:31 am Leo
25th 1:21 am Virgo
27th 0:53 am Libra
29th 1:10 am Scorpio
31st 4:13 am Sagittarius

April 1975
1st 11:13 am Capricorn
4th 9:45 am Aquarius
7th 10:16 am Pisces
9th 10:44 pm Aries
11th 9:51 am Taurus
14th 7:13 pm Gemini
17th 2:27 am Cancer
19th 7:11 am Leo
21st 9:40 am Virgo
23rd 10:41 am Libra
25th 11:43 am Scorpio
27th 2:29 pm Sagittarius
29th 8:12 pm Capricorn

May 1975
2nd 5:36 am Aquarius
4th 5:35 pm Pisces
6th 6:01 am Aries
9th 5:00 pm Taurus
12th 1:43 am Gemini
14th 8:05 am Cancer
16th 12:35 pm Leo
18th 3:44 pm Virgo
20th 6:04 pm Libra
22nd 8:26 pm Scorpio
24th 11:51 pm Sagittarius
27th 5:35 am Capricorn
29th 2:14 pm Aquarius

June 1975
1st 1:33 am Pisces
3rd 2:01 pm Aries
6th 1:19 am Taurus
8th 3:17 am Gemini
10th 6:43 am Cancer
12th 9:10 pm Leo
14th 11:40 pm Virgo
16th 2:59 pm Libra
19th 7:37 am Scorpio
21st 9:31 am Sagittarius
23rd 10:34 pm Capricorn
25th 9:35 pm Aquarius
28th 10:03 am Pisces
30th   pm Aries

July 1975
3rd 9:51 am Taurus
5th 6:55 pm Gemini
8th 0:22 am Cancer
10th 2:49 am Leo
12th 3:56 am Virgo
14th 5:24 am Libra
16th 8:26 am Scorpio
18th 1:35 pm Sagittarius
20th 8:46 pm Capricorn
23rd 5:58 am Aquarius
25th 4:50 pm Pisces
28th 5:27 am Aries
30th 5:53 pm Taurus

August 1975
2nd 3:50 am Gemini
4th 10:11 am Cancer
6th 12:40 pm Leo
8th 12:53 pm Virgo
10th 12:54 pm Libra
12th 2:34 pm Scorpio
14th 7:02 pm Sagittarius
17th 2:26 am Capricorn
19th 12:11 pm Aquarius
21st 11:32 pm Pisces
24th 12:02 pm Aries
27th 0:44 am Taurus
29th 11:49 am Gemini
31st 7:33 pm Cancer

Moon Tables

September 1975

2nd 11:08 pm Leo
4th 11:30 pm Virgo
6th 10:38 pm Libra
8th 10:47 pm Scorpio
11th 1:41 am Sagittarius
13th 8:15 am Capricorn
15th 5:53 pm Aquarius
18th 5:32 am Pisces
20th 6:08 pm Aries
23rd 6:43 am Taurus
25th 6:12 pm Gemini
28th 3:05 am Cancer
30th 8:16 am Leo

October 1975

2nd 10:00 am Virgo
4th 9:41 am Libra
6th 9:13 am Scorpio
8th 10:42 am Sagittarius
10th 3:35 pm Capricorn
13th 0:10 am Aquarius
15th 11:42 am Pisces
18th 0:20 am Aries
20th 12:42 pm Taurus
22nd 11:52 pm Gemini
25th 8:54 am Cancer
27th 3:16 pm Leo
29th 6:44 pm Virgo
31st 7:55 pm Libra

November 1975

2nd 8:10 pm Scorpio
4th 9:13 pm Sagittarius
7th 0:47 am Capricorn
9th 8:06 am Aquarius
11th 6:45 pm Pisces
14th 7:17 am Aries
16th 7:37 pm Taurus
19th 6:12 am Gemini
21st 2:33 pm Cancer
23rd 8:47 pm Leo
26th 1:05 am Virgo
28th 3:47 am Libra
30th 5:38 am Scorpio

December 1975

2nd 7:37 am Sagittarius
4th 11:04 am Capricorn
6th 5:18 pm Aquarius
9th 2:55 am Pisces
11th 3:09 pm Aries
14th 3:40 am Taurus
16th 2:10 pm Gemini
18th 9:49 pm Cancer
21st 2:53 am Leo
23rd 6:27 am Virgo
25th 9:27 am Libra
27th 12:29 pm Scorpio
29th 3:55 pm Sagittarius
31st 8:19 pm Capricorn

January 1976

3rd 2:35 am Aquarius
5th 11:40 am Pisces
7th 11:22 pm Aries
10th 12:09 pm Taurus
12th 11:21 pm Gemini
15th 6:57 am Cancer
17th 11:13 am Leo
19th 1:25 pm Virgo
21st 3:12 pm Libra
23rd 5:50 pm Scorpio
25th 9:52 pm Sagittarius
28th 3:25 am Capricorn
30th 10:38 am Aquarius

February 1976

1st 7:50 pm Pisces
4th 7:20 am Aries
6th 8:14 pm Taurus
9th 8:13 am Gemini
11th 4:55 pm Cancer
13th 9:31 pm Leo
15th 10:50 pm Virgo
17th 11:15 pm Libra
20th 0:15 am Scorpio
22nd 3:20 am Sagittarius
24th 8:58 am Capricorn
26th 4:50 pm Aquarius
29th 2:44 am Pisces

March 1976

2nd 2:24 pm Aries
5th 3:19 am Taurus
7th 3:55 pm Gemini
10th 1:58 am Cancer
12th 7:52 am Leo
14th 9:56 am Virgo
16th 9:45 am Libra
18th 9:22 am Scorpio
20th 10:39 am Sagittarius
22nd 2:54 pm Capricorn
24th 10:20 pm Aquarius
27th 8:35 am Pisces
29th 8:35 pm Aries

April 1976

1st 9:34 am Taurus
3rd 10:15 pm Gemini
6th 9:04 am Cancer
8th 4:33 pm Leo
10th 8:15 pm Virgo
12th 8:54 pm Libra
14th 8:16 pm Scorpio
16th 8:18 pm Sagittarius
18th 10:45 pm Capricorn
21st 4:51 am Aquarius
23rd 2:31 pm Pisces
26th 2:36 am Aries
28th 3:36 pm Taurus

May 1976

1st 4:02 am Gemini
3rd 2:51 pm Cancer
5th 11:08 pm Leo
8th 4:18 am Virgo
10th 6:37 am Libra
12th 7:03 am Scorpio
14th 7:06 am Sagittarius
16th 8:37 am Capricorn
18th 1:10 pm Aquarius
20th 9:30 pm Pisces
23rd 9:09 am Aries
25th 10:08 pm Taurus
28th 10:19 am Gemini
30th 8:37 pm Cancer

June 1976

2nd 4:35 am Leo
4th 10:17 am Virgo
6th 1:56 pm Libra
8th 3:57 pm Scorpio
10th 5:07 pm Sagittarius
12th 6:47 pm Capricorn
14th 10:32 pm Aquarius
17th 5:49 am Pisces
19th 4:35 pm Aries
22nd 5:22 am Taurus
24th 5:35 pm Gemini
27th 3:27 am Leo
29th 10:36 am Leo

July 1976

1st 3:44 pm Virgo
3rd 7:33 pm Libra
5th 10:32 pm Scorpio
8th 1:06 am Sagittarius
10th 3:50 am Capricorn
12th 7:57 am Aquarius
14th 2:41 pm Pisces
17th 0:40 am Aries
19th 1:11 pm Taurus
22nd 1:40 am Gemini
24th 11:35 am Cancer
26th 6:16 pm Leo
28th 10:22 pm Virgo
31st 1:13 am Libra

August 1976

2nd 3:56 am Scorpio
4th 7:04 am Sagittarius
6th 10:56 am Capricorn
8th 3:59 pm Aquarius
10th 11:00 pm Pisces
13th 8:52 am Aries
15th 9:06 pm Taurus
18th 9:52 am Gemini
20th 8:31 pm Cancer
23rd 3:28 am Leo
25th 7:01 am Virgo
27th 8:42 am Libra
29th 10:06 am Scorpio
31st 12:32 pm Sagittarius

September 1976

2nd 4:32 pm Capricorn
4th 10:20 pm Aquarius
7th 6:14 am Pisces
9th 4:20 pm Aries
12th 4:31 am Taurus
14th 5:31 pm Gemini
17th 5:03 am Cancer
19th 1:06 pm Leo
21st 5:13 pm Virgo
23rd 6:27 pm Libra
25th 6:34 pm Scorpio
27th 7:24 pm Sagittarius
29th 10:15 pm Capricorn

October 1976

2nd 3:51 am Aquarius
4th 12:12 pm Pisces
6th 10:51 pm Aries
9th 11:12 am Taurus
12th 0:14 am Gemini
14th 12:21 pm Cancer
16th 9:49 pm Leo
19th 3:23 am Virgo
21st 5:24 am Libra
23rd 5:17 am Scorpio
25th 4:52 am Sagittarius
27th 5:50 am Capricorn
29th 10:11 am Aquarius
31st 5:56 pm Pisces

November 1976

3rd 4:47 am Aries
5th 5:23 pm Taurus
8th 6:20 am Gemini
10th 6:27 pm Cancer
13th 4:34 am Leo
15th 11:40 am Virgo
17th 3:30 pm Libra
19th 4:29 pm Scorpio
21st 4:06 pm Sagittarius
23rd 4:09 pm Capricorn
25th 6:36 pm Aquarius
28th 0:50 am Pisces
30th 11:06 am Aries

December 1976

2nd 11:42 pm Taurus
5th 12:36 pm Gemini
8th 0:21 am Cancer
10th 10:09 am Leo
12th 5:53 pm Virgo
14th 11:13 pm Libra
17th 2:02 am Scorpio
19th 2:54 am Sagittarius
21st 3:14 am Capricorn
23rd 4:53 am Aquarius
25th 9:43 am Pisces
27th 6:37 pm Aries
30th 6:45 am Taurus

January 1977

1st 7:43 pm Gemini
4th 7:10 am Cancer
6th 4:19 pm Leo
8th 11:24 pm Virgo
11th 4:47 am Libra
13th 8:43 am Scorpio
15th 11:18 am Sagittarius
17th 1:04 pm Capricorn
19th 3:17 pm Aquarius
21st 7:35 pm Pisces
24th 3:24 am Aries
26th 2:43 pm Taurus
29th 3:38 am Gemini
31st 3:18 pm Cancer

February 1977

3rd 0:13 am Leo
5th 6:17 am Virgo
7th 10:36 am Libra
9th 2:04 pm Scorpio
11th 5:12 pm Sagittarius
13th 8:15 pm Capricorn
15th 11:46 pm Aquarius
18th 4:49 am Pisces
20th 12:28 pm Aries
22nd 11:06 pm Taurus
25th 11:51 am Gemini
28th 0:04 am Cancer

March 1977

2nd 9:22 am Leo
4th 3:16 pm Virgo
6th 6:35 pm Libra
8th 8:39 pm Scorpio
10th 10:43 pm Sagittarius
13th 1:42 am Capricorn
15th 6:03 am Aquarius
17th 12:09 pm Pisces
19th 8:25 pm Aries
22nd 7:08 am Taurus
24th 7:40 pm Gemini
27th 8:15 am Cancer
29th 6:38 pm Leo

April 1977

1st 1:25 am Virgo
3rd 4:39 am Libra
5th 5:41 am Scorpio
7th 6:12 am Sagittarius
9th 7:45 am Capricorn
11th 11:28 am Aquarius
13th 5:52 pm Pisces
16th 2:54 am Aries
18th 2:04 pm Taurus
21st 2:38 am Gemini
23rd 3:24 pm Cancer
26th 2:43 am Leo
28th 10:48 am Virgo
30th 3:09 pm Libra

Why Does He Say One Thing and Do Another?

May 1977		June 1977		July 1977		August 1977	
2nd	4:22 am Scorpio	1st	2:54 am Sagittarius	2nd	1:01 pm Aquarius	1st	1:26 am Pisces
4th	4:01 pm Sagittarius	3rd	2:09 am Capricorn	4th	3:38 pm Pisces	3rd	6:59 am Aries
6th	3:59 pm Capricorn	5th	2:47 am Aquarius	6th	10:06 pm Aries	5th	4:21 pm Taurus
8th	6:05 pm Aquarius	7th	6:42 am Pisces	9th	8:37 am Taurus	8th	4:30 am Gemini
10th	11:29 pm Pisces	9th	2:40 pm Aries	11th	9:15 pm Gemini	10th	5:03 pm Cancer
13th	8:33 am Aries	12th	1:57 am Taurus	14th	9:48 am Cancer	13th	5:55 am Leo
15th	8:05 pm Taurus	14th	2:51 pm Gemini	16th	8:51 pm Leo	15th	12:24 pm Virgo
18th	8:50 am Gemini	17th	3:28 am Cancer	19th	5:56 am Virgo	17th	6:48 pm Libra
20th	9:35 pm Cancer	19th	2:50 pm Leo	21st	1:06 pm Libra	19th	11:36 pm Scorpio
23rd	9:10 am Leo	22nd	0:28 am Virgo	23rd	6:10 pm Scorpio	22nd	3:03 am Sagittarius
25th	6:27 pm Virgo	24th	7:30 am Libra	25th	9:03 pm Capricorn	24th	5:29 am Capricorn
28th	0:29 am Libra	26th	11:36 am Scorpio	27th	10:14 pm Capricorn	26th	7:41 am Aquarius
30th	2:55 am Scorpio	28th	12:58 pm Sagittarius	29th	11:04 pm Aquarius	28th	10:50 am Pisces
		30th	12:48 pm Capricorn			30th	4:15 pm Aries

September 1977		October 1977		November 1977		December 1977	
2nd	0:51 am Taurus	1st	8:34 pm Gemini	3rd	5:01 am Leo	2nd	11:03 pm Virgo
4th	12:28 pm Gemini	4th	9:09 am Cancer	5th	3:12 pm Virgo	5th	7:13 am Libra
7th	1:02 am Cancer	6th	8:57 pm Leo	7th	9:50 pm Libra	7th	11:27 am Scorpio
9th	12:10 pm Leo	9th	5:55 am Virgo	10th	0:42 am Scorpio	9th	12:18 pm Sagittarius
11th	8:33 pm Virgo	11th	11:25 am Libra	12th	1:04 am Sagittarius	11th	11:28 am Capricorn
14th	2:07 am Libra	13th	2:09 pm Scorpio	14th	0:52 am Capricorn	13th	11:06 am Aquarius
16th	5:45 am Scorpio	15th	3:28 pm Sagittarius	16th	2:02 am Aquarius	15th	1:16 pm Pisces
18th	8:29 am Sagittarius	17th	4:53 pm Capricorn	18th	6:02 am Pisces	17th	7:16 pm Aries
20th	11:05 am Capricorn	19th	7:38 pm Aquarius	20th	1:17 pm Aries	20th	4:57 am Taurus
22nd	2:14 pm Aquarius	22nd	0:25 am Pisces	22nd	11:09 pm Taurus	22nd	4:53 pm Gemini
24th	6:32 pm Pisces	24th	7:37 am Aries	25th	10:49 am Gemini	25th	5:29 am Cancer
27th	0:41 am Aries	26th	4:54 pm Taurus	27th	11:20 pm Cancer	27th	5:51 pm Leo
29th	9:24 am Taurus	29th	4:07 am Gemini	30th	11:51 am Leo	29th	5:11 am Virgo
		31st	4:41 pm Cancer				

January 1978		February 1978		March 1978		April 1978	
1st	2:27 pm Libra	2nd	7:11 am Sagittarius	1st	1:00 am Sagittarius	2nd	0:05 am Aquarius
3rd	8:32 pm Scorpio	4th	8:48 am Capricorn	3rd	3:57 pm Capricorn	4th	3:21 am Pisces
5th	11:02 pm Sagittarius	6th	9:06 am Aquarius	5th	5:51 pm Aquarius	6th	7:55 am Aries
7th	10:54 pm Capricorn	8th	9:52 am Pisces	7th	7:47 pm Pisces	8th	2:25 pm Taurus
9th	10:06 pm Aquarius	10th	1:03 pm Aries	9th	11:10 pm Aries	10th	11:29 pm Gemini
11th	10:52 pm Pisces	12th	7:54 pm Taurus	12th	5:21 am Taurus	13th	11:01 am Cancer
14th	3:09 am Aries	15th	6:27 am Gemini	14th	2:52 pm Gemini	15th	11:32 pm Leo
16th	11:37 am Taurus	17th	6:56 pm Cancer	17th	2:50 am Cancer	18th	10:41 am Virgo
18th	11:08 pm Gemini	20th	7:09 am Leo	19th	3:11 pm Leo	20th	6:51 pm Libra
21st	11:51 am Cancer	22nd	5:39 pm Virgo	22nd	1:50 am Virgo	22nd	11:41 pm Scorpio
24th	0:04 am Leo	25th	2:03 am Libra	24th	9:40 am Libra	25th	2:01 am Sagittarius
26th	10:54 am Virgo	27th	8:27 am Scorpio	26th	3:00 pm Scorpio	27th	3:30 am Capricorn
28th	8:07 pm Libra			28th	6:38 pm Sagittarius	29th	5:31 am Aquarius
31st	3:02 am Scorpio			30th	9:25 pm Capricorn		

May 1978		June 1978		July 1978		August 1978	
1st	9:03 am Pisces	2nd	3:52 am Taurus	1st	7:40 pm Gemini	3rd	2:11 am Leo
3rd	2:29 pm Aries	4th	1:56 pm Gemini	4th	7:35 am Cancer	5th	2:28 pm Virgo
5th	9:53 pm Taurus	7th	1:31 am Cancer	6th	8:13 pm Leo	8th	1:28 am Libra
8th	7:22 am Gemini	9th	2:08 pm Leo	9th	8:42 am Virgo	10th	10:07 am Scorpio
10th	6:44 pm Cancer	12th	2:34 am Virgo	11th	7:46 pm Libra	12th	3:38 pm Sagittarius
13th	7:16 am Leo	14th	12:51 pm Libra	14th	3:43 am Scorpio	14th	5:59 pm Capricorn
15th	7:14 pm Virgo	16th	7:24 pm Scorpio	16th	7:44 am Sagittarius	16th	6:14 pm Aquarius
18th	4:22 am Libra	18th	9:50 pm Sagittarius	18th	8:30 am Capricorn	18th	6:07 pm Pisces
20th	9:35 am Scorpio	20th	9:52 pm Capricorn	20th	7:44 am Aquarius	20th	7:32 pm Aries
22nd	11:28 am Sagittarius	22nd	9:11 pm Aquarius	22nd	7:31 am Pisces	23rd	0:06 am Taurus
24th	11:43 am Capricorn	24th	9:59 pm Pisces	24th	9:52 am Aries	25th	8:36 am Gemini
26th	12:15 pm Aquarius	27th	1:46 am Aries	26th	3:56 pm Taurus	27th	7:59 pm Cancer
28th	2:42 pm Pisces	29th	9:26 am Taurus	29th	1:33 am Gemini	30th	8:39 am Leo
30th	7:56 pm Aries			31st	1:20 pm Cancer		

September 1978		October 1978		November 1978		December 1978	
1st	8:47 pm Virgo	1st	2:14 pm Libra	2nd	10:02 am Sagittarius	1st	8:44 pm Capricorn
4th	7:14 am Libra	3rd	9:47 pm Scorpio	4th	12:40 pm Capricorn	3rd	9:36 pm Aquarius
6th	3:36 pm Scorpio	6th	3:06 am Sagittarius	6th	3:04 pm Aquarius	5th	11:56 pm Pisces
8th	9:38 pm Sagittarius	8th	6:51 am Capricorn	8th	6:07 pm Pisces	8th	3:41 am Aries
11th	1:19 am Capricorn	10th	9:42 am Aquarius	10th	10:12 pm Aries	10th	9:53 am Taurus
13th	3:08 am Aquarius	12th	12:13 pm Pisces	13th	3:36 am Taurus	12th	5:37 pm Gemini
15th	4:10 am Pisces	14th	3:06 pm Aries	15th	10:48 am Gemini	15th	3:51 am Cancer
17th	5:52 am Aries	16th	7:23 pm Taurus	17th	8:16 pm Cancer	17th	3:38 pm Leo
19th	9:47 am Taurus	19th	2:05 am Gemini	20th	8:10 am Leo	20th	4:32 am Virgo
21st	4:50 pm Gemini	21st	11:55 am Cancer	22nd	8:56 pm Virgo	22nd	4:35 pm Libra
24th	3:33 am Cancer	24th	0:04 am Leo	25th	8:03 am Libra	25th	1:30 am Scorpio
26th	4:01 pm Leo	26th	12:29 pm Virgo	27th	3:33 pm Scorpio	27th	6:03 am Sagittarius
29th	4:10 am Virgo	28th	10:51 pm Libra	29th	7:20 pm Sagittarius	29th	7:13 am Capricorn
		31st	5:49 am Scorpio			31st	6:55 am Aquarius

Moon Tables

January 1979
2nd 7:12 am Pisces
4th 9:47 am Aries
6th 3:23 pm Taurus
8th 11:43 pm Gemini
11th 10:16 am Cancer
13th 10:17 pm Leo
16th 11:10 am Virgo
18th 11:40 pm Libra
21st 9:45 am Scorpio
23rd 4:02 pm Sagittarius
25th 6:23 pm Capricorn
27th 6:11 pm Aquarius
29th 5:27 pm Pisces
31st 6:15 am Aries

February 1979
2nd 10:05 am Taurus
5th 5:37 am Gemini
7th 4:08 pm Cancer
10th 4:28 am Leo
12th 5:18 pm Virgo
15th 5:35 am Libra
17th 4:09 pm Scorpio
19th 11:51 pm Sagittarius
22nd 3:58 am Capricorn
24th 5:10 am Aquarius
26th 4:53 am Pisces
28th 4:57 am Aries

March 1979
2nd 7:14 am Taurus
4th 1:04 pm Gemini
6th 10:36 pm Cancer
9th 10:49 am Leo
11th 11:44 pm Virgo
14th 11:40 am Libra
16th 9:50 pm Scorpio
19th 5:36 am Sagittarius
21st 10:53 am Capricorn
23rd 1:50 pm Aquarius
25th 3:04 pm Pisces
27th 3:49 am Aries
29th 5:40 pm Taurus
31st 10:09 pm Gemini

April 1979
3rd 6:27 am Cancer
5th 5:59 pm Leo
8th 6:52 am Virgo
10th 6:45 pm Libra
13th 4:15 am Scorpio
15th 11:16 am Sagittarius
17th 4:22 pm Capricorn
19th 8:01 pm Aquarius
21st 10:41 pm Pisces
24th 0:52 am Aries
26th 3:30 am Taurus
28th 7:53 am Gemini
30th 3:16 pm Cancer

May 1979
3rd 1:57 am Leo
5th 2:41 pm Virgo
8th 2:48 am Libra
10th 12:07 pm Scorpio
12th 6:23 pm Sagittarius
14th 10:27 pm Capricorn
17th 1:26 am Aquarius
19th 4:19 am Pisces
21st 7:31 am Aries
23rd 11:22 am Taurus
25th 4:31 pm Gemini
27th 11:51 pm Cancer
30th 10:11 am Leo

June 1979
1st 10:41 pm Virgo
4th 11:08 am Libra
6th 9:03 pm Scorpio
9th 3:14 am Sagittarius
11th 6:23 am Capricorn
13th 8:08 am Aquarius
15th 9:59 am Pisces
17th 12:56 pm Aries
19th 5:21 pm Taurus
21st 11:24 pm Gemini
24th 7:27 am Cancer
26th 5:50 pm Leo
29th 6:15 am Virgo

July 1979
1st 7:06 pm Libra
4th 5:53 am Scorpio
6th 12:50 pm Sagittarius
8th 4:04 pm Capricorn
10th 4:59 pm Aquarius
12th 5:26 pm Pisces
14th 7:00 pm Aries
16th 10:45 pm Taurus
19th 5:03 am Gemini
21st 1:44 pm Cancer
24th 0:32 am Leo
26th 1:02 pm Virgo
29th 2:05 am Libra
31st 1:42 pm Scorpio

August 1979
2nd 10:03 pm Sagittarius
5th 2:21 am Capricorn
7th 3:27 am Aquarius
9th 3:06 am Pisces
11th 3:12 am Aries
13th 5:26 am Taurus
15th 10:47 am Gemini
17th 7:21 pm Cancer
20th 6:32 am Leo
22nd 7:13 pm Virgo
25th 8:13 am Libra
27th 8:11 pm Scorpio
30th 5:36 am Sagittarius

September 1979
1st 11:28 am Capricorn
3rd 1:55 pm Aquarius
5th 2:02 pm Pisces
7th 1:31 pm Aries
9th 2:17 pm Taurus
11th 5:59 pm Gemini
14th 1:27 am Cancer
16th 12:28 pm Leo
19th 1:15 am Virgo
21st 2:10 pm Libra
24th 1:55 am Scorpio
26th 11:33 am Sagittarius
28th 6:36 pm Capricorn
30th 10:48 pm Aquarius

October 1979
3rd 0:23 am Pisces
5th 0:27 am Aries
7th 0:45 am Taurus
9th 3:09 am Gemini
11th 9:14 am Cancer
13th 7:13 pm Leo
16th 7:51 am Virgo
18th 8:44 pm Libra
21st 8:00 am Scorpio
23rd 5:07 pm Sagittarius
26th 0:11 am Capricorn
28th 5:15 am Aquarius
30th 8:26 am Pisces

November 1979
1st 10:08 am Aries
3rd 11:16 am Taurus
5th 1:30 pm Gemini
7th 6:27 pm Cancer
10th 3:16 am Leo
12th 3:21 pm Virgo
15th 4:15 am Libra
17th 3:26 pm Scorpio
19th 11:56 pm Sagittarius
22nd 6:00 am Capricorn
24th 10:35 am Aquarius
26th 2:16 pm Pisces
28th 5:16 pm Aries
30th 7:54 pm Taurus

December 1979
2nd 11:02 pm Gemini
5th 4:03 am Cancer
7th 12:13 pm Leo
9th 11:52 pm Virgo
12th 12:27 pm Libra
15th 0:08 am Scorpio
17th 8:32 am Sagittarius
19th 1:51 pm Capricorn
21st 5:12 pm Aquarius
23rd 7:50 pm Pisces
25th 10:40 pm Aries
28th 2:08 am Taurus
30th 6:34 am Gemini

January 1980
1st 12:33 pm Cancer
3rd 8:49 pm Leo
6th 7:50 am Virgo
8th 8:37 pm Libra
11th 8:50 am Scorpio
13th 6:12 pm Sagittarius
15th 11:51 pm Capricorn
18th 2:25 am Aquarius
20th 3:33 am Pisces
22nd 4:54 am Aries
24th 7:36 am Taurus
26th 12:14 pm Gemini
28th 7:05 pm Cancer
31st 4:11 am Leo

February 1980
2nd 3:23 pm Virgo
5th 4:04 am Libra
7th 4:43 pm Scorpio
10th 3:15 am Sagittarius
12th 10:06 am Capricorn
14th 1:14 pm Aquarius
16th 1:52 pm Pisces
18th 1:45 pm Aries
20th 2:39 pm Taurus
22nd 6:03 pm Gemini
25th 0:36 am Cancer
27th 10:14 am Leo
29th 9:54 pm Virgo

March 1980
3rd 10:40 am Libra
5th 11:24 pm Scorpio
8th 10:35 am Sagittarius
10th 6:59 pm Capricorn
12th 11:46 pm Aquarius
15th 1:10 am Pisces
17th 0:41 am Aries
19th 0:13 am Taurus
21st 1:49 am Gemini
23rd 7:00 am Cancer
25th 4:02 pm Leo
28th 3:49 am Virgo
30th 4:43 pm Libra

April 1980
2nd 5:21 am Scorpio
4th 4:34 pm Sagittarius
7th 1:41 am Capricorn
9th 7:56 am Aquarius
11th 11:03 am Pisces
13th 11:39 am Aries
15th 11:12 am Taurus
17th 11:47 am Gemini
19th 3:18 pm Cancer
21st 10:54 pm Leo
24th 10:14 am Virgo
26th 11:11 pm Libra
29th 11:34 am Scorpio

May 1980
1st 10:23 pm Sagittarius
4th 7:13 am Capricorn
6th 2:01 pm Aquarius
8th 6:31 pm Pisces
10th 8:44 pm Aries
12th 9:25 pm Taurus
14th 10:09 pm Gemini
17th 0:53 am Cancer
19th 7:19 am Leo
21st 5:35 pm Virgo
24th 6:12 am Libra
26th 6:37 pm Scorpio
29th 5:04 am Sagittarius
31st 1:13 pm Capricorn

June 1980
2nd 7:28 pm Aquarius
5th 0:10 am Pisces
7th 3:23 am Aries
9th 5:30 am Taurus
11th 7:25 am Gemini
13th 10:35 am Cancer
15th 4:26 pm Leo
18th 1:49 am Virgo
20th 1:56 pm Libra
23rd 2:27 am Scorpio
25th 12:58 pm Sagittarius
27th 8:45 pm Capricorn
30th 2:03 am Aquarius

July 1980
2nd 5:48 am Pisces
4th 8:48 am Aries
6th 11:32 am Taurus
8th 2:36 pm Gemini
10th 6:48 pm Cancer
13th 1:04 am Leo
15th 10:15 am Virgo
17th 9:55 pm Libra
20th 10:32 am Scorpio
22nd 9:40 pm Sagittarius
25th 5:42 am Capricorn
27th 10:32 am Aquarius
29th 1:10 pm Pisces
31st 2:55 pm Aries

August 1980
2nd 4:58 pm Taurus
4th 8:12 pm Gemini
7th 1:14 am Cancer
9th 8:28 am Leo
11th 5:58 pm Virgo
14th 5:33 am Libra
16th 6:14 pm Scorpio
19th 6:04 am Sagittarius
21st 3:06 pm Capricorn
23rd 8:30 pm Aquarius
25th 10:42 pm Pisces
27th 11:12 pm Aries
29th 11:42 pm Taurus

Why Does He Say One Thing and Do Another?

September 1980				October 1980				November 1980				December 1980			
1st	1:53 am	Gemini		2nd	7:59 pm	Leo		1st	12:21 pm	Virgo		1st	7:14 am	Libra	
3rd	6:44 am	Cancer		5th	6:20 am	Virgo		4th	0:30 am	Libra		3rd	7:59 pm	Scorpio	
5th	2:26 pm	Leo		7th	6:31 pm	Libra		6th	1:18 pm	Scorpio		6th	7:55 am	Sagittarius	
8th	0:32 am	Virgo		10th	7:15 am	Scorpio		9th	1:25 am	Sagittarius		8th	6:09 pm	Capricorn	
10th	12:24 pm	Libra		12th	7:38 pm	Sagittarius		11th	12:13 pm	Capricorn		11th	2:34 am	Aquarius	
13th	1:07 am	Scorpio		15th	6:34 am	Capricorn		13th	9:08 pm	Aquarius		13th	8:50 am	Pisces	
15th	1:26 pm	Sagittarius		17th	2:49 pm	Aquarius		16th	3:18 am	Pisces		15th	1:18 pm	Aries	
17th	11:45 pm	Capricorn		19th	7:28 pm	Pisces		18th	6:18 am	Aries		17th	3:33 pm	Taurus	
20th	6:26 am	Aquarius		21st	8:40 pm	Aries		20th	6:48 am	Taurus		19th	4:40 pm	Gemini	
22nd	9:22 am	Pisces		23rd	7:55 pm	Taurus		22nd	6:29 am	Gemini		21st	6:05 pm	Cancer	
24th	9:36 am	Aries		25th	7:19 pm	Gemini		24th	7:23 am	Cancer		23rd	9:35 pm	Leo	
26th	8:55 am	Taurus		27th	9:02 pm	Cancer		26th	11:28 am	Leo		26th	4:35 am	Virgo	
28th	9:25 am	Gemini		30th	2:40 am	Leo		28th	7:40 pm	Virgo		28th	3:06 pm	Libra	
30th	12:51 pm	Cancer										31st	3:34 am	Scorpio	

January 1981				February 1981				March 1981				April 1981			
2nd	3:38 pm	Sagittarius		1st	10:31 am	Capricorn		3rd	3:47 am	Aquarius		1st	6:37 pm	Pisces	
5th	1:39 am	Capricorn		3rd	5:51 pm	Aquarius		5th	8:07 am	Pisces		3rd	8:22 pm	Aries	
7th	9:09 am	Aquarius		5th	10:20 pm	Pisces		7th	9:45 am	Aries		5th	8:03 pm	Taurus	
9th	2:39 pm	Pisces		8th	1:02 am	Aries		9th	10:23 am	Taurus		7th	7:50 pm	Gemini	
11th	6:42 pm	Aries		10th	3:12 am	Taurus		11th	11:46 am	Gemini		9th	9:35 pm	Cancer	
13th	9:45 pm	Taurus		12th	5:53 am	Gemini		13th	3:10 pm	Cancer		12th	2:39 am	Leo	
16th	0:17 am	Gemini		14th	9:46 am	Cancer		15th	9:05 pm	Leo		14th	10:59 am	Virgo	
18th	3:09 am	Cancer		16th	3:14 pm	Leo		18th	5:22 am	Virgo		16th	9:38 pm	Libra	
20th	7:24 am	Leo		18th	10:34 pm	Virgo		20th	3:53 pm	Libra		19th	9:40 am	Scorpio	
22nd	2:06 pm	Virgo		21st	8:14 am	Libra		23rd	3:15 am	Scorpio		21st	10:15 pm	Sagittarius	
24th	11:44 pm	Libra		23rd	7:55 pm	Scorpio		25th	3:51 pm	Sagittarius		24th	10:30 am	Capricorn	
27th	11:48 am	Scorpio		26th	8:26 am	Sagittarius		28th	3:51 am	Capricorn		26th	8:56 pm	Aquarius	
30th	0:10 am	Sagittarius		28th	7:43 pm	Capricorn		30th	1:09 pm	Aquarius		29th	3:54 am	Pisces	

May 1981				June 1981				July 1981				August 1981			
1st	6:53 am	Aries		1st	4:49 pm	Gemini		1st	2:59 am	Cancer		1st	6:58 pm	Virgo	
3rd	6:58 am	Taurus		3rd	4:43 pm	Cancer		3rd	4:51 am	Leo		4th	2:26 am	Libra	
5th	6:03 am	Gemini		5th	6:47 pm	Leo		5th	9:32 am	Virgo		6th	1:01 pm	Scorpio	
7th	6:22 am	Cancer		8th	0:26 am	Virgo		7th	5:45 pm	Libra		9th	1:23 am	Sagittarius	
9th	9:46 am	Leo		10th	9:09 am	Libra		10th	5:02 am	Scorpio		11th	1:17 pm	Capricorn	
11th	4:59 pm	Virgo		12th	9:55 pm	Scorpio		12th	5:35 pm	Sagittarius		13th	10:56 pm	Aquarius	
14th	3:25 am	Libra		15th	10:32 am	Sagittarius		15th	5:18 am	Capricorn		16th	5:32 am	Pisces	
16th	3:39 pm	Scorpio		17th	10:21 pm	Capricorn		17th	2:50 pm	Aquarius		18th	9:48 am	Aries	
19th	4:14 am	Sagittarius		20th	8:34 am	Aquarius		19th	10:25 pm	Pisces		20th	12:45 pm	Taurus	
21st	4:19 pm	Capricorn		22nd	4:42 pm	Pisces		22nd	3:44 am	Aries		22nd	3:20 pm	Gemini	
24th	2:59 am	Aquarius		24th	10:18 pm	Aries		24th	7:18 am	Taurus		24th	6:18 pm	Cancer	
26th	11:01 am	Pisces		27th	1:16 am	Taurus		26th	9:42 am	Gemini		26th	10:12 pm	Leo	
28th	3:39 pm	Aries		29th	2:22 am	Gemini		28th	11:43 am	Cancer		29th	3:35 am	Virgo	
30th	5:08 pm	Taurus						30th	2:25 pm	Leo		31st	11:07 am	Libra	

September 1981				October 1981				November 1981				December 1981			
2nd	9:13 pm	Scorpio		2nd	5:01 pm	Sagittarius		1st	12:46 pm	Capricorn		1st	7:07 am	Aquarius	
5th	9:24 am	Sagittarius		5th	5:47 am	Capricorn		4th	0:50 am	Aquarius		3rd	2:19 pm	Pisces	
7th	9:48 pm	Capricorn		7th	4:57 pm	Aquarius		6th	9:46 am	Pisces		5th	11:49 pm	Aries	
10th	7:54 am	Aquarius		10th	0:32 am	Pisces		8th	2:33 pm	Aries		8th	2:29 am	Taurus	
12th	2:29 pm	Pisces		12th	3:59 am	Aries		10th	3:41 pm	Taurus		10th	2:29 am	Gemini	
14th	5:53 pm	Aries		14th	4:43 am	Taurus		12th	3:00 pm	Gemini		12th	1:42 am	Cancer	
16th	7:30 pm	Taurus		16th	4:43 am	Gemini		14th	2:40 pm	Cancer		14th	2:09 am	Leo	
18th	9:01 pm	Gemini		18th	5:55 am	Cancer		16th	4:36 pm	Leo		16th	5:41 am	Virgo	
20th	11:40 pm	Cancer		20th	9:39 am	Leo		18th	9:55 pm	Virgo		18th	1:03 pm	Libra	
23rd	4:11 am	Leo		22nd	4:07 pm	Virgo		21st	6:34 am	Libra		20th	11:38 pm	Scorpio	
25th	10:32 am	Virgo		25th	0:56 am	Libra		23rd	5:38 pm	Scorpio		23rd	12:11 pm	Sagittarius	
27th	6:43 pm	Libra		27th	11:40 am	Scorpio		26th	6:01 am	Sagittarius		26th	0:58 am	Capricorn	
30th	4:56 am	Scorpio		29th	11:50 pm	Sagittarius		28th	6:52 pm	Capricorn		28th	12:51 pm	Aquarius	
												30th	11:01 pm	Pisces	

January 1982				February 1982				March 1982				April 1982			
2nd	6:29 am	Aries		2nd	8:19 pm	Gemini		1st	1:49 am	Gemini		2nd	1:39 pm	Leo	
4th	10:17 am	Taurus		4th	10:17 pm	Cancer		4th	4:49 am	Cancer		4th	6:20 pm	Virgo	
6th	12:46 pm	Gemini		6th	11:50 pm	Leo		6th	7:51 am	Leo		7th	0:26 am	Libra	
8th	1:01 pm	Cancer		9th	2:16 am	Virgo		8th	11:29 am	Virgo		9th	8:37 am	Scorpio	
10th	1:24 pm	Leo		11th	7:05 am	Libra		10th	4:37 pm	Libra		11th	7:08 pm	Sagittarius	
12th	3:42 pm	Virgo		13th	3:20 pm	Scorpio		13th	0:17 am	Scorpio		14th	7:42 am	Capricorn	
14th	9:19 pm	Libra		16th	2:44 am	Sagittarius		15th	11:05 am	Sagittarius		16th	8:16 pm	Aquarius	
17th	6:48 am	Scorpio		18th	3:34 pm	Capricorn		17th	11:46 pm	Capricorn		19th	6:15 am	Pisces	
19th	6:50 pm	Sagittarius		21st	3:11 am	Aquarius		20th	11:48 am	Aquarius		21st	12:17 pm	Aries	
22nd	7:49 am	Capricorn		23rd	12:04 pm	Pisces		22nd	8:57 pm	Pisces		23rd	2:55 pm	Taurus	
24th	7:22 pm	Aquarius		25th	6:14 pm	Aries		25th	2:35 am	Aries		25th	3:48 pm	Gemini	
27th	4:47 am	Pisces		27th	10:32 pm	Taurus		27th	5:38 am	Taurus		27th	4:44 pm	Cancer	
29th	11:55 am	Aries						29th	7:44 am	Gemini		29th	7:10 pm	Leo	
31st	5:02 pm	Taurus						31st	10:10 am	Cancer					

42

Moon Tables

May 1982
1st 11:44 pm Virgo
4th 6:34 am Libra
6th 3:26 pm Scorpio
9th 2:18 am Sagittarius
11th 2:51 pm Capricorn
14th 3:44 am Aquarius
16th 2:42 pm Pisces
18th 10:03 pm Aries
21st 1:20 am Taurus
23rd 1:54 am Gemini
25th 1:38 am Cancer
27th 2:28 am Leo
29th 5:46 am Virgo
31st 12:06 pm Libra

June 1982
2nd 9:12 pm Scorpio
5th 8:33 am Sagittarius
7th 9:11 pm Capricorn
10th 10:06 am Aquarius
12th 9:43 pm Pisces
15th 6:16 am Aries
17th 11:01 am Taurus
19th 12:31 pm Gemini
21st 12:13 pm Cancer
23rd 11:50 am Leo
25th 1:41 pm Virgo
27th 6:34 pm Libra
30th 3:03 am Scorpio

July 1982
2nd 2:27 pm Sagittarius
5th 3:15 am Capricorn
7th 4:01 pm Aquarius
10th 3:33 am Pisces
12th 12:45 pm Aries
14th 6:56 pm Taurus
16th 10:03 pm Gemini
18th 10:46 pm Cancer
20th 10:36 pm Leo
22nd 11:21 pm Virgo
25th 2:47 am Libra
27th 10:04 am Scorpio
29th 8:49 pm Sagittarius

August 1982
1st 9:36 am Capricorn
3rd 10:17 pm Aquarius
6th 9:21 am Pisces
8th 6:20 pm Aries
11th 1:00 am Taurus
13th 5:21 am Gemini
15th 7:39 am Cancer
17th 8:42 am Leo
19th 9:44 am Virgo
21st 12:27 pm Libra
23rd 6:25 pm Scorpio
26th 4:13 am Sagittarius
28th 4:41 pm Capricorn
31st 5:22 am Aquarius

September 1982
2nd 4:07 pm Pisces
5th 0:24 am Aries
7th 6:26 am Taurus
9th 10:57 am Gemini
11th 2:18 pm Cancer
3th 4:46 pm Leo
15th 6:50 pm Virgo
17th 10:05 pm Libra
20th 3:36 am Scorpio
22nd 12:35 pm Sagittarius
25th 0:32 am Capricorn
27th 1:19 pm Aquarius
30th 0:19 am Pisces

October 1982
2nd 8:02 am Aries
4th 1:07 pm Taurus
6th 4:38 pm Gemini
8th 7:40 pm Cancer
10th 10:45 pm Leo
13th 2:10 am Virgo
15th 6:26 am Libra
17th 12:26 pm Scorpio
19th 9:05 pm Sagittarius
22nd 8:41 am Capricorn
24th 9:36 pm Aquarius
27th 9:08 am Pisces
29th 5:21 pm Aries
31st 10:03 pm Taurus

November 1982
3rd 0:23 am Gemini
5th 1:58 am Cancer
7th 4:12 am Leo
9th 7:43 am Virgo
11th 12:48 pm Libra
13th 7:44 pm Scorpio
16th 4:55 am Sagittarius
18th 4:23 pm Capricorn
21st 5:21 am Aquarius
23rd 5:41 pm Pisces
26th 3:04 am Aries
28th 8:28 am Taurus
30th 10:34 am Gemini

December 1982
2nd 10:58 am Cancer
4th 11:29 am Leo
6th 1:37 pm Virgo
8th 6:14 pm Libra
11th 1:33 am Scorpio
13th 11:30 am Sagittarius
15th 11:16 pm Capricorn
18th 12:13 pm Aquarius
21st 0:56 am Pisces
23rd 11:30 am Aries
25th 6:33 pm Taurus
27th 9:48 pm Gemini
29th 10:12 pm Cancer
31st 9:33 pm Leo

January 1983
2nd 9:51 pm Virgo
5th 0:45 am Libra
7th 7:20 am Scorpio
9th 5:16 pm Sagittarius
12th 5:27 am Capricorn
14th 6:26 pm Aquarius
17th 7:01 am Pisces
19th 6:05 pm Aries
22nd 2:34 am Taurus
24th 7:36 am Gemini
26th 9:24 am Cancer
28th 9:09 am Leo
30th 8:38 am Virgo

February 1983
1st 9:53 am Libra
3rd 2:37 pm Scorpio
5th 11:29 pm Sagittarius
8th 11:35 am Capricorn
11th 0:41 am Aquarius
13th 12:50 pm Pisces
15th 11:46 pm Aries
18th 8:28 am Taurus
20th 2:48 pm Gemini
22nd 6:29 pm Cancer
24th 7:46 pm Leo
26th 7:49 pm Virgo
28th 8:31 pm Libra

March 1983
2nd 11:51 pm Scorpio
5th 7:18 am Sagittarius
7th 6:30 pm Capricorn
10th 7:29 am Aquarius
12th 7:44 pm Pisces
15th 5:58 am Aries
17th 2:02 pm Taurus
19th 8:18 pm Gemini
22nd 0:53 am Cancer
24th 3:43 am Leo
26th 5:19 am Virgo
28th 6:50 am Libra
30th 10:02 am Scorpio

April 1983
1st 4:24 pm Sagittarius
4th 2:30 am Capricorn
6th 3:06 pm Aquarius
9th 3:29 am Pisces
11th 1:32 pm Aries
13th 8:56 pm Taurus
16th 2:12 am Gemini
18th 6:12 am Cancer
20th 9:25 am Leo
22nd 12:11 pm Virgo
24th 3:04 pm Libra
26th 7:07 pm Scorpio
29th 1:29 am Sagittarius

May 1983
1st 11:04 am Capricorn
3rd 11:09 pm Aquarius
6th 11:41 am Pisces
8th 10:14 pm Aries
11th 5:33 am Taurus
13th 9:59 am Gemini
15th 12:45 pm Cancer
17th 3:00 pm Leo
19th 5:37 pm Virgo
21st 9:12 pm Libra
24th 2:18 am Scorpio
26th 9:30 am Sagittarius
28th 7:09 pm Capricorn
31st 7:01 am Aquarius

June 1983
2nd 7:42 pm Pisces
5th 6:55 am Aries
7th 2:59 pm Taurus
9th 7:34 pm Gemini
11th 9:30 pm Cancer
13th 10:21 pm Leo
15th 11:37 pm Virgo
18th 2:38 am Libra
20th 8:02 am Scorpio
22nd 3:57 pm Sagittarius
25th 2:09 am Capricorn
27th 2:07 pm Aquarius
30th 2:51 am Pisces

July 1983
2nd 2:44 pm Aries
5th 0:05 am Taurus
7th 5:37 am Gemini
9th 7:47 am Cancer
11th 7:53 am Leo
13th 7:45 am Virgo
15th 9:15 am Libra
17th 1:43 pm Scorpio
19th 9:32 pm Sagittarius
22nd 8:12 am Capricorn
24th 8:26 pm Aquarius
27th 9:10 am Pisces
29th 9:21 pm Aries

August 1983
1st 7:33 am Taurus
3rd 2:38 pm Gemini
5th 6:06 pm Cancer
7th 6:35 pm Leo
9th 5:50 pm Virgo
11th 5:55 pm Libra
13th 8:46 pm Scorpio
16th 3:36 am Sagittarius
18th 2:01 pm Capricorn
21st 2:26 am Aquarius
23rd 3:09 pm Pisces
26th 3:07 am Aries
28th 1:35 pm Taurus
30th 9:47 pm Gemini

September 1983
2nd 2:51 am Cancer
4th 4:45 am Leo
6th 4:36 am Virgo
8th 4:16 am Libra
10th 5:54 am Scorpio
12th 11:14 am Sagittarius
14th 8:35 pm Capricorn
17th 8:45 am Aquarius
19th 9:29 pm Pisces
22nd 9:09 am Aries
24th 7:11 pm Taurus
27th 3:23 am Gemini
29th 9:21 am Cancer

October 1983
1st 12:52 pm Leo
3rd 2:14 pm Virgo
5th 2:44 pm Libra
7th 4:11 pm Scorpio
9th 8:24 pm Sagittarius
12th 4:33 am Capricorn
14th 4:03 pm Aquarius
17th 4:40 am Pisces
19th 4:16 pm Aries
22nd 1:46 am Taurus
24th 9:07 am Gemini
26th 2:45 pm Cancer
28th 6:49 pm Leo
30th 9:32 pm Virgo

November 1983
1st 11:32 pm Libra
4th 1:55 am Scorpio
6th 6:14 am Sagittarius
8th 1:37 pm Capricorn
11th 0:12 am Aquarius
13th 12:41 pm Pisces
16th 0:37 am Aries
18th 10:04 am Taurus
20th 4:42 pm Gemini
22nd 9:09 pm Cancer
25th 0:19 am Leo
27th 3:03 am Virgo
29th 5:57 am Libra

December 1983
1st 9:44 am Scorpio
3rd 2:50 pm Sagittarius
5th 10:30 pm Capricorn
8th 8:44 am Aquarius
10th 8:54 pm Pisces
13th 9:15 am Aries
15th 7:31 pm Taurus
18th 2:23 am Gemini
20th 6:00 am Cancer
22nd 7:43 am Leo
24th 9:03 am Virgo
26th 11:22 am Libra
28th 3:26 pm Scorpio
30th 9:44 pm Sagittarius

Why Does He Say One Thing and Do Another?

January 1984		February 1984		March 1984		April 1984	
2nd	6:11 am Capricorn	3rd	11:23 am Pisces	1st	5:30 pm Pisces	2nd	11:54 pm Taurus
4th	4:32 pm Aquarius	6th	0:04 am Aries	4th	6:07 am Aries	5th	10:01 am Gemini
7th	4:35 am Pisces	8th	12:03 pm Taurus	6th	6:08 pm Taurus	7th	5:56 pm Cancer
9th	5:15 pm Aries	10th	9:37 pm Gemini	9th	4:28 am Gemini	9th	11:01 pm Leo
12th	4:34 am Taurus	13th	3:19 am Cancer	11th	11:43 am Cancer	12th	1:10 am Virgo
14th	12:35 pm Gemini	15th	5:07 am Leo	13th	3:17 pm Leo	14th	1:30 am Libra
16th	4:43 pm Cancer	17th	4:32 am Virgo	15th	3:44 pm Virgo	16th	1:42 am Scorpio
18th	5:48 pm Leo	19th	3:42 am Libra	17th	2:54 pm Libra	18th	3:46 am Sagittarius
20th	5:37 pm Virgo	21st	4:48 am Scorpio	19th	2:54 pm Scorpio	20th	9:16 am Capricorn
22nd	6:11 pm Libra	23rd	9:28 am Sagittarius	21st	5:46 pm Sagittarius	22nd	6:30 pm Aquarius
24th	9:07 pm Scorpio	25th	5:52 pm Capricorn	24th	0:36 am Capricorn	25th	6:26 am Pisces
27th	3:14 am Sagittarius	28th	5:03 am Aquarius	26th	11:10 am Aquarius	27th	7:00 pm Aries
29th	12:15 pm Capricorn			28th	11:36 pm Pisces	30th	6:27 am Taurus
31st	11:10 pm Aquarius			31st	12:12 pm Aries		

May 1984		June 1984		July 1984		August 1984	
2nd	3:59 pm Gemini	1st	5:50 am Cancer	2nd	7:26 pm Virgo	1st	4:04 am Libra
4th	11:25 pm Cancer	3rd	10:16 am Leo	4th	9:26 pm Libra	3rd	6:07 am Scorpio
7th	4:41 am Leo	5th	1:25 pm Virgo	7th	0:28 am Scorpio	5th	10:33 am Sagittarius
9th	7:58 am Virgo	7th	4:02 pm Libra	9th	5:04 am Sagittarius	7th	5:27 pm Capricorn
11th	9:52 am Libra	9th	6:48 pm Scorpio	11th	11:25 am Capricorn	10th	2:26 am Aquarius
13th	11:24 am Scorpio	11th	10:26 pm Sagittarius	13th	7:43 pm Aquarius	12th	1:14 pm Pisces
15th	1:54 pm Sagittarius	14th	3:51 am Capricorn	16th	6:12 am Pisces	15th	1:27 am Aries
17th	6:46 pm Capricorn	16th	11:45 am Aquarius	18th	6:26 pm Aries	17th	2:11 pm Taurus
20th	2:57 am Aquarius	18th	10:19 pm Pisces	21st	6:51 am Taurus	20th	1:30 am Gemini
22nd	2:10 pm Pisces	21st	10:49 am Aries	23rd	5:06 pm Gemini	22nd	9:14 am Cancer
25th	2:38 am Aries	23rd	10:37 pm Taurus	25th	11:44 pm Cancer	24th	12:55 pm Leo
27th	2:10 pm Taurus	26th	7:59 am Gemini	28th	2:39 am Leo	26th	1:31 pm Virgo
29th	11:21 pm Gemini	28th	2:04 pm Cancer	30th	3:28 am Virgo	28th	12:59 pm Libra
		30th	5:27 pm Leo			30th	1:27 pm Scorpio

September 1984		October 1984		November 1984		December 1984	
1st	4:34 pm Sagittarius	1st	5:31 am Capricorn	2nd	7:52 am Pisces	2nd	3:43 am Aries
3rd	10:55 pm Capricorn	3rd	2:07 pm Aquarius	4th	8:21 pm Aries	4th	4:20 pm Taurus
6th	8:13 am Aquarius	6th	1:18 am Pisces	7th	8:52 am Taurus	7th	3:23 am Gemini
8th	7:25 pm Pisces	8th	1:50 pm Aries	9th	8:09 pm Gemini	9th	11:53 am Cancer
11th	7:46 am Aries	11th	2:27 am Taurus	12th	5:28 am Cancer	11th	6:06 pm Leo
13th	8:32 pm Taurus	13th	2:12 pm Gemini	14th	12:30 pm Leo	13th	10:35 pm Virgo
16th	8:22 am Gemini	15th	12:00 pm Cancer	16th	5:04 pm Virgo	16th	1:52 am Libra
18th	5:32 pm Cancer	18th	6:38 am Leo	18th	7:28 pm Libra	18th	4:27 am Scorpio
20th	10:47 pm Leo	20th	9:52 am Virgo	20th	8:31 pm Scorpio	20th	7:00 am Sagittarius
23rd	0:19 am Virgo	22nd	10:31 am Libra	22nd	9:35 pm Sagittarius	22nd	10:24 am Capricorn
24th	11:41 pm Libra	24th	10:11 am Scorpio	25th	0:19 am Capricorn	24th	3:52 pm Aquarius
26th	11:04 pm Scorpio	26th	10:49 am Sagittarius	27th	6:12 am Aquarius	27th	0:20 am Pisces
29th	0:31 am Sagittarius	28th	2:11 pm Capricorn	29th	3:38 pm Pisces	29th	11:52 am Aries
		30th	9:16 pm Aquarius				

January 1985		February 1985		March 1985		April 1985	
1st	0:36 am Taurus	2nd	5:56 am Cancer	1st	3:19 pm Cancer	2nd	10:21 am Virgo
3rd	11:57 am Gemini	4th	10:58 am Leo	3rd	9:27 pm Leo	4th	10:53 am Libra
5th	8:16 pm Cancer	6th	1:08 pm Virgo	5th	11:44 pm Virgo	6th	10:13 am Scorpio
8th	1:28 am Leo	8th	2:13 pm Libra	7th	11:49 pm Libra	8th	10:22 am Sagittarius
10th	4:40 am Virgo	10th	3:52 pm Scorpio	9th	11:47 pm Scorpio	10th	1:03 pm Capricorn
12th	7:14 am Libra	12th	7:12 pm Sagittarius	12th	1:31 am Sagittarius	12th	7:06 pm Aquarius
14th	10:09 am Scorpio	15th	0:27 am Capricorn	14th	5:58 am Capricorn	15th	4:32 am Pisces
16th	1:50 pm Sagittarius	17th	7:39 am Aquarius	16th	1:14 pm Aquarius	17th	4:19 pm Aries
18th	6:31 pm Capricorn	19th	4:40 pm Pisces	18th	10:50 pm Pisces	20th	5:11 am Taurus
21st	0:39 am Aquarius	22nd	3:45 am Aries	21st	10:21 am Aries	22nd	5:59 pm Gemini
23rd	9:06 am Pisces	24th	4:28 pm Taurus	23rd	11:07 pm Taurus	25th	5:23 am Cancer
25th	8:06 pm Aries	27th	5:09 am Gemini	26th	12:01 pm Gemini	27th	2:06 pm Leo
28th	8:53 am Taurus			28th	11:13 pm Cancer	29th	7:21 pm Virgo
30th	9:00 pm Gemini			31st	6:47 am Leo		

May 1985		June 1985		July 1985		August 1985	
1st	9:21 pm Libra	2nd	7:34 am Sagittarius	1st	6:23 pm Capricorn	2nd	12:37 pm Pisces
3rd	9:17 pm Scorpio	4th	8:37 am Capricorn	3rd	9:38 pm Aquarius	4th	9:44 pm Aries
5th	8:58 pm Sagittarius	6th	11:58 am Aquarius	6th	3:44 am Pisces	7th	9:42 am Taurus
7th	10:13 pm Capricorn	8th	6:51 pm Pisces	8th	1:24 pm Aries	9th	10:31 pm Gemini
10th	2:41 am Aquarius	11th	5:26 am Aries	11th	1:44 am Taurus	12th	9:24 am Cancer
12th	10:50 am Pisces	13th	6:12 pm Taurus	13th	2:21 pm Gemini	14th	4:53 pm Leo
14th	10:26 pm Aries	16th	6:43 am Gemini	16th	0:53 am Cancer	16th	9:14 pm Virgo
17th	11:23 am Taurus	18th	5:19 pm Cancer	18th	8:22 am Leo	18th	11:43 pm Libra
19th	12:00 pm Gemini	21st	1:31 am Leo	20th	1:26 pm Virgo	21st	1:51 am Scorpio
22nd	11:01 am Cancer	23rd	7:29 am Virgo	22nd	5:09 pm Libra	23rd	4:37 am Sagittarius
24th	7:50 pm Leo	25th	11:44 am Libra	24th	8:16 pm Scorpio	25th	8:26 am Capricorn
27th	2:04 am Virgo	27th	2:34 pm Scorpio	26th	11:12 pm Sagittarius	27th	1:33 pm Aquarius
29th	5:37 am Libra	29th	4:29 pm Sagittarius	29th	2:21 am Capricorn	29th	8:25 pm Pisces
31st	7:05 am Scorpio			31st	6:28 am Aquarius		

Moon Tables

September 1985
1st 5:43 am Aries
3rd 5:28 pm Taurus
6th 6:26 am Gemini
8th 6:07 pm Cancer
11th 2:25 am Leo
13th 6:49 am Virgo
15th 8:33 am Libra
17th 9:17 am Scorpio
19th 10:43 am Sagittarius
21st 1:52 pm Capricorn
23rd 7:13 pm Aquarius
26th 2:51 am Pisces
28th 12:44 pm Aries

October 1985
1st 0:34 am Taurus
3rd 1:35 pm Gemini
6th 1:58 am Cancer
8th 11:28 am Leo
10th 5:05 pm Virgo
12th 7:10 pm Libra
14th 7:12 pm Scorpio
16th 7:07 pm Sagittarius
18th 8:37 pm Capricorn
21st 0:55 am Aquarius
23rd 8:31 am Pisces
25th 6:48 pm Aries
28th 6:50 am Taurus
30th 7:58 pm Gemini

November 1985
2nd 8:29 am Cancer
4th 7:01 pm Leo
7th 2:17 am Virgo
9th 5:48 am Libra
11th 6:30 am Scorpio
13th 5:54 am Sagittarius
15th 5:57 am Capricorn
17th 8:32 am Aquarius
19th 2:48 pm Pisces
22nd 0:44 am Aries
24th 1:08 pm Taurus
27th 2:07 am Gemini
29th 2:20 pm Cancer

December 1985
2nd 0:59 am Leo
4th 9:09 am Virgo
6th 2:28 pm Libra
8th 4:54 pm Scorpio
10th 5:12 pm Sagittarius
12th 5:02 pm Capricorn
14th 6:20 pm Aquarius
16th 10:52 pm Pisces
19th 7:42 am Aries
21st 7:42 pm Taurus
24th 8:44 am Gemini
26th 8:42 pm Cancer
29th 6:42 am Leo
31st 2:40 pm Virgo

January 1986
2nd 8:43 pm Libra
5th 0:44 am Scorpio
7th 2:47 am Sagittarius
9th 3:43 am Capricorn
11th 5:05 am Aquarius
13th 8:45 am Pisces
15th 4:09 pm Aries
18th 3:16 am Taurus
20th 4:12 pm Gemini
23rd 4:14 am Cancer
25th 1:45 pm Leo
27th 8:51 pm Virgo
30th 2:09 am Libra

February 1986
1st 6:18 am Scorpio
3rd 9:31 am Sagittarius
5th 12:02 pm Capricorn
7th 2:38 pm Aquarius
9th 6:36 pm Pisces
12th 1:22 am Aries
14th 11:42 am Taurus
17th 0:18 am Gemini
19th 12:38 pm Cancer
21st 10:25 pm Leo
24th 4:58 am Virgo
26th 9:07 am Libra
28th 12:06 pm Scorpio

March 1986
2nd 2:53 pm Sagittarius
4th 5:57 pm Capricorn
6th 9:43 pm Aquarius
9th 2:50 am Pisces
11th 10:07 am Aries
13th 8:06 pm Taurus
16th 8:24 am Gemini
18th 9:05 pm Cancer
21st 7:35 am Leo
23rd 2:36 pm Virgo
25th 6:22 pm Libra
27th 8:06 pm Scorpio
29th 9:22 pm Sagittarius
31st 11:26 pm Capricorn

April 1986
3rd 3:13 am Aquarius
5th 9:06 am Pisces
7th 5:14 pm Aries
10th 3:37 am Taurus
12th 3:52 pm Gemini
15th 4:42 am Cancer
17th 4:06 pm Leo
20th 0:25 am Virgo
22nd 4:48 am Libra
24th 6:15 am Scorpio
26th 6:18 am Sagittarius
28th 6:45 am Capricorn
30th 9:11 am Aquarius

May 1986
2nd 2:35 pm Pisces
4th 11:01 pm Aries
7th 10:00 am Taurus
9th 10:25 pm Gemini
12th 11:17 am Cancer
14th 11:14 pm Leo
17th 8:41 am Virgo
19th 2:36 pm Libra
21st 4:59 pm Scorpio
23rd 4:55 pm Sagittarius
25th 4:15 pm Capricorn
27th 5:05 pm Aquarius
29th 8:58 pm Pisces

June 1986
1st 4:46 am Aries
3rd 3:48 pm Taurus
6th 4:26 am Gemini
8th 5:14 pm Cancer
11th 5:09 am Leo
13th 3:14 pm Virgo
15th 10:37 pm Libra
18th 2:34 am Scorpio
20th 3:34 am Sagittarius
22nd 3:00 am Capricorn
24th 2:53 am Aquarius
26th 5:18 am Pisces
28th 11:41 am Aries
30th 9:55 pm Taurus

July 1986
3rd 10:33 am Gemini
5th 11:20 pm Cancer
8th 10:52 am Leo
10th 8:47 pm Virgo
13th 4:37 am Libra
15th 9:53 am Scorpio
17th 12:30 pm Sagittarius
19th 1:08 pm Capricorn
21st 1:20 pm Aquarius
23rd 3:03 pm Pisces
25th 8:06 pm Aries
28th 5:14 am Taurus
30th 5:20 pm Gemini

August 1986
2nd 6:03 am Cancer
4th 5:24 pm Leo
7th 2:44 am Virgo
9th 10:02 am Libra
11th 3:34 pm Scorpio
13th 7:14 pm Sagittarius
15th 9:21 pm Capricorn
17th 10:44 pm Aquarius
20th 0:52 am Pisces
22nd 5:30 am Aries
24th 1:40 pm Taurus
27th 1:01 am Gemini
29th 1:38 pm Cancer

September 1986
1st 1:07 am Leo
3rd 10:02 am Virgo
5th 4:32 pm Libra
7th 9:11 pm Scorpio
10th 0:41 am Sagittarius
12th 3:27 am Capricorn
14th 6:07 am Aquarius
16th 9:29 am Pisces
18th 2:36 pm Aries
20th 10:25 pm Taurus
23rd 9:15 am Gemini
25th 9:44 pm Cancer
28th 9:36 am Leo
30th 6:55 pm Virgo

October 1986
3rd 1:03 am Libra
5th 4:34 am Scorpio
7th 6:48 am Sagittarius
9th 8:54 am Capricorn
11th 11:47 am Aquarius
13th 4:05 pm Pisces
15th 10:14 pm Aries
18th 6:37 am Taurus
20th 5:15 pm Gemini
23rd 5:36 am Cancer
25th 6:00 pm Leo
28th 4:18 am Virgo
30th 11:00 am Libra

November 1986
1st 2:16 pm Scorpio
3rd 3:18 pm Sagittarius
5th 3:51 pm Capricorn
7th 5:31 pm Aquarius
9th 9:30 pm Pisces
12th 4:16 am Aries
14th 1:26 pm Taurus
17th 0:26 am Gemini
19th 12:46 pm Cancer
22nd 1:24 am Leo
24th 12:41 pm Virgo
26th 8:57 pm Libra
29th 1:13 am Scorpio

December 1986
1st 2:07 am Sagittarius
3rd 1:29 am Capricorn
5th 1:24 am Aquarius
7th 3:52 am Pisces
9th 9:55 am Aries
11th 7:12 pm Taurus
14th 6:42 am Gemini
16th 7:09 pm Cancer
19th 7:43 am Leo
21st 7:28 pm Virgo
24th 4:50 am Libra
26th 11:00 am Scorpio
28th 1:14 pm Sagittarius
30th 12:53 pm Capricorn

January 1987
1st 11:58 am Aquarius
3rd 12:43 pm Pisces
5th 4:57 pm Aries
8th 1:16 am Taurus
10th 12:42 pm Gemini
13th 1:19 am Cancer
15th 1:45 pm Leo
18th 1:14 am Virgo
20th 11:05 am Libra
22nd 6:28 pm Scorpio
24th 10:35 pm Sagittarius
26th 11:42 pm Capricorn
28th 11:17 pm Aquarius
30th 11:26 pm Pisces

February 1987
2nd 2:12 am Aries
4th 8:50 am Taurus
6th 7:26 pm Gemini
9th 7:56 am Cancer
11th 8:22 pm Leo
14th 7:25 am Virgo
16th 4:43 pm Libra
19th 0:05 am Scorpio
21st 5:08 am Sagittarius
23rd 7:55 am Capricorn
25th 9:08 am Aquarius
27th 10:09 am Pisces

March 1987
1st 12:41 pm Aries
3rd 6:16 pm Taurus
6th 3:28 am Gemini
8th 3:25 pm Cancer
11th 3:55 am Leo
13th 2:53 pm Virgo
15th 11:36 pm Libra
18th 5:56 am Scorpio
20th 10:30 am Sagittarius
22nd 1:47 pm Capricorn
24th 4:18 pm Aquarius
26th 7:05 pm Pisces
28th 10:13 pm Aries
31st 3:49 am Taurus

April 1987
2nd 12:20 pm Gemini
4th 11:34 pm Cancer
7th 12:02 pm Leo
9th 11:29 pm Virgo
12th 8:02 am Libra
14th 1:39 pm Scorpio
16th 5:01 pm Sagittarius
18th 7:22 pm Capricorn
20th 9:45 pm Aquarius
23rd 1:03 am Pisces
25th 5:42 am Aries
27th 12:08 pm Taurus
29th 8:45 pm Gemini

Why Does He Say One Thing and Do Another?

May 1987
2nd 7:41 am Cancer
4th 8:07 pm Leo
7th 8:05 am Virgo
9th 5:26 pm Libra
11th 11:09 pm Scorpio
14th 1:42 am Sagittarius
16th 2:38 am Capricorn
18th 3:45 am Aquarius
20th 6:27 am Pisces
22nd 11:27 am Aries
24th 6:41 pm Taurus
27th 3:56 am Gemini
29th 3:01 pm Cancer

June 1987
1st 3:27 am Leo
3rd 3:54 pm Virgo
6th 2:22 am Libra
8th 9:01 am Scorpio
10th 11:49 am Sagittarius
12th 12:04 pm Capricorn
14th 11:49 am Aquarius
16th 1:00 pm Pisces
18th 5:02 pm Aries
21st 0:10 am Taurus
23rd 9:38 am Gemini
25th 9:22 pm Cancer
28th 9:52 am Leo
30th 10:33 pm Virgo

July 1987
3rd 9:50 am Libra
5th 5:58 pm Scorpio
7th 10:03 pm Sagittarius
9th 10:42 pm Capricorn
11th 9:50 pm Aquarius
13th 9:38 pm Pisces
16th 0:02 am Aries
18th 6:09 am Taurus
20th 3:36 pm Gemini
23rd 3:14 am Cancer
25th 3:50 pm Leo
28th 4:25 am Virgo
30th 3:56 pm Libra

August 1987
2nd 1:08 am Scorpio
4th 6:42 am Sagittarius
6th 8:47 am Capricorn
8th 8:36 am Aquarius
10th 8:04 am Pisces
12th 9:14 am Aries
14th 1:44 pm Taurus
16th 10:01 pm Gemini
19th 9:21 am Cancer
21st 9:58 pm Leo
24th 10:23 am Virgo
26th 9:35 pm Libra
29th 6:47 am Scorpio
31st 1:20 pm Sagittarius

September 1987
2nd 5:00 pm Capricorn
4th 6:19 pm Aquarius
6th 6:37 pm Pisces
8th 7:36 pm Aries
10th 10:57 pm Taurus
13th 5:59 am Gemini
15th 4:25 pm Cancer
18th 4:50 am Leo
20th 5:13 pm Virgo
23rd 3:57 am Libra
25th 12:28 pm Scorpio
27th 6:48 pm Sagittarius
29th 11:08 pm Capricorn

October 1987
2nd 1:50 am Aquarius
4th 3:39 am Pisces
6th 5:36 am Aries
8th 8:50 am Taurus
10th 3:07 pm Gemini
13th 0:30 am Cancer
15th 12:34 pm Leo
18th 1:06 am Virgo
20th 11:47 am Libra
22nd 7:39 pm Scorpio
25th 0:57 am Sagittarius
27th 4:32 am Capricorn
29th 7:27 am Aquarius
31st 10:20 am Pisces

November 1987
2nd 1:41 pm Aries
4th 6:04 pm Taurus
7th 0:15 am Gemini
9th 9:12 am Cancer
11th 8:45 pm Leo
14th 9:28 am Virgo
16th 8:46 pm Libra
19th 4:43 am Scorpio
21st 9:13 am Sagittarius
23rd 11:31 am Capricorn
25th 1:13 pm Aquarius
27th 3:43 pm Pisces
29th 7:38 pm Aries

December 1987
2nd 1:06 am Taurus
4th 8:16 am Gemini
6th 5:22 pm Cancer
9th 4:40 am Leo
11th 5:29 pm Virgo
14th 5:36 am Libra
16th 2:35 pm Scorpio
18th 7:29 pm Sagittarius
20th 9:06 pm Capricorn
22nd 9:21 pm Aquarius
24th 10:12 pm Pisces
27th 1:07 am Aries
29th 6:40 am Taurus
31st 2:32 pm Gemini

January 1988
3rd 0:18 am Cancer
5th 11:49 am Leo
8th 0:35 am Virgo
10th 1:13 pm Libra
12th 11:39 pm Scorpio
15th 5:53 am Sagittarius
17th 8:10 am Capricorn
19th 8:02 am Aquarius
21st 7:31 am Pisces
23rd 8:37 am Aries
25th 12:43 pm Taurus
27th 8:06 pm Gemini
30th 6:14 am Cancer

February 1988
1st 6:08 pm Leo
4th 6:54 am Virgo
6th 7:35 pm Libra
9th 6:38 am Scorpio
11th 2:30 pm Sagittarius
13th 6:32 pm Capricorn
15th 7:23 pm Aquarius
17th 6:44 pm Pisces
19th 6:38 pm Aries
21st 8:54 pm Taurus
24th 2:45 am Gemini
26th 12:16 pm Cancer
29th 0:12 am Leo

March 1988
2nd 1:07 pm Virgo
5th 1:33 am Libra
7th 12:25 pm Scorpio
9th 8:58 pm Sagittarius
12th 2:29 am Capricorn
14th 5:06 am Aquarius
16th 5:42 am Pisces
18th 5:47 am Aries
20th 7:09 am Taurus
22nd 11:27 am Gemini
24th 7:30 pm Cancer
27th 6:55 am Leo
29th 7:50 pm Virgo

April 1988
1st 8:04 am Libra
3rd 6:25 pm Scorpio
6th 2:29 am Sagittarius
8th 8:17 am Capricorn
10th 12:08 pm Aquarius
12th 2:23 pm Pisces
14th 3:47 pm Aries
16th 5:33 pm Taurus
18th 9:12 pm Gemini
21st 4:08 am Cancer
23rd 2:38 pm Leo
26th 3:17 am Virgo
28th 3:36 pm Libra

May 1988
1st 1:39 am Scorpio
3rd 8:50 am Sagittarius
5th 1:53 pm Capricorn
7th 5:36 pm Aquarius
9th 8:40 pm Pisces
11th 11:24 pm Aries
14th 2:23 am Taurus
16th 6:35 am Gemini
18th 1:10 pm Cancer
20th 10:53 pm Leo
23rd 11:39 am Virgo
25th 11:50 pm Libra
28th 10:02 am Scorpio
30th 4:54 pm Sagittarius

June 1988
1st 8:59 pm Capricorn
3rd 11:35 pm Aquarius
6th 2:02 am Pisces
8th 5:06 am Aries
10th 9:05 am Taurus
12th 2:18 pm Gemini
14th 9:22 pm Cancer
17th 7:00 am Leo
19th 7:04 pm Virgo
22nd 7:56 am Libra
24th 6:56 pm Scorpio
27th 2:15 am Sagittarius
29th 5:57 am Capricorn

July 1988
1st 7:31 am Aquarius
3rd 8:36 am Pisces
5th 10:42 am Aries
7th 2:31 pm Taurus
9th 8:18 pm Gemini
12th 4:12 am Cancer
14th 2:15 pm Leo
17th 2:18 am Virgo
19th 3:20 pm Libra
22nd 3:11 am Scorpio
24th 11:36 am Sagittarius
26th 4:02 pm Capricorn
28th 5:22 pm Aquarius
30th 5:24 pm Pisces

August 1988
1st 5:57 pm Aries
3rd 8:28 pm Taurus
6th 1:45 am Gemini
8th 9:56 am Cancer
10th 8:29 pm Leo
13th 8:48 am Virgo
15th 9:52 pm Libra
18th 10:08 am Scorpio
20th 7:52 pm Sagittarius
23rd 1:47 am Capricorn
25th 4:02 am Aquarius
27th 4:01 am Pisces
29th 3:31 am Aries
31st 4:25 am Taurus

September 1988
2nd 8:17 am Gemini
4th 3:41 pm Cancer
7th 2:16 am Leo
9th 2:49 pm Virgo
12th 3:51 am Libra
14th 4:05 pm Scorpio
17th 2:25 am Sagittarius
19th 9:40 am Capricorn
21st 1:38 pm Aquarius
23rd 2:47 pm Pisces
25th 2:30 pm Aries
27th 2:32 pm Taurus
29th 4:47 pm Gemini

October 1988
1st 10:39 pm Cancer
4th 8:33 am Leo
6th 9:01 pm Virgo
9th 10:03 am Libra
11th 9:57 pm Scorpio
14th 7:57 am Sagittarius
16th 3:42 pm Capricorn
18th 9:03 pm Aquarius
20th 11:58 pm Pisces
23rd 0:58 am Aries
25th 1:22 am Taurus
27th 2:56 am Gemini
29th 7:33 am Cancer
31st 4:08 pm Leo

November 1988
3rd 4:02 am Virgo
5th 5:03 pm Scorpio
8th 4:44 am Scorpio
10th 2:03 pm Sagittarius
12th 9:11 pm Capricorn
15th 2:35 am Aquarius
17th 6:32 am Pisces
19th 9:11 am Aries
21st 11:02 am Taurus
23rd 1:15 pm Gemini
25th 5:24 pm Cancer
28th 0:52 am Leo
30th 12:02 pm Virgo

December 1988
2nd 0:57 am Libra
5th 12:47 pm Scorpio
7th 9:53 pm Sagittarius
10th 4:05 am Capricorn
12th 8:25 am Aquarius
14th 11:52 am Pisces
16th 3:03 pm Aries
18th 6:12 pm Taurus
20th 9:44 pm Gemini
23rd 2:36 am Cancer
25th 10:01 am Leo
27th 8:28 pm Virgo
30th 9:09 am Libra

Moon Tables

January 1989
1st   9:33 pm Scorpio
4th   7:07 am Sagittarius
6th   1:09 pm Capricorn
8th   4:29 pm Aquarius
10th 6:31 pm Pisces
12th 8:37 pm Aries
14th 11:38 pm Taurus
17th 3:59 am Gemini
19th 10:01 am Cancer
21st 6:05 pm Leo
24th 4:34 am Virgo
26th 5:02 pm Libra
29th 5:46 am Scorpio
31st 4:24 pm Sagittarius

February 1989
2nd 11:28 pm Capricorn
5th   2:48 am Aquarius
7th   3:52 am Pisces
9th   4:19 am Aries
11th 5:48 am Taurus
13th 9:28 am Gemini
15th 3:45 pm Cancer
18th 0:33 am Leo
20th 11:37 am Virgo
23rd 0:06 am Libra
25th 12:56 pm Scorpio
28th 0:29 am Sagittarius

March 1989
2nd   8:53 am Capricorn
4th   1:31 pm Aquarius
6th   2:56 pm Pisces
8th   2:36 pm Aries
10th 2:29 pm Taurus
12th 4:22 pm Gemini
14th 9:29 pm Cancer
17th 6:17 am Leo
19th 5:42 pm Virgo
22nd 6:24 am Libra
24th 7:11 pm Scorpio
27th 6:52 am Sagittarius
29th 4:22 pm Capricorn
31st 10:45 pm Aquarius

April 1989
3rd   1:36 am Pisces
5th   1:50 am Aries
7th   1:07 am Taurus
9th   1:32 am Gemini
11th 5:02 am Cancer
13th 12:35 pm Leo
15th 11:40 pm Virgo
18th 12:33 pm Libra
21st 1:14 am Scorpio
23rd 12:58 pm Sagittarius
25th 10:16 pm Capricorn
28th 5:31 am Aquarius
30th 10:00 am Pisces

May 1989
2nd 11:49 am Aries
4th 11:55 am Taurus
6th 12:08 pm Gemini
8th   2:27 pm Cancer
10th 8:27 pm Leo
13th 6:33 am Virgo
15th 7:09 pm Libra
18th 7:47 am Scorpio
20th 6:51 pm Sagittarius
23rd 3:54 am Capricorn
25th 10:59 am Aquarius
27th 4:10 pm Pisces
29th 7:25 pm Aries
31st 8:50 pm Taurus

June 1989
2nd 10:04 pm Gemini
5th   0:19 am Cancer
7th   5:33 am Leo
9th   2:35 pm Virgo
12th 2:32 am Libra
14th 3:11 pm Scorpio
17th 2:12 am Sagittarius
19th 10:39 pm Capricorn
21st 4:56 pm Aquarius
23rd 9:37 pm Pisces
26th 1:08 am Aries
28th 3:47 am Taurus
30th 6:10 am Gemini

July 1989
2nd   9:23 am Cancer
4th   2:43 pm Leo
6th 11:06 pm Virgo
9th 10:32 am Libra
11th 11:10 pm Scorpio
14th 10:28 am Sagittarius
16th 6:59 pm Capricorn
19th 0:36 am Aquarius
21st 4:07 am Pisces
23rd 6:42 am Aries
25th 9:13 am Taurus
27th 12:19 pm Gemini
29th 4:35 pm Cancer
31st 10:43 pm Leo

August 1989
3rd   7:22 am Virgo
5th   6:30 pm Libra
8th   7:04 am Scorpio
10th 7:00 pm Sagittarius
13th 4:13 am Capricorn
15th 9:54 am Aquarius
17th 12:43 pm Pisces
19th 1:59 pm Aries
21st 3:14 pm Taurus
23rd 5:43 pm Gemini
25th 10:15 pm Cancer
28th 5:16 am Leo
30th 2:33 pm Virgo

September 1989
2nd   1:49 am Libra
4th   2:24 pm Scorpio
7th   2:50 am Sagittarius
9th   1:08 pm Capricorn
11th 7:59 pm Aquarius
13th 11:06 pm Pisces
15th 11:38 pm Aries
17th 11:23 pm Taurus
20th 0:17 am Gemini
22nd 3:53 am Cancer
24th 10:48 am Leo
26th 8:35 pm Virgo
29th 8:17 am Libra

October 1989
1st   8:54 pm Scorpio
4th   9:29 am Sagittarius
6th   8:43 pm Capricorn
9th   5:02 am Aquarius
11th 9:32 am Pisces
13th 10:38 am Aries
15th 9:53 am Taurus
17th 9:23 am Gemini
19th 11:15 am Cancer
21st 4:52 pm Leo
24th 2:16 am Virgo
26th 2:12 pm Libra
29th 2:56 am Scorpio
31st 3:23 pm Sagittarius

November 1989
3rd   2:47 am Capricorn
5th 12:06 pm Aquarius
7th   6:21 pm Pisces
9th   9:06 pm Aries
11th 9:08 pm Taurus
13th 8:19 pm Gemini
15th 8:54 pm Cancer
18th 0:46 am Leo
20th 8:58 am Virgo
22nd 8:27 pm Libra
25th 9:12 am Scorpio
27th 9:30 pm Sagittarius
30th 8:25 am Capricorn

December 1989
2nd   5:40 pm Aquarius
5th   0:48 am Pisces
7th   5:09 am Aries
9th   6:56 am Taurus
11th 7:15 am Gemini
13th 7:53 am Cancer
15th 10:47 am Leo
17th 5:24 pm Virgo
20th 3:47 am Libra
22nd 4:18 pm Scorpio
25th 4:35 am Sagittarius
27th 3:08 pm Capricorn
29th 11:38 pm Aquarius

January 1990
1st   6:09 am Pisces
3rd 10:54 am Aries
5th   2:05 pm Taurus
7th   4:01 pm Gemini
9th   5:54 pm Cancer
11th 9:04 pm Leo
14th 2:50 am Virgo
16th 12:21 pm Libra
19th 0:16 am Scorpio
21st 12:41 pm Sagittarius
23rd 11:27 pm Capricorn
26th 7:22 am Aquarius
28th 12:48 pm Pisces
30th 4:32 pm Aries

February 1990
1st   7:28 pm Taurus
3rd 10:13 pm Gemini
6th   1:28 am Cancer
8th   5:55 am Leo
10th 12:17 pm Virgo
12th 9:10 pm Libra
15th 8:35 am Scorpio
17th 9:05 pm Sagittarius
20th 8:25 am Capricorn
22nd 4:48 pm Aquarius
24th 9:48 pm Pisces
27th 0:16 am Aries

March 1990
1st   1:44 am Taurus
3rd   3:39 am Gemini
5th   7:06 am Cancer
7th 12:28 pm Leo
9th   7:49 pm Virgo
12th 5:11 am Libra
14th 4:27 pm Scorpio
17th 4:56 am Sagittarius
19th 4:59 pm Capricorn
22nd 2:28 am Aquarius
24th 8:03 am Pisces
26th 10:11 am Aries
28th 10:27 am Taurus
30th 10:46 am Gemini

April 1990
1st 12:55 pm Cancer
3rd   5:53 pm Leo
6th   1:43 am Virgo
8th 11:46 am Libra
10th 11:18 pm Scorpio
13th 11:49 am Sagittarius
16th 0:16 am Capricorn
18th 10:48 am Aquarius
20th 5:53 pm Pisces
22nd 8:56 pm Aries
24th 9:01 pm Taurus
26th 8:13 pm Gemini
28th 8:42 pm Cancer

May 1990
1st   0:09 am Leo
3rd   7:21 am Virgo
5th   5:30 pm Libra
8th   5:24 am Scorpio
10th 5:56 pm Sagittarius
13th 6:21 am Capricorn
15th 5:28 pm Aquarius
18th 1:53 am Pisces
20th 6:28 am Aries
22nd 7:40 am Taurus
24th 7:01 am Gemini
26th 6:38 am Cancer
28th 8:35 am Leo
30th 2:13 pm Virgo

June 1990
1st 11:31 pm Libra
4th 11:24 am Scorpio
6th 12:00 pm Sagittarius
9th 12:21 pm Capricorn
11th 11:09 pm Aquarius
14th 7:57 am Pisces
16th 1:51 pm Aries
18th 4:40 pm Taurus
20th 5:14 pm Gemini
22nd 5:12 pm Cancer
24th 6:29 pm Leo
26th 10:43 pm Virgo
29th 6:51 am Libra

July 1990
1st   6:02 pm Scorpio
4th   6:35 am Sagittarius
6th   6:39 pm Capricorn
9th   5:05 am Aquarius
11th 1:28 pm Pisces
13th 7:35 pm Aries
15th 11:29 pm Taurus
18th 1:32 am Gemini
20th 2:46 am Cancer
22nd 4:33 am Leo
24th 8:23 am Virgo
26th 3:24 pm Libra
29th 1:40 am Scorpio
31st 1:59 pm Sagittarius

August 1990
3rd   2:08 am Capricorn
5th 12:16 pm Aquarius
7th   7:54 pm Pisces
10th 1:15 am Aries
12th 4:56 am Taurus
14th 7:43 am Gemini
16th 10:14 am Cancer
18th 1:15 pm Leo
20th 5:37 pm Virgo
23rd 0:19 am Libra
25th 9:50 am Scorpio
27th 9:59 pm Sagittarius
30th 10:21 am Capricorn

47

Why Does He Say One Thing and Do Another?

September 1990
1st 8:49 pm Aquarius
4th 4:03 am Pisces
6th 8:21 am Aries
8th 10:56 am Taurus
10th 1:07 pm Gemini
12th 3:56 pm Cancer
14th 7:55 pm Leo
17th 1:20 am Virgo
19th 8:38 am Libra
21st 6:09 pm Scorpio
24th 5:54 am Sagittarius
26th 6:37 pm Capricorn
29th 5:51 am Aquarius

October 1990
1st 1:37 pm Pisces
3rd 5:38 pm Aries
5th 7:05 pm Taurus
7th 7:48 pm Gemini
9th 9:31 pm Cancer
12th 1:17 am Leo
14th 7:24 am Virgo
16th 3:30 pm Libra
19th 1:25 am Scorpio
21st 1:13 pm Sagittarius
24th 2:04 am Capricorn
26th 2:11 pm Aquarius
28th 11:23 pm Pisces
31st 4:11 am Aries

November 1990
2nd 5:30 am Taurus
4th 5:07 am Gemini
6th 5:10 am Cancer
8th 7:28 am Leo
10th 12:52 pm Virgo
12th 9:10 pm Libra
15th 7:42 am Scorpio
17th 7:40 pm Sagittarius
22nd 9:08 am Aquarius
25th 7:27 am Pisces
27th 2:00 pm Aries
29th 4:33 pm Taurus

December 1990
1st 4:21 pm Gemini
3rd 3:30 pm Cancer
5th 4:05 pm Leo
7th 7:42 pm Virgo
10th 3:02 am Libra
12th 1:29 pm Scorpio
15th 1:43 am Sagittarius
17th 2:35 pm Capricorn
20th 2:59 am Aquarius
22nd 1:45 pm Pisces
24th 9:43 pm Aries
27th 2:07 am Taurus
29th 2:24 am Gemini
31st 3:04 am Cancer

January 1991
2nd 2:57 am Leo
4th 5:01 am Virgo
6th 10:39 am Libra
8th 8:01 pm Scorpio
11th 8:07 am Sagittarius
13th 8:59 pm Capricorn
16th 9:02 am Aquarius
18th 7:22 pm Pisces
21st 3:27 am Aries
23rd 8:57 am Taurus
25th 12:04 pm Gemini
27th 1:23 pm Cancer
29th 2:05 pm Leo
31st 3:48 pm Virgo

February 1991
2nd 8:05 pm Libra
5th 4:03 am Scorpio
7th 3:24 pm Sagittarius
10th 4:14 am Capricorn
12th 4:13 pm Aquarius
15th 1:58 am Pisces
17th 9:09 am Aries
19th 2:23 pm Taurus
21st 6:09 pm Gemini
23rd 8:56 pm Cancer
25th 11:13 pm Leo
28th 1:52 am Virgo

March 1991
2nd 6:06 am Libra
4th 1:13 pm Scorpio
6th 11:34 pm Sagittarius
9th 12:13 pm Capricorn
12th 0:29 am Aquarius
14th 10:05 am Pisces
16th 4:34 pm Aries
18th 8:39 pm Taurus
20th 11:36 pm Gemini
23rd 2:28 am Cancer
25th 5:44 am Leo
27th 9:43 am Virgo
29th 2:52 pm Libra
31st 10:02 pm Scorpio

April 1991
3rd 8:02 am Sagittarius
5th 8:21 pm Capricorn
8th 8:57 am Aquarius
10th 7:14 pm Pisces
13th 1:48 am Aries
15th 5:03 am Taurus
17th 6:42 am Gemini
19th 8:18 am Cancer
21st 11:06 am Leo
23rd 3:32 pm Virgo
25th 9:36 pm Libra
28th 5:36 am Scorpio
30th 3:46 pm Sagittarius

May 1991
3rd 3:56 am Capricorn
5th 4:50 pm Aquarius
8th 4:01 am Pisces
10th 11:29 am Aries
12th 3:03 pm Taurus
14th 3:50 pm Gemini
16th 4:16 pm Cancer
18th 5:33 pm Leo
20th 9:02 pm Virgo
23rd 3:10 am Libra
25th 11:44 am Scorpio
27th 10:21 pm Sagittarius
30th 10:42 am Capricorn

June 1991
1st 11:42 pm Aquarius
4th 11:34 am Pisces
6th 8:22 pm Aries
9th 1:12 am Taurus
11th 2:35 am Gemini
13th 2:16 am Cancer
15th 2:12 am Leo
17th 4:05 am Virgo
19th 9:06 am Libra
21st 5:21 pm Scorpio
24th 4:18 am Sagittarius
26th 4:50 pm Capricorn
29th 5:46 am Aquarius

July 1991
1st 5:48 pm Pisces
4th 3:31 am Aries
6th 9:48 am Taurus
8th 12:38 pm Gemini
10th 1:02 pm Cancer
12th 12:37 pm Leo
14th 1:17 pm Virgo
16th 4:39 pm Libra
18th 11:41 pm Scorpio
21st 10:19 am Sagittarius
23rd 10:57 pm Capricorn
26th 11:48 am Aquarius
28th 11:34 pm Pisces
31st 9:18 am Aries

August 1991
2nd 4:29 pm Taurus
4th 8:53 pm Gemini
6th 10:48 pm Cancer
8th 11:10 pm Leo
10th 11:36 pm Virgo
13th 1:54 am Libra
15th 7:39 am Scorpio
17th 5:14 pm Sagittarius
20th 5:34 am Capricorn
22nd 6:27 pm Aquarius
25th 5:49 am Pisces
27th 2:59 pm Aries
30th 10:00 pm Taurus

September 1991
1st 3:03 am Gemini
3rd 6:19 am Cancer
5th 8:14 am Leo
7th 9:39 am Virgo
9th 11:57 am Libra
11th 4:48 pm Scorpio
14th 1:17 am Sagittarius
16th 1:05 pm Capricorn
19th 1:56 am Aquarius
21st 1:17 pm Pisces
23rd 9:56 pm Aries
26th 3:59 am Taurus
28th 8:25 am Gemini
30th 11:57 am Cancer

October 1991
2nd 2:50 pm Leo
4th 5:46 pm Virgo
6th 9:03 pm Libra
9th 2:03 am Scorpio
11th 10:03 am Sagittarius
13th 9:12 pm Capricorn
16th 10:04 am Aquarius
18th 9:52 pm Pisces
21st 6:30 am Aries
23rd 11:53 am Taurus
25th 3:08 pm Gemini
27th 5:37 pm Cancer
29th 8:21 pm Leo
31st 11:48 pm Virgo

November 1991
3rd 4:14 am Libra
5th 10:13 am Scorpio
7th 6:26 pm Sagittarius
10th 5:20 am Capricorn
12th 6:08 pm Aquarius
15th 6:31 am Pisces
17th 4:04 pm Aries
19th 9:49 pm Taurus
22nd 0:23 am Gemini
24th 1:26 am Cancer
26th 2:38 am Leo
28th 5:14 am Virgo
30th 9:50 am Libra

December 1991
2nd 4:36 pm Scorpio
5th 1:34 am Sagittarius
7th 12:45 pm Capricorn
10th 1:28 am Aquarius
12th 2:18 pm Pisces
15th 1:06 am Aries
17th 8:05 am Taurus
19th 11:18 am Gemini
21st 11:41 am Cancer
23rd 11:41 am Leo
25th 12:28 pm Virgo
27th 3:42 pm Libra
29th 10:05 pm Scorpio

Key Phrases for the Moon Signs

The following phrases indicate each moon sign's essential emotional needs. They can be very helpful tools for remembering each moon sign's most salient emotional issue.

MOON IN ARIES I need lots of ego strokes and to get what I want exactly when I want it.

MOON IN TAURUS I need stability and a sound, secure future.

MOON IN GEMINI I need someone exciting who turns on my mind.

MOON IN CANCER I need to have all of my emotional needs met.

MOON IN LEO I need a love that awes me.

MOON IN VIRGO I need someone who meets all of my standards.

MOON IN LIBRA I need a harmonious, flowing, sharing partnership.

MOON IN SCORPIO I need passion, intensity, and a soulful sort of intimacy.

MOON IN SAGITTARIUS I need adventure and to feel fully alive.

MOON IN CAPRICORN I need material and deep emotional security.

MOON IN AQUARIUS I need a best friend who allows me freedom.

MOON IN PISCES I need a soul mate who makes time stop.

The Moon in
Aries Man

Who He Is Emotionally

The moon in Aries man has a wild, restless spirit that spurs him on impulsively toward the first direction that happens to occur to him. Impulsive, impatient, and often possessing little staying power, he seeks excitement and tends to put his needs first before all other considerations. A rambunctious child at heart, he is always revved up and ready to go. Hot with life and his own anticipation, the moon in Aries man wants to burn.

Ambitious, aggressive, assertive, and enterprising, he has emotional energy to give away. The moon in Aries man doesn't look before he leaps and loves living that way. Courageous, competitive, and always primed for a challenge, he gives off sparks and sometimes strokes of lightning. A thrill seeker who can't sit still for very long, he is a man who must always test new ground. Entranced by novelty and caught up in momentary satisfaction, he may be poor at following through on a previous commitment, should something sparkly snag his attention.

Fearless and full of wild initiative, the moon in Aries man makes a great fighter pilot; however, as a person, he is often more primed for excitement than sensitivity. He wants exactly what he wants when he wants it. Since he has a low frustration tolerance, he is not prepared to be patient and to wait things out. Putting immediate gratification at the top of his list of priorities, he can be something of a caution when he doesn't get his way. Sometimes reckless, self-centered, and certainly very testy, he can have the speed and unpredictability of a ricocheted bullet. Where did this sheer velocity come from? It is likely that both his temper and his interest will be gone before you can come upon an answer.

In the area of love he loves the chase but often gets bored with the prize. The moon in Aries man is fired up by conquest. The excitement of a hot new sexual encounter can make him forget what time it is or where he's supposed to be. A new fling is one of his favorite things. The moon in Aries man is turned on by chills and thrills and needs a strong dose of constant excitement. As a child, he probably had to be tied down. As an adult, he won't allow it. Wild and full of wanderlust, he wants to feel the flame—if only for a little while.

Even if he is the Virgo sun, shy type, this man will be attracted to wild fire sign women who will be restless and provocative. However, should he have an Aries sun, he could be double trouble. Wild, unruly

Marlon Brando is such a combination. Whatever his sun sign, the moon in Aries man wants nothing less than the world on his own terms, and given his ability to make waves, he often gets it.

How He Feels

Quick to anger, he also calms down in record time. Feelings don't linger too long with the moon in Aries man. He suffers the risk of moving and thinking and feeling too fast.

Sometimes irritable, insensitive, and shallow, he blowtorches his way through a bad moment. When busy, impatient, or seriously emotionally compromised, his words can be both clipped and cutting.

The moon in Aries man doesn't brood about the meaning of things. They fly past him and he by them, and before he knows it, it's all a new experience and the past has been forgotten. Because he is so fast-moving and impulsive, this man can promise things in one moment and forget them the next. He can also behave like a completely different person from one day to the next, all depending on how much his moods affect him.

Usually, the moon in Aries man is competitive, not compassionate. Heavy emotional scenes annoy him and emotional demands can make him shut you out completely. Needing a lot of space, he can't bear to feel confined. At all times he needs to be freed up to do his own thing and feel the wind in his face thrusting him in a completely new and exciting direction.

How He Shows His Feelings

Honest, direct, and very much to the point, the moon in Aries man can be blunt, tactless, and have the kind of candor that can wreak incredible damage. This is not a man who walks around brooding and holding feelings inside. He tells it like it is. Whether anyone really wants to hear it or not is completely beside the point.

Sexual and impulsive, this guy finds the bedroom to be a comfort zone. The moon in Aries man gives his all to his passion of the moment, and in that moment it may all seem like the very first time. As enthusiastic as a teenager just given a car, he will hold nothing back when he believes that he's in love. However, how long these passionate feelings last depends on how mature he happens to be and how much he yearns for change and variety.

His Dark Side

When immature, he can be arrogant and headstrong, cruel and argumentative. When the moon in Aries man is unevolved, he can be a big baby. Reckless, restless, petulant, and impatient, he can act like a race car headed for a brick wall.

His irritability can completely control him and his impatience and desire for novelty consume him. When emotionally immature, he can be faithless and full of so much restless energy that he will never finish anything he starts. Selfish, shallow, insensitive, and self-indulgent, he lives only for self-gratification, not noticing who he hurts and certainly not caring. Having poor self-restraint, little self-awareness, and a very quick temper, this is a man who can be like a bomb going off. However, it must also be said that his little explosions never last long.

His Bright Side

He can be wildly romantic, masculine, and courageous. He is also self-confident. He knows what he wants, and he'll get it no matter what. Rushing in where heroes fear to tread, he can be the biggest dragon slayer.

The moon in Aries man can be exciting, enthusiastic, and brimming with life. Sexual, passionate, and full of energy, he knows how to direct it to get the desired results. For the right person, he can be a challenging, highly charged lover who electrifies life.

His Attitude Toward Relationships

The moon in Aries man loves falling in love with love. However, he is poor at sustaining his feelings. Hot, passionate, and a man of the moment, when all aflame he is an avid pursuer. However, once he has the prize in hand, he may get bored.

Sometimes needing novelty and a challenge even more than a relationship, he is known to stray, especially when feeling settled. Because he hates being confined and passionately loves his freedom, he is happiest with someone as restless as he is who is more of a playmate than a serious, security-oriented person.

This is a man who writes his own rules, and this sometimes leads to very selfish behavior. The moon in Aries man is not the most mature type. He needs a lot of room to roam and a lot of time to grow up. Often jealous and possessive, he can demand a fidelity that he would never be able to fulfill himself. He can be thoughtless, inconsiderate, and belligerent when challenged. Because of this, this is a man who makes challenging and risky relationship material. However, should he have sown all his wild oats and found a truly compatible person, he can be an exciting partner.

His Romance Factor

When caught up in a passionate love, the moon in Aries man can be wildly romantic. Each time he falls in love it's as if it's for the first time. However, down the road, when a relationship settles into a routine, demands are made and something is expected of him, his attention may wane.

During this phase he is not the type to want to talk things out. The moon in Aries man has no patience for problem times unless the bumps personally challenge him. If he is bored, he will back away. However, if his boat is rocked and he is made jealous, he will get fired up all over again. The moon in Aries man has to feel fire in his veins to feel fully alive and completely in love. He has something of a chewing gum attitude toward romance. When the sweetness goes, you throw it all away and get a new piece.

This man needs a larger-than-life vision to pursue. Essentially, he is in love with his own feelings of being in love. Whoever serves as a catalyst must keep the flame going if she is going to stay in the light. The moon in Aries man can easily be a love-them-and-leave-them kind of guy. It takes him a long time to grow up and value a person, and even then, someone has to have a strong effect on him to make him want to commit. Someone has to be a large enough light to make him want to stretch, and until he wants to stretch, he'll never grow.

His Reality Factor

His reality is of his own making. A typical moon in Aries comment might be "Don't confuse me with the facts!" Basically, this man believes what he wants to believe, what is convenient, and what suits his personal purposes.

He can be completely irrational, defensive, combative, and terribly unfair. He doesn't care how he behaves if it gets him what he wants. The moon in Aries man will twist the truth to serve himself. He can also have the kind of candor that can almost kill you.

His Fear Factor

This is a man who tends to be fearless. Arrogant, confident, and rather combative, he does not think in terms of abandonment or pain. With a shrug he can leave the past behind and never look back. Jealousy fuels him and loss leaves him only looking for a new person. Even if he is upset, the moon in Aries man does not stay in darkness for very long. His style is to keep on moving, living, and conquering.

How He Relates to Fire Sign Women
(Aries, Leo, Sagittarius)

Here he is in his own element and it is one that will challenge him and give him the sort of excitement he needs. The fire sign woman is as restless and excitement seeking as he is. She is also headstrong, temperamental, passionate, and impatient. Both romantic and impulsive, she will move to the same beat and be willing to take the action anywhere. He may have to stretch to get her attention, and it will spur him on. Neither one of them can bear being bored, and there is no danger of this here. This can be a very exciting and fulfilling match.

How He Relates to Air Sign Women
(Gemini, Libra, Aquarius)

Initially, she will rise to his challenge. However, the cool, detached air sign woman may not be as hot as this man's moon sign ideally requires. While he lives his romantic life on impulse, she has to think everything out before she makes a move. The sense of timing is very different here for these two people. He wants magnetic sparks and blind passion. She will go along with the flow but mentally has to try to sort everything out. At a certain point, he may feel that he is pushing her along and it isn't really worth it. Sometimes this balance of opposites can work, but it takes a very special pair to pull it off.

How He Relates to Earth Sign Women
(Taurus, Virgo, Capricorn)

The sensual, sexual earth sign woman will be set on fire by his breathtaking, breakneck tactics. However, she will not give him the challenge that he needs to stick around for the long haul. She will want to tie him down, and he will feel it and want to flee. He lives in the moment while she looks far down the road for future security. Ultimately, she will be a threat to his freedom-loving ways. He does not want to feel responsible to another person, and she will want to hold him accountable. This sort of situation is simply not what the moon in Aries man is looking for and is one fraught with friction, frustration, and irritation.

How He Relates to Water Sign Women
(Cancer, Scorpio, Pisces)

This man's effect on the sensual water sign woman will be steamy. He won't understand her, but she will have something he needs: real passion. She will be frustrated by his flightiness, but it is likely she will still hold on for the emotional excitement. There is a lot of friction and conflict here, but there can also be intense feeling. It could be that the moon in Aries man is in over his head. How long he is willing to stay there depends on how exciting the water sign woman happens to be.

The Moon in
Taurus Man

Who He Is Emotionally

The moon in Taurus man is the steadiest and most practical of the twelve moon signs. Emotionally solid as the earth, this man lives on the surface of life and is essentially very straightforward and uncomplicated.

Possessing enormous common sense, even in complex emotional situations, he is able to sort things out and make things simple. The moon in Taurus man can reduce layers of emotion to the simple facts. Consequently, he is not one to get blown out of the water by moods, misunderstandings, or bad times. He is the most stable of the moon signs. Likewise, he likes to live in stability and serenity and builds his life toward that end.

The moon in Taurus man has a strong material side and in this realm is very security conscious. He is shrewd with money and instinctively knows how to make it and prudently handle it. At all times this man has two feet on the ground and knows exactly where he is going. There are moments when this may lead him to be a bit boring and predictable. However, it also means that even during bad times, this is a man who would never go bankrupt.

The moon in Taurus man gravitates toward what is tangible. He is often not at ease with anything mystical or esoteric. However, there can be great exceptions to this, based on other strong influences in the horoscope. The great psychiatrist Carl Jung, who had a moon in Taurus, had a strong empirical involvement with mysticism, studying and measuring in a methodical way its overall psychological value. Generally speaking, grounded in the day-to-day details and often having a strong affinity with mother earth and nature, the moon in Taurus man knows how to get back to basics.

He also loves beauty and has a strongly developed sensual side that involves all of the senses. The moon in Taurus man responds strongly to food, sex, scent, and often fine music. His sensual nature brings him great comfort. Comfort and creature comforts are extremely important to his well-being, so important that he may very well create them through such endeavors as cooking, building furniture, or playing music, etc.

The moon in Taurus man always marries, usually has a family, and is very financially responsible to the life he takes on. He is one person who has no problems with commitment, although he may be slow at first to make up his mind to make that vow. Once committed, he will be faithful, unless other strong influences in the horoscope indicate otherwise. The moon in Taurus man excels at staying power for whatever he seriously takes on. Affectionate, faithful, dependable, and always moving forward in the most constructive direction, he knows not only where he's going but is also confident that he'll get there in his own time, and he always does.

How He Feels

The moon in Taurus man is more practical and task-oriented than emotional. Although he can be very loving, his mind gets caught up in the material realm, work, and the tasks at hand, often to the exclusion of conscious feeling.

This is a man who is solid, enduring, and matter-of-fact. He does not delve, probe, brood, or get caught up in convolutions of thought and feeling like some of the other moon signs. When a problem arises, he tries to find a sound solution instead of getting caught up in an emotional crisis. That is why he would make a good emergency room doctor or a corporate head like Lee Iacocca, who was the head of the Chrysler Corporation and a man known for his extraordinary organizational and leadership abilities.

Stable, logical, and very well organized, the moon in Taurus man never loses his head. During busy times it might overshadow his heart; however, this may also be the key to his stability.

How He Shows His Feelings

Not terribly emotional and usually very involved with his work and other responsibilities, the moon in Taurus man is generally not emotionally expressive. He lives in a world of practical considerations and things that need to be dealt with. He also gets caught up in the flow of a repetitive day-to-day routine, which can also work to have a deadening effect on his feelings.

In general, he is more comfortable giving a hug than going into a long emotional dialogue. More physically affectionate than verbally expressive, he is more comfortable in bed than sitting across the table from you, expounding on his feelings.

His Dark Side

The moon in Taurus man can sometimes be so ultra-conservative that he can become narrow-minded and rigid in his attitudes. Ronald Reagan has a moon in Taurus. This can lead him into ruts and completely unconscious behavior. When living on this level he can be shallow and insensitive, so lost in meaningless details that he doesn't see any deeper, more significant issues.

He can be so money-oriented that he loses sight of the larger picture. More material than spiritual, he can put an enormous amount of energy and time into the act of finding a bargain to save a few pennies. Money can take on more meaning than it should to this man, especially when it starts to control his decisions, responses, and sense of reality.

The moon in Taurus man can get so grounded in the solid things of this earth that he never questions or explores a higher meaning. Consequently, the men who go in this direction never grow and their world becomes shallow and sterile.

His Bright Side

In general, he is stable and dependable, loyal and committed. He is also sensual and affectionate and has a strong aesthetic sense.

The moon in Taurus man is very often creative. He can also be a great cook, good at conjuring creature comforts, and very pleasure-loving.

He can be a brick in a time of crisis and can make complicated emotional matters simple. His way of looking at the world can conserve a lot of emotional energy and eliminate a lot of confusion. Overall, his strength and stability can be very reassuring.

His Attitude Toward Relationships

This is a man who is almost always marriage-oriented. The moon in Taurus man needs a wife with whom he shares a domestic setting. Like the moon in Cancer man, a home base is important to him as are children.

Although at first he may be slow to commit—this is a man who looks before he leaps—he will be loyal and loving once he has made up his mind. Solid, dependable, and sure to create a marriage that is financially secure, he will probably stay married forever. The moon in Taurus man needs permanence, roots, and the right kind of domestic situation to send him serenely off into the larger world to make money.

His Romance Factor

When the time is right, he can be very romantic, remembering birthdays and anniversaries with flowers and presents and larger-than-life plans. The moon in

Taurus man can be very pleasure-oriented when he makes time for it.

He can also be sensual, affectionate, and full of physical love. This is a man most comfortable expressing himself physically. He will probably be too busy to be romantic every day, but when he does aspire to it, he can come through with flair and enthusiasm.

His Reality Factor

The moon in Taurus man might be the most realistic of all the moon signs. Having a sound, practical approach to life and all its big and little problems, he looks at a situation as it is, not how he would like it to be ideally. Pragmatic and to the point, he deals with the black-and-white sides of an issue, not probing beneath the surface for the gray, which might confuse the entire picture. In general, the moon in Taurus man is clear-cut and addresses the obvious. While this is definitely a judgment strength, it can also diminish the expression of a deep, soulful creativity.

His Fear Factor

Solid, stable, and centered in the earth, the moon in Taurus man is not generally fearful. His world is so well organized around practical details that he feels very much in control.

Positive, plodding, and not one to probe beneath the surface, he is not weighed down with neurotic fears of betrayal or abandonment. Basically, he lives life from day to day, trusting in himself and in the status quo of his existence.

How He Relates to Fire Sign Women
(Aries, Leo, Sagittarius)

The restless, flamboyant fire sign woman is not one to have patience for the moon in Taurus man's pace. While he needs stability and serenity, she demands that life be full of excitement and novelty. Her casual spending patterns could give him cardiac arrest; his conservative ways could make her nearly die from boredom. This combination won't even last long enough for him to give her some sound advice on everything she is doing wrong.

How He Relates to Air Sign Women
(Gemini, Libra, Aquarius)

This is likely to be a rather neutral combination that holds no particular chemistry or intense friction either. The air sign woman likes to learn, explore, and experience new intellectual and spiritual vistas, while the moon in Taurus man is very tied to routine and tradition with his feet firmly on the ground. His inability to expand his life's horizons or go deeper or wider may frustrate her, while her occasional coldness may threaten him. Essentially, this couple has few forces that will hold them together and most likely won't sustain their mutual interests for very long.

How He Relates to Earth Sign Women
(Taurus, Virgo, Capricorn)

Both in this pairing have serious security requirements as well as stability needs. They are grounded in the material, practical realm and look at life from a similar viewpoint. The earth sign woman wants all the things that the moon in Taurus man can provide her with naturally: security, sex, and money. In turn, she is just the sort of person with whom he can plan a sane and stable future. Both seek a serene domestic foundation from which they can raise a family. These two have the potential of building a long-lasting future together, making each other feel secure and comforted.

How He Relates to Water Sign Women
(Cancer, Scorpio, Pisces)

He may not understand her; however, he has the innate ability to help her make things more simple, which the water sign woman has problems doing on her own. She will be attracted to his strength, staying power, and sense of determination. He will be captivated by the mysterious and compelling nature of her sensuous, feminine ways. This can be a powerful sexual connection; however, the water sign woman may eventually yearn for a deeper, more soulful kind of communication.

The Moon in
Gemini Man

Who He Is Emotionally

The moon in Gemini man is ruled by his head and often has a hard time connecting to his heart. By nature he needs a lot of change, variety, diversity, and stimulation to keep his demanding cerebral side happy. Therefore, he responds to humor, cleverness, quick-wittedness, and sparkling conversation that keeps his mind moving. Emotionally detached and needing a challenge, he is most taken with a woman who can be equal to his personality and maybe even dazzle and outdistance him with her own wit.

This is a man who might say one thing and do another, only because he feels so completely different from day to day. He might not even be aware of it but his quicksilver mind demands a wide range of stimuli or else his attention will fade away. He can be quite fickle and a challenge to pin down. However, he is also winsome and can be a charming companion for the restless sort of woman who is simply interested in having a good time with no strings attached.

He is a friendly sort of fellow who is initially most entranced by someone great to talk to. However, it might also be said that because he is so friendly, open, and curious, he finds that many people usually interest him in a lot of different ways. He is capable of carrying on several relationships at the same time since he likes the feeling that he is going places both mentally and physically. Restless, changeable, curious, and inquisitive, he often has a large repertoire of interests that he pursues in his own haphazard fashion, sometimes merely dabbling superficially and losing his enthusiasm in midstream.

The mind here is always moving in overdrive and forever thinking ahead. The moon in Gemini man has a hard time staying in the present unless he gets lost in a perfect conversation that fascinates him so much he forgets what time it is. Easily bored, he cannot bear belabored points, long-drawn-out detailed stories, or intense emotional scenes that he feels drain the life right out of him. When bored, trapped, or seriously confronted, this is a man who will take flight. He is fond of the easy way out and, if compromised, won't communicate or return phone calls.

Freedom-loving and yearning to experience a strong degree of novelty and variety, the moon in Gemini man can be a trifle flighty. This man needs his space as well as time spent traveling around in his different dimensions. Anyone trying to close in on him or tie him down is in store for some serious disappointments. When it comes to commitment, he takes it slow and can have a hard time when it comes to monogamy. Independent and always wondering what's around the corner, he often feels he can't be cramped into conforming to someone else's expectations or routine. One part of him may indeed want a relationship, but his Gemini moon will still demand that he remain free.

The moon in Gemini man is best off with a woman who is a friend with whom he loves to talk and share similar interests. Personal respect and intellectual compatibility are on the top of his list for the perfect lover. Security-seeking women who are diminished by the capriciousness of a forgotten phone call are not for him. To enjoy a Gemini moon man you have to be able to live in the moment and like doing that. Then one day you may find that one moment at a time has turned into a lifetime.

How He Feels

The moon in Gemini man thinks before he feels. His life is one long thought that keeps changing through time and space. His nature is cool and detached and his emotions superficial. Because of this he is acutely uncomfortable with intense emotional displays.

Life can fly past him since he doesn't hold on to feelings for very long. The positive aspect of his nature is that he can let go and move on after a bad experience. The negative aspect is that he can also be emotionally fickle. Unless there are other influences in his chart, the moon in Gemini man has a tendency to not be very compassionate. Basically, this is because he doesn't have the depth to really understand other people's feelings, and he also doesn't want to get trapped by any pain.

This man is very mercurial and can't really understand emotional consistency. Therefore, if he promises one thing in one moment and days later finds his circumstances have changed, he will change with them and most likely will not deliver. Needless to say, this man is not the most emotionally dependable. Usually, he also doesn't feel guilt or remorse about putting people in painful predicaments. His emotional range doesn't extend to include strong empathy. It is too fast moving and needful of freedom and space.

This is a man who can be emotionally cool or even cold, depending on what is coming at him. Any strong emotional demands or heavy emotional displays have an adverse effect on him, making him close up and cut off. On the other hand, humor and quick-wittedness expand his feelings and free him to be himself in the moment. A butterfly of sorts, he soars through mental space and settles wherever it seems convenient. Emotionally, he will stay there until he gets bored. Then he moves quickly on to a new person, place, idea, or possibility. The moon in Gemini man is in love with novelty. It brings little bursts of excitement through his heart that have a way of playing with his brain, the center of his natural focus. To get to his heart you have to go through his mind and make him feel fully alive.

How He Shows His Feelings

Because he has a tendency to think rather than feel, the moon in Gemini man is logical, articulate, and reasonable in most situations. He will try to talk things out and make sense out of nonsense and is often amazingly successful at doing so. This can be a great plus to his personality since it can cool down an argument and create a workable compromise. In general, he is not one to get lost in the eye of the emotional storm. The moon in Gemini man does not easily lose his mind to either minor or major differences.

Sometimes he can't feel, especially if drowned out by someone else's emotional maelstrom. Raw, angry emotion can make him cut off, and teary-eyed episodes take all his patience. The moon in Gemini man can be frosty when he feels forced into places he doesn't want to be. His emotional comfort zone drives him to keep things cool, light, and breezy. This emotional reaction is his escape hatch and it's something he needs to have at all times.

When emotionally involved, he'll communicate by talking about his plans and ideas or by sharing activities that are stimulating or fun. The moon in Gemini man likes to have a good time and keep it light and lively. For him loving someone's company means falling in love. However, he won't get down on his knees and make dramatic declarations. He'll just keep calling.

It must be mentioned that this man can also be emotionally changeable and run from hot to cold in record time. If he feels bored, closed in, or that a situation is getting too predictable, this is the time when the air around him may cool and he may disappear. The moon in Gemini man can be quite ruthless about this sort of behavior and curiously devoid of guilt or compassion. His disappearing acts are knee-jerk responses to situations he finds boring and unbearable. The moon in Gemini man's emotional survival mechanism sometimes renders him so detached that he isn't capable of making a strong connection with anyone. He tends to be a Peter Pan type who needs a lot of time to grow up and become comfortable feeling more deeply.

His Dark Side

His darkest quality is that he can be emotionally capricious and so uncaring. He can also be very inconsistent, saying one thing and doing another, and potentially leave another person feeling very unloved. His restless nature and need for change and variety can make him a feckless flirt who has a tendency to be unfaithful.

The moon in Gemini man's superficial nature often makes him skim over people's feelings and never commit deeply to anything or anyone. Consequently, he can be very irresponsible and flighty, needing only to be free to race on to the next idea, challenge, person, or pursuit that captures his fancy. He can be consumed by the purely inconsequential and have serious problems following through on anything. His tendency to lose interest in something or someone who once seemed so important can be a problem that he doesn't easily overcome. Basically, this stems from the fact that he won't see the need to change. He may never see that his nature is inconvenient to other people. All that he knows is that it makes his life colorful and interesting. In order to feel satisfied, this man must see the world in his own way and live in it on his own terms.

His Bright Side

The typical moon in Gemini man excels at communication. He is clever, imaginative, curious, intelligent, and usually a lot of fun. He is also emotionally flexible and open to change, different ways of looking at life, and lots of different kinds of people. This man can let go of negative emotional experiences and doesn't allow resentments or grudges to grind him down.

He can have a bright, perky personality that is often the life of the party. He also has a sense of humor that can sometimes compensate for his lack of sensitivity. His verbal, witty style can make him both amusing and entertaining. The moon in Gemini man tends to be a people person who is a bright light in social scenes and who can set the tone for a scintillating evening. He can be a most charming dazzler who is spontaneous, free, fearless, and full of a zest for life that brings on endless adventures.

His intelligence and curiosity can open doors to new, interesting experiences, and his desire for learning can lead to lots of exciting interests that he is only too willing to share.

His Attitude Toward Relationships

He is a cool, detached, freedom-loving sort who simply thrives on challenge, stimulation, and diversity. The moon in Gemini man can be happy with a lot of women. However, should he try to settle down with one, she has to have different sides to her personality that make her interesting and intellectually vital to him.

Because he is easily bored, he needs to feel entertained, amused, stimulated, and challenged. Even then, his head may turn. Since he has a deep-seated fear of commitment, his behavior may be inconsistent and more puzzling than perfectly romantic. The moon in Gemini man doesn't feel compelled to be in a relationship. He has a fear of being suffocated that often causes him to hold back and give mixed signals. A woman with too many emotional needs, demands, and expectations will make him take flight, afraid that she might entrap him.

He is best off with a friend who is as restless, as curious, and as requiring of stimulation as he is. The moon in Gemini man is most happy sharing this aspect of himself. To him this is more important than sex. His sexual response to a woman is often triggered by how much she makes him think. A woman with the best body who has nothing interesting to say will only bore him. The moon in Gemini man needs a mate who is an equal partner, capable of making his mind stretch. Otherwise, he has no problem pursuing different kinds of women in his restless quest for novelty and diversity.

His Romance Factor

This is not a man who is sentimental or emotional. However, if he is talked to in the right way, he is open to creating his own version of romantic moments based on his love of travel and adventure. Spontaneously, he might produce plane tickets or make reservations for the ballet or a play. The moon in Gemini man likes to do things that make him think or are challenging. That could include ballooning, skydiving, or long, scenic rides in the country. However, his timing never runs on schedule, nor is it particularly influenced by calendar dates. The moon in Gemini man does things in his own way at his own convenience. He does not spend his time dreaming over ways in which to please a loved one—at least not for very long. It is more likely that he will be off at his computer, working on some creative writing or law brief, and not remember his own birthday. It might be said that the moon in Gemini man is romantically absent-minded. However, there is hope for the woman smart enough to know how to get him thinking in the right direction.

His Reality Factor

He is smart, cool, logical, and highly reality-oriented. At times he can be too pragmatic about emotional issues. The moon in Gemini man must see things through his head. In the process, his heart can get lost or tucked way out of sight. Basically, his sense of reality dictates how things should be, and often he doesn't understand the deeper layers of an emotional situation. He can also get so lost in minor details that he misses the larger and more complex picture. The moon in Gemini man responds to what's on the surface. He doesn't delve, probe, or direct his attention to the more profound elements of an issue. Therefore, his emotional reality might be missing a number of nuances. His picture of life tends to be rather tidy and eliminates such intimidating elements as fear, confusion, or the painful complexities of the human condition. A lot of careful communication is needed for him to extend his understanding. However, he *is* flexible and, if approached in the right way, will always lend a willing ear.

His Fear Factor

The moon in Gemini man is afraid of being trapped and suffocated. He needs to feel he has a lot of space around him all of the time. When he senses that his space is invaded, threatened, or his freedom thwarted, he can feel out of control and will remedy that by fleeing. This is a man who is also afraid of intense emotion. It drowns him and takes his breath away. This moon is an air sign and needs a lot of oxygen to keep moving in its preferred direction. Therefore, this man may never lose the desire to cut loose and create more space for himself.

How He Relates to Fire Sign Women
(Aries, Leo, Sagittarius)

The moon in Gemini man fans the fire sign woman's flame, and in turn, she feeds his freedom-loving nature. Restless, spirited, and independent herself, she comes even more alive when affected by his spontaneous, clever, and amusing ways. He will entertain and delight her, and she will take up the challenge that he'll pose. This combination can be one of passion, fulfilling communication, and adventure for both involved, providing the moon in Gemini man plays by some rules. His capricious ways will not be considered in any way tolerable by the fire sign woman. This woman has a temper and is not afraid to show it, should she feel out of control. She is not one to be slighted, nor will she fade away sitting by the phone. Impulsive and impatient by nature, she will cut loose in record time or quickly turn the tables. Then the moon in Gemini man might suddenly realize that he has feelings after all.

How He Relates to Air Sign Women
(Gemini, Libra, Aquarius)

The air sign woman is a natural match for this man, providing she doesn't have a water moon (Cancer, Scorpio, or Pisces). Here there can be a meeting of the minds that is mutually compatible and highly stimulating. The air sign woman also spends a lot of time in her head and has a way of analyzing emotional situations instead of getting emotional, which is a moon in Gemini man's dream come true. She is also curious, loves new ideas and new experiences. There is a potential for excellent communication here and steady growth through shared interests. The air sign woman could be the buddy, soul mate, and unpossessive lover who captures the moon in Gemini man's heart. At the very least, she may help him find it.

How He Relates to Earth Sign Women
(Taurus, Virgo, Capricorn)

The earth sign woman needs security and stability while the moon in Gemini man needs freedom and space. This is the beginning of many sorts of conflicts that might make this match a truly challenging one. The moon in Gemini man hates feeling tied down, and that is what the earth sign woman will do her best to accomplish. She wants a seven-year plan that will assure her of all future securities, whereas he needs to know that, in a certain sense, he will always be free. He needs to feel that he can go in any direction at any given time, and she will want a complete agenda of where he might be going. With this kind of woman the moon in Gemini man will feel stifled and the earth sign woman will feel insecure and frustrated. Both will be on edge, and it can be a cutting one.

How He Relates to Water Sign Women
(Cancer, Scorpio, Pisces)

These two natures are terribly different and could suffer from tremendous miscommunication if they try to come together. The water sign woman has emotional depth that the moon in Gemini man can't fathom. She also has a need for emotional security that might make the moon in Gemini man very uncomfortable. While he is capable of being faithful, he hates to feel that he *has* to be because someone has taken his choices away from him. He will not understand her moods or what is happening when she withdraws. Likewise, he will be stumped by the needs that she expects him to meet quite intuitively. He will feel drowned by her emotions; she will feel iced by his behavior. This is clearly a case of two people coming from such different inner worlds that it could be a very problematic match.

The Moon in
Cancer Man

Who He Is Emotionally

The moon in Cancer man is the most sensitive of the twelve moon signs, whether or not he openly shows it. Kind, caring, compassionate, and empathetic, he is most definitely a man of feeling.

Because the moon rules Cancer, it is especially powerful in this sign. Likewise, the feelings of the moon in Cancer man are very powerful and close to the surface. Unlike a number of other moon signs, this is a man who is in touch with his feelings. His emotional nature is a conscious part of who he is. Likewise, consciously and unconsciously, he lives through it.

Closeness, intimacy, and his desire to nurture are central issues in his life. The moon in Cancer man always marries, has a family, and is a very involved father. However, often he also cares for needy souls who happen to surround him, some stray animals who show up and anyone else who might look like they need it. The moon in Cancer man is sympathetic. Being supersensitive himself, he also understands vulnerability. He is like a sponge for the sadness of his immediate world and wishes to make everything better.

Romantic, sentimental, and highly security-oriented, he needs to know where he stands early on in a love relationship. At first shy and reticent about revealing himself, the moon in Cancer man will hold back, watch and wait and listen until he feels secure. His style is to feel a situation out and then proceed with caution.

Sometimes moody, changeable, and emotionally subjective, his supersensitive feelings can overwhelm him and make him feel the need to withdraw. Highly receptive to the emotional atmosphere surrounding him, he can unconsciously reflect the feelings of others and take on their moods.

The emotional needs are strong in this sign. This is a man who must have the give-and-take of love and affection for his happiness. Power, wealth, and fame mean little if he has no one to come home to. A home base and a mutually supportive love relationship are the keys to his soul. Once he finds the right someone to satisfy this yearning he has for closeness, he will be unquestionably faithful. The moon in Cancer man doesn't have to search the world to satisfy some craving for excitement like some other moon sign men. He is happiest at home with the right partner who can provide him with all the love that he needs.

How He Feels

He is sensitive and emotional, sentimental and deeply instinctive. He is so in touch with his own feelings that he is completely comfortable with the feelings of everyone around him.

Warm, affectionate, loving, and caring, the moon in Cancer man is fully present in emotional situations. His emotions can go very deep and, whether positive or negative, are long-lasting.

When hurt, he may withdraw for a bit to lick his wounds and brood about how slighted he feels in the situation. However, unlike a lot of other moon signs, he won't cut himself off. At a certain point he will emerge from his shell and be willing to communicate. The moon in Cancer is very similar to the moon in Scorpio in that it may forgive, but it will never forget. In between, both can hold a grudge like a torch that inflames their own sense of justice.

How He Shows His Feelings

When deeply connected, the moon in Cancer man is openly affectionate and will share his feelings in his own time and way. Quite conscious and sensitive to everything around him, he knows what he feels and it simply flows forth.

Unlike a number of other moon signs, he doesn't repress painful moments or erect elaborate defenses to cope emotionally. When hurt, he will withdraw for a time. When angry, he may be passive-aggressive or piercingly sarcastic. The moon in Cancer man can have a lacerating sense of humor that he uses to express hostility.

Whatever the situation, he usually makes his emotions felt by those around him. The moon in Cancer man is so full of feeling that there is nowhere he can really go to hide it. Whether positive or negative, his feelings often overflow, and he is suddenly at the mercy of the rushing current.

His Dark Side

When very immature, he can be self-centered and needy, changeable and moody. The immature moon in Cancer man is reactive rather than responsive and overly sensitive to misperceived slights. He can be extremely thin-skinned as well as childish and petulant, blowing petty occurrences completely out of proportion.

In love, he can be both jealous and possessive, to the point where he is smothering. However, usually if his needs are met, he doesn't drift to this extreme.

His Bright Side

He is kind and caring, loving and thoughtful. The moon in Cancer man loves to give and receive love. Empathetic, intuitive, and strongly instinctive, he has a sensibility that sometimes borders on being psychic.

He can be a warm, sensitive lover and a deeply committed, nurturing father. Once he has a strong home base, he will never take it for granted. He will find ways to be warm and caring and show his love the value he holds in his heart.

His Attitude Toward Relationships

The moon in Cancer man is the most relationship-oriented of all the moon signs. Love, affection, home, and family are all extremely important to him.

Both romantic and sentimental, he is more sensual than passionately sexual. Having a sense of nostalgia and a very strong memory, he will thoughtfully honor all the personal holidays and private occasions that are pertinent to the relationship.

When the moon in Cancer man finds the woman with whom he deeply wants to share a life, he feels grateful. Life without love means little to him. Because of that, he is always conscious of the importance of what he has and how much he wants to hold on to it. He will show his feelings through physical affection, sexual passion, and, from time to time, a deep baring of his soul.

His Romance Factor

The moon in Cancer man can be an old-fashioned romantic who honors all special personal occasions and is good at creating intimate moments.

More inclined to an intimate candlelit dinner at home than an impersonal restaurant setting, he may even do the cooking. Compliments and fine wine will flow through the evening. He'll probably even remember flowers.

The moon in Cancer man takes the all-or-nothing approach to love. Emotionally and physically he is warm, receptive, open, expressive, and cuddly. Completely comfortable with the feminine side of his nature, he can be a sensual lover, friend, soul mate, and life partner who is prepared to be committed for a lifetime.

His Reality Factor

The immature moon in Cancer man can be extremely hypersensitive and self-centered, misperceiving slights and taking things the wrong way. Sometimes suspicious, jealous and paranoid, he does have a tendency to lose objectivity in a situation when he becomes overly emotional. The moon in Cancer man needs to always pause, put things in perspective, and work at not taking things so personally.

His Fear Factor

Jealousy can be one of this man's demons. His biggest fear is either not finding the love of his life or finding her and losing her. Like the man with the moon in Scorpio, abandonment and betrayal are two of the moon in Cancer man's deepest fears. Security is essential to his well-being, and once he has found his meaningful connection, he will do everything he can to maintain it.

How He Relates to Fire Sign Women
(Aries, Leo, Sagittarius)

The restless, freedom-loving fire sign woman wants novelty, excitement, and adventure. Security isn't in her vocabulary. Furthermore, she tends to live in the moment and can't bear the thought of being tied down. Her impatient, impulsive ways will only inspire insecurity in the moon in Cancer man. His need for a family and a strong home base will suffocate her. Her need for freedom at all costs will probably cause him to back off and begin to be self-protective. In this connection, it might be the best thing he could do. Even if there is an initial attraction here, the temperaments are so different that there will be definite problems down the road.

How He Relates to Air Sign Women
(Gemini, Libra, Aquarius)

The emotionally detached air sign woman can be hard to pin down. She lives in her head, while the moon in Cancer man is anchored in his feelings. It is likely that she won't understand the depth of his sensitivity. Likewise, he will be chilled by some of her cool responses. This pairing can give rise to communication problems and different ways of approaching the world that clash completely. Both are working toward fulfilling quite different needs. Essentially, the air sign woman needs a lot of breathing space while the moon in Cancer man needs to merge intimately with his love. In the long run these differences can prove to be divisive.

How He Relates to Earth Sign Women
(Taurus, Virgo, Capricorn)

The steady, reliable earth sign woman has similar security needs to the moon in Cancer man and shares his desire for a strong nurturing home base. Both will want to build a family and create a close-knit life together. Their similar needs, values, and outlook on life should give this couple a basis for a sound foundation that holds much potential for staying power.

How He Relates to Water Sign Women
(Cancer, Scorpio, Pisces)

The moon in Cancer man will merge with the sensitive water sign woman. Both are intuitive, emotional, caring, and supportive. Both require a strong feeling of security and intimacy for their overall sense of well-being. These two have the potential for a romantic, sensual, deeply emotional union. Coming together, this couple could also find a spiritual connection that brings them a great deal of fulfillment on the soul level.

The Moon in
Leo Man

Who He Is Emotionally

The moon in Leo man is a positive, expansive person with a great *joie de vivre* and a strong confidence in his own abilities. Pleasure-loving, prideful, generous, magnanimous, and usually ambitious, he wants the world to shine and to send him only the best that life has to offer.

There are basically two types of Leo moon men. One is ruled by his heart. The other exists at the mercy of his ego. Sometimes, of course, both collide.

The ego-oriented man wants to advertise an enviable face to the world and get the kind of feedback that makes him feel larger than life. Given to bragging and spurred on by the need to show off, he is highly status-conscious and controlled by his overwhelming need to look superior at all times and in all situations.

This moon in Leo man doesn't have the courage or maturity to look deeper into himself. His values are shallow as he lives on the surface of life.

The more evolved moon in Leo man lives life through his heart, not his ego. Warm, affectionate, a great friend, and deeply loving, he can be kind, giving, spiritually motivated, and a true seeker of higher truths and the meaning his life has in the greater scheme of things.

However, both types have a zest for life and all its big and little pleasures. For all Leo moon types, love is a big priority. The Leo moon man needs to love and feel loved, even if his pride won't allow him to show it. Ambitious, often power-oriented, and usually highly personable, he is at a loss without love, even in a sea of worldly treasures.

Being passionately in love is this man's favorite activity, although it can also drive him to lose his mind. The moon in Leo man in love is very emotional. He lends himself fully to the experience, often with a dramatic intensity. He is grand, is drawn to luxury, and will lavish beauty and imagination upon his love along with a lot of energy. Usually creative, he can be both indulgent and inventive with his attentions.

Idealistic and dramatic, he will dream up glamorous, romantic scenarios that he will play out in larger-than-life ways. The moon in Leo man loves fine wines, champagne, upscale restaurants, beautiful things, and settings worthy of a king. If he finds the right woman, he will treat her like a queen. However, in return, he expects her to prove herself worthy, impress him, and make him look good.

How He Feels

The moon in Leo man has a tendency to be romantic, flamboyant, and indulgent. Having a big heart that embraces everything important to him, this man finds many ways to bring that to bear in life.

His heart has to be in everything he successfully undertakes. Leo is the sign ruling the heart. Therefore, he is at his best when he is warm rather than prideful and deeply feeling for others rather than needing to attract admiration to himself.

Optimistic and sometimes emotionally naive, he can be fooled by flattery because he wants so strongly to believe it. Craving feedback and ego enhancement from the outside world, the moon in Leo man may assign too much power to how his performance is being viewed by others. This man has a drive and determination to succeed in anything he seriously undertakes. However, when he uses his success as a prime factor in determining how he feels about himself, he is setting himself up for a potentially bad payoff.

The moon in Leo man needs to establish strong spiritual and humanistic values that become personally important to him in his life as opposed to valuing only those experiences that make him look good to the world. This might involve some sacrifice. However, gaining this insight and using it successfully will make his relationship with himself authentic. What can come from this discovery is something so truly inspiring that it can change the entire course of his life for the better. When he is able to live more fully from his higher ideals, the quality of the love that he is capable of experiencing and attracting will also be of a higher, richer quality.

How He Shows His Feelings

He is open and demonstrative and often bold and dramatic. If deeply wounded, this man may hold his feelings inside and hide them away from the world. However, he can be very expressive about what is positive and moves him.

Emotionally speaking, the moon in Leo man is pure and uncomplicated. At times his ego may interfere with the higher flow of his feelings, but in the long run, his heart will come through. When it does, there is a warmth here that can be extremely penetrating. The heart of the moon in Leo man can radiate like the sun. If directed at you, you may have the experience of a deep, soulful contact. This can be a subtle feeling that is still very powerful.

The moon in Leo man won't hold his emotions back unless he is hurt and his pride demands it. He shows his positive feelings with words, flowers, flamboyant gestures, physical affection, and passion. A man of his word, he comes through with what he promises and won't give mixed messages like a lot of other moon signs. Usually prepared to follow through on what he promises, the moon in Leo man is a man of his word. Straightforward and to the point, he puts himself on the line and has enough of a sense of honor that compels him to stick to his word.

His Dark Side

When the moon in Leo man is emotionally immature, he can be arrogant, selfish, egotistical, and egocentric. Demanding and controlling, he is completely fixed on getting his way. Status-conscious and concerned with making a superior impression, he can be a snob who drops names, talks incessantly about himself, and chats up a list of expensive toys to which his life is attached.

This sort of man takes himself too seriously and can be so shallow and self-absorbed that he doesn't even hear himself. He can also be so concerned with his own ego needs that his behavior toward others is unconscious and inconsiderate. Living through his ego and not his heart, this sort of moon in Leo man is so needy of admiration that he will go to any lengths to get it. In his determination to get attention, he may become a ladies' man who loves them and leaves them as soon as the initial glow of love wears off.

His Bright Side

Positive, upbeat, optimistic, and pleasure-loving, he is the grand master of the good life. The moon in Leo man knows how to have fun, and he does it with flair. Generous, kind, loving, and often compassionate, he has a powerful heart that, when operating to its full capacity, has a way of making magic.

Romantic, affectionate, loyal, and loving, the moon in Leo man has the potential to be warm and magnanimous, sparkling and witty. He has a childlike love of life as well as a scintillating sense of humor. Sophisticated and full of *savoir faire,* he has great taste and a worldly sense of glamour. Creative, imaginative, and in touch with his feelings, he can both give and receive love in a way that can make the world around him seem like a better place.

His Attitude Toward Relationships

Both romantic and idealistic, the moon in Leo man is happiest when in love. Love elevates him beyond the mundane and gives him a sense of greater meaning. It can also motivate him to accomplish more ambitious goals.

The moon in Leo man needs a woman he can feel proud of and put on a pedestal. In turn, she also has to pay homage to him and give the connection an importance and attention that makes it seem mythological. Both beauty and brains are important to the moon in Leo man. However, initially, he is often galvanized by energy, personality, and humor.

Because his dream is to achieve the best in the best of all possible worlds, he can set himself up for some severe disappointment, should his fantasy fall through. The moon in Leo man can find himself in fated, fatal attractions that sometimes splinter into tiny pieces and devastate him emotionally. When he falls deeply in love, it is with his head, heart, and soul, and when deeply hurt, it may take him years to recover. Often mythologizing the entire romantic connection, he can experience a breakup like a drama of mythic proportions that will hold its special place forever in his heart.

However, eventually, the moon in Leo man must love again. When he does, he will be loyal, loving, affectionate, and romantic. He will rebuild his faith and put forth his best for the woman he finds worthy of him, and the meaning that he gets from the deep sense of union he finds with her will be its own reward.

His Romance Factor

This man can turn special occasions into celebrations, and he can make a small moment into a major event. The moon in Leo man is extremely romantic, and on the lady of his life he will shower the light of his heart.

Champagne, candlelight, fine wines, and flowers will be part of his repertoire. This man is magnanimous and has a taste for the best in life. He will bring this to bear in his romance with full regalia. He won't care about the cost as long as every detail contributes to the drama. However, the woman must warrant star treatment and be a goddess in his eyes who deserves such grand attention.

His Reality Factor

The moon in Leo man can be both manipulated and led astray. When uninvolved, he can judge a situation fairly objectively. However, when in love or when his dreams are at stake, he is led around by his heart.

The battle between his head and his heart is often a hard one. When madly in love, he stands somewhere in the middle, torn apart and struggling to take control.

His Fear Factor

The moon in Leo man can be very jealous and possessive. He also fears looking like a fool and needs to know that he is standing on terra firma.

This is a man who is superserious about betrayal. When truly involved, he takes everything to heart. On the deepest level, he fears the loss of love or the possibility that he will never really find it. Deep within himself he is wise enough to know that life without love has no meaning, and because he wants to make the most of his life, he will put it on his list of serious priorities.

How He Relates to Fire Sign Women
(Aries, Leo, Sagittarius)

The fire sign woman is wild, romantic, and full of life. She needs the same sparkle, excitement, and larger-than-life experiences as the moon in Leo man. He will love her energy, vivacity, and flash. She will love his romantic gestures, sensibilities, and sense of luxury and beauty. Both are idealistic and share a view of a life filled with love and endless possibilities. This is an ideal combination that can create much joy and need for celebration.

How He Relates to Air Sign Women
(Gemini, Libra, Aquarius)

This airy woman will fan his fire with her breezy personality and witty ways. He will delight her with his childlike sense of humor, and she will add dash to his life with her perky personality. Both share an enthusiasm for novelty, adventure, and great conversation. Her independent, individualistic ways will challenge him to come closer. Together they will go in style and make a life together that is scintillating and exciting.

How He Relates to Earth Sign Women
(Taurus, Virgo, Capricorn)

She will adore his style but will dampen his personality and potential. The moon in Leo man needs spontaneity and excitement, and this woman may be too tied down to the ground. She will enjoy the fruits of his flamboyant ways but may also find him hopelessly impractical. He will find her too fixed and immobile to fly the way he wants to go. Restless, impatient, and easily bored, the moon in Leo man may find that this pairing seriously falls short of his excitement quota.

How He Relates to Water Sign Women
(Cancer, Scorpio, Pisces)

Although it is likely that he will never understand her, the sensuality and passion a moon in Leo man finds with a water sign woman may compensate for what is left unsaid. Her ability to surrender both emotionally and sexually will touch him deep in his soul. His romantic razzle-dazzle will win her. There will be a lot of feeling exchanged between these two, though it is anyone's guess as to how long the passion will last.

The Moon in
Virgo Man

Who He Is Emotionally

The key word for the moon in Virgo man is discriminating. He is practical rather than emotional and reasonable rather than deeply feeling. Conventional and somewhat constrictive, he is disciplined, duty-bound and highly security-oriented.

Work tends to come before pleasure with this man who must attend to business details often to the detriment of emotional matters. A great moon for a lawyer, surgeon, accountant, or president (both John F. Kennedy and Lyndon Johnson had this moon), it can pose problems in the initial stages of a romance, providing that he allows the romance to reach the initial stages.

This man is critical and not in touch with his deeper feelings. Furthermore, he highly validates his own way of thinking and wants the world to change according to his belief system. This might be the most difficult moon sign when it comes to the subject of love and compassion. The emotional range here is rather narrow, and anyone who gets close to the moon in Virgo man will soon feel his limits.

This man can be calculating, controlled, and a worrywart over petty matters. Because he feels he always has to be busy and cannot kick back and smell the flowers, he is a hard man to relate to in any relaxed way. He can be a highly obsessive-compulsive person who doesn't know how to calm down. This can put a big damper on his ability to create a deeper connection with a woman, and it often does.

On the positive side, he can be caring and conscientious. The moon in Virgo man can also be helpful in practical ways. His nature is serious, industrious, and persevering. Honest and sincere, he is someone to be counted on. His big problem is that he cannot let go of minor preoccupations long enough to discover, explore, and share the best of himself.

More comfortable on the work scene than having dinner by candlelight, this man is driven by the need to accomplish for accomplishment's sake. His goal may not even be a major accomplishment and often isn't. However, it still fulfills his sense of purpose and deep work ethic. Often assigning small details the importance of major life issues, this man finds a way to always be preoccupied. Living life in this manner, he can have a hard time when it comes time to open up and love someone.

How He Feels

The moon in Virgo man doesn't tend to feel emotions deeply. Logical, practical, and realistic, he thinks and feels along utilitarian lines. Both critical and discriminating, he is always seeing the imperfections in a situation or person and spends a lot of time trying to sort them out or eradicate them altogether.

With what is often a narrow, judgmental outlook and a value system that puts an emphasis on efficiency and productivity, he is not at home with the feelings of other people. Likewise, he is not in touch with his own.

The moon in Virgo man's feelings are deeply buried. He is out of touch with old childhood wounds and painful moments that evoked in him deep embarrassment or vulnerability. Consequently, as an adult, he has little compassion for the feeling realm. He puts his emphasis on trying to make small things perfect, on being efficient and turning out a product without a single flaw.

His sensitivity to "flaws," both material and physical, often makes the moon in Virgo man someone difficult to be with. Also health- and diet-conscious, he will notice those five extra pounds and won't be shy about constructive criticism.

He is without sympathy for a person who persists on a path not focused on the goal of perfection. Essentially intolerant of other ways of thinking and feeling, he will criticize and act as if he has the power to make everything that is too fat, flawed, excessive, or emotional go away.

The moon in Virgo man likes things to be clean, tidy, cut-and-dried. Heavy emotional displays disturb him. Emotional demands provoke in him the need for distance. Seeing the world from a singular dimension, he doesn't understand the complexities of other people. Therefore, he is often out of touch with the words or behavior that a person might need most.

Nevertheless, this man is conscientious in his own way and wants to be of help in most situations. He can be counted on in a crisis, and even if his responses may seem completely emotionally inappropriate, he does mean well. The moon in Virgo man simply thinks that the entire world should live as he would, and seeing the world from a small place that seems very secure and controllable, he is hard put to have a more profound emotional response. The moon in Virgo man's ignorance is his bliss, and his personal opinions he sees as his present to the world.

How He Shows His Feelings

The moon in Virgo man doesn't really show his feelings. He lives on the surface in a comfort zone of controlled and controlling activity, details, deadlines, disciplined regimes, and perhaps exercise.

Although he can occasionally be high-strung, when angry this man usually tends to be passive-aggressive, preferring to communicate through omission.

When in love, the moon in Virgo man is more comfortable giving a practical little gift than talking about his feelings. He can be physically affectionate but shies away from deep emotional displays. Often articulate, he can be witty, clever, and constantly offering his constructive advice. As annoying as his comments may seem, he is sincere about trying to improve a situation, person, or predicament.

His Dark Side

His narrow, petty outlook and small-minded judgmental ways sometimes make the moon in Virgo man a challenge to be with. When he operates on an immature level, he can be so constrictive and compulsive that he effectively cuts off the lines of communication.

Often this man does not really listen. That is because he is listening to the voice in his own head. When overtaken by the negative aspects of his moon sign, he tends to worry about ridiculous things, to hold on to grudges, and to be completely self-righteous. This is a man who finds it close to impossible to say "I'm sorry. I was wrong." Blind to his own personal bias, he is determined to be right, regardless of the issue, the situation, or the sort of destructiveness he might be creating with his narrow-minded attitudes.

The worst part of the dark side of the moon in Virgo man is his pettiness. He can measure out his life in endless inconsequential details and in tiny, meaningless acts, never looking for a larger purpose and never searching for something deeper.

His Bright Side

He can be intelligent, witty, and well meaning. He can also be solicitous, kind, caring, loyal, and utterly dependable. The moon in Virgo man will bring you tea when you're sick. He will also drive you to the doctor. He will give you vitamins and an umbrella for your birthday, and though this is far from a favorite romantic fantasy, you can depend on him to come through.

His Attitude Toward Relationships

Because he is so security-conscious, the moon in Virgo man usually marries. Best off with someone who is as earthbound as he is, he is a monogamous person who will be loyal and faithful. In turn, he expects the same. He can be very jealous, won't tolerate betrayal, and will be slow to forgive, should he discover an indiscretion. This man needs to feel that he can fully trust before he takes a woman seriously and that she is worthy of his hard-won respect.

Usually critical, predictable, and consistent, he can also be kind, caring, devoted, and happy to be of help. However, it is not likely that he will be flexible and open to change in the face of problems. Compassion and deep communication are two of the areas that prove to be most challenging for him. Since these two factors are key to a successful relationship, the moon in Virgo man carries with him a lot of relationship baggage that is confusing, befuddling, and burdensome. When he is able to take an honest and courageous look at the limitations his attitudes impose and change the constrictive tendencies within himself into a more constructive and open-minded awareness, he will be on the road to a relationship that has more possibility and dimension.

Then he will be capable of a partnership that is based on a deeper, compassionate human love, which can evolve over time.

His Romance Factor

It is the moon in Virgo man's impulse to put all romantic considerations behind his work schedule. He is not naturally romantic. However, he is sexual and sensual. He can be an earthy and erotic lover who is wholehearted and enthusiastic. However, in a period of afterglow he may also be found phoning the office. Having strong workaholic tendencies, this man often has a lot on his mind and his detached behavior makes it clear it's not particularly you.

His Reality Factor

The moon in Virgo man bases his life on what he believes to be sound logic. He is realistic, not fantasy-oriented. He is practical, not poetic. His tendency is to reduce emotional issues into reasonable plans of action that produce sound results. He believes in doing, not feeling, in acting smartly, not acting out. The implication of emotional complications eludes him completely. What he sees is what he gets. Consequently, sometimes he gets very little.

He has to learn to be more open and less judgmental. He also has to work on seeing the larger picture and on not getting lost in the petty details. When he can be compassionate and less critical, he will get so much more from his love connection.

His Fear Factor

He fears chaos, intense emotional scenes, sheer vulnerability, and being out of control. On an unconscious level, he also fears his own anger, which may build up and surface on occasion. The moon in Virgo man fears feeling like a fool, more so than many other of the signs. That is because he doesn't trust himself without all his armor. His routines, schedules, time-efficient plans, and absorption in work details help him make the world look obvious and simple. They are his best defense against feeling vulnerable in a life where he can't relax or trust a lot of people.

How He Relates to Fire Sign Women
(Aries, Leo, Sagittarius)

This is a match that may not last through dinner. The fire sign woman wants to have fun. Fun is something the moon in Virgo man doesn't really understand. It will not be long before he will bore her to the point that she loses all patience. The desire to escape this man will quickly become her first priority while he may find her flighty ways more than he can take.

How He Relates to Air Sign Women
(Gemini, Libra, Aquarius)

The air sign woman may have some tolerance for the moon in Virgo man's anal retentive behavior—up to a point. She, too, requires order in her world. However, she also needs stimulation, mental excitement, and quality communication. Too much laundry list talk leaves her cold. Ideally, she wants to expand her boundaries. He wants to contain them. At a certain point she will feel closed in by his small-minded ways unless he has grown to be more open-minded and receptive to other points of view.

How He Relates to Earth Sign Women
(Taurus, Virgo, Capricorn)

The earth sign woman shares this man's security needs and similarly sees the importance of organization, routine, and planning. Instinctively, she will understand his compulsive need for control. Both will be grounded in the day-to-day duties of sharing a life together. Here there are common goals, mutual compatibility, and a basis for sound communication. This union can prove to be both satisfying and secure.

How He Relates to Water Sign Women
(Cancer, Scorpio, Pisces)

The water sign woman needs intimacy and emotional reassurance. The cool moon in Virgo man is content with security, stability, control, and order. His detached, matter-of-fact manner has a tendency to turn her off. She desires someone who will make her feel, and most likely she won't find it here. In turn, he may decide that she is far too emotional for his liking and may also feel threatened by the uncertainty of her moods.

The Moon in
Libra Man

Who He Is Emotionally

He is a sociable sort of guy with an easygoing manner and a great eye for beauty. The moon in Libra man was made for the good life. He desires beauty, harmony, and a little piece of heaven in all his experiences. Hating conflict, which can seriously undermine his sense of stability and comfort, the moon in Libra man may quickly disappear from the scene of an intense dispute. Above all, this man seeks balance and a sense of well-being that supports his pleasure-loving attitude toward life.

Libra, being an air sign, brings him a focus that is more cerebral than emotional. Therefore, he is more reflective and deliberate than compassionate and deeply intuitive. In an attempt to distance himself from intense emotions, he can be downright cold in the middle of some messy emotional display. The moon in Libra man is more comfortable with reason than emotion, and even his caring gestures usually are driven by an idea rather than a deep feeling.

Ugliness and disorder disturb him, whether he sees them in a person's personality or the surrounding environment. Luxury, creature comforts, and a pleasant place to come home to are high on his list of what he loves best. This is a man who must be in an environment that works for him, not against him. The same is true of his choice of a life partner.

Being rational and able to see two sides of an issue, this man can be a clever peacemaker and negotiator. However, he does not want to be forced to live in that role. He needs a woman who is positive, easygoing and not given to dramatic or hysterical emotional displays. In the face of such discord, he will disappear, and it might be into the arms of some new dazzling beauty who has caught his eye. The moon in Libra man can resort to both shallow and changeable behavior when seriously challenged. He does not want to be upset by personal behavior or circumstance. Life to him must be lived from a perspective of peace, not demanding emotional intensity.

Although he can be something of a flirt who flits from one female to another, he will eventually choose to share his life with a partner. Romantic and generous, he can be fun to be with, always preferring to focus on the bright and the beautiful and never forgetting to be grateful for all his good times.

How He Feels

Like the moon in Gemini man, this man thinks before he feels. The moon in Libra man is rational and rea-

124

sonable, rather than deeply emotive. Therefore, his emotional range is fairly limited and his feelings can be fleeting.

Because he tends to be more cool and friendly than deeply feeling, he can also be uncomfortable with the feelings of others. Being an air sign, which rules thinking and communication, the moon in Libra man is more at home with clever conversation than an intense outpouring of emotion. He can be charming when flirting but is often a bit detached when it comes to taking into consideration the feelings of others. When cornered, he can cut himself off and seem like someone who is not quite as charming as he initially appeared.

All air sign moons seek freedom, and they demonstrate that in how they respond to life. This man may seem easygoing and fully capable of handling most anything that comes his way, but he can be easily suffocated and intimidated by too much intensity. The moon in Libra man may mask this under his easygoing veneer. However, this need will surface in time, and he will see to it that it is honored. As a result, this man has his own sense of space and timing. If pushed for too much closeness too soon, he will be so acutely uncomfortable that he will probably back off. Like all air sign moons he needs breathing space, and he will see to it that he gets it, no matter what he has to do and where he has to go to find it.

How He Shows His Feelings

The moon in Libra man is very romantic and communicative. When in love, he is big on beautiful gestures like flowers and nights out at fine restaurants.

He will compliment you over candlelight and offer clever cheery conversation. On special occasions, he may break out the champagne and think up magical things to do that will make the evening unique and really memorable.

In the case of a quarrel, he will talk things out reasonably, trying to come to the most agreeable solution. Because he is able to see both sides of a situation, the moon in Libra man can also be a convincing and nonthreatening communicator who keeps things so clear that they seem to be easily resolved. At all costs he will maneuver the conversation away from meanness and ugliness, sorting out differences and keeping everything civilized.

His Dark Side

The moon in Libra man can be a feckless womanizer who is in love with love. The need for excitement and novelty can send him into a stream of pretty faces that he often forgets in record time.

This is a man who can be fickle, cold, and emotionally shallow. He can also be far more interested in the appearance of a woman than what she has to offer emotionally, spiritually, and intellectually. Generally, the moon in Libra is comfortable just focusing on the surface. What looks good gets his attention, but what keeps his attention is what strongly appeals to his comfort zone of pleasure, peace, harmony, and beauty.

During bad times he can completely cut off and show little or no compassion. To preserve his sense of harmony, he can be amazingly deaf to someone else's distraught feelings.

His Bright Side

He can be charming, witty, sociable, and gregarious. He is great at parties and is a person who can plan the perfect romantic event. Because the moon in Libra man so loves beauty and pleasure, he intuitively knows how to create it. Therefore, he can be fun, funny, and full of life.

He can also be creative and bring this to bear in a relationship in all kinds of ways, from thinking up wonderful surprises to planning romantic weekend getaways. Being thoughtful, reflective, and articulate, he can express himself in ways that can simplify and sort out a heavy emotional situation. His ability to be a peacemaker and negotiate a workable solution makes him very easy to be around.

His Attitude Toward Relationships

Although he can be a flirt and a playboy, eventually the moon in Libra man will want to settle down and is most happy in a harmonious relationship. This man is the marrying type and will always choose in the long run to go in the direction of commitment.

Libra is the sign of relationship; therefore, having a partner will always be a priority. As someone who would rather share a life than live alone, he will see to it that there is always someone on the scene to fulfill that need.

Easygoing and good at minimizing emotional problems, this man can be a pleasant partner who is easy to get along with. However, he can also get lazy and complacent and may need some gentle prodding to grow in the relationship.

The moon in Libra man can be dependent, not so much on his partner but on the comfort of the relationship itself. The danger here is that this man can subtly depersonalize his partner, her needs, and her problems. This can cause a big conflict with a woman who requires a deeper spiritual interaction and a lot of emotional understanding.

His Romance Factor

The moon in Libra man is very romantic and attuned to all the nuances that can turn an evening into a special event. He loves candlelit dinners, moonlit walks, and grand, glamorous occasions. He will contribute his special touch of creativity to enhance all the beauty that surrounds such moments.

He'll remember birthdays, anniversaries, and Valentine's Day. He'll buy flowers and presents and wine and dine the woman of his choice. Fine restaurants, good music, and cultural entertainment are likely to be part of his romantic repertoire. He will compliment his lover, be openly appreciative of his lover's appearance, and will probably open doors and do little things to make his woman feel beautiful. In turn, he expects that she is refined, graceful, lovely, and worthy of all his romantic ideals. Ideally, he wants a woman who is a complement to him, someone he can show off, a shining jewel of a person who is also a gracious, feminine partner.

His Reality Factor

The moon in Libra man is cool, objective, and tends to take his time, weigh things out, and fully examine both sides of a situation before taking action. At the same time, he is idealistic and has a fantasy life based on his ideals.

Like all air sign moons, this man approaches a situation through rational means and sometimes the deeper emotional issues suffer as a result. His sense of reality comes from observation and deliberation, not deep intuition. Nevertheless, he is not one to deny feelings. More likely, he will try to tidy them up and put them in their proper place. His style is to analyze a situation so that it sounds reasonable, is perfectly understandable, and seems to make such sense that everything loses its emotional charge.

His Fear Factor

The moon in Libra man fears fights, heavy emotional confrontations, ugly scenes, and situations that seem hopelessly out of control. Disharmony of all kinds brings out the worst in him. Being trapped in any disarray, emotional or physical, unsettles him and sends him into such enormous anxiety that he feels he has to defend himself against it. His defense is flight, not fight, and in his escape mode he may burn some bridges behind him.

How He Relates to Fire Sign Women
(Aries, Leo, Sagittarius)

The fire sign woman is famed for her quick temper, which could cause a nervous twitch in the moon in

Libra man. Initially, he will be attracted to her confidence, energy, and sheer enthusiasm for life. He will also admire her style and the way she conducts herself. However, her temperament will be challenging, should he cross her in any way. He can help her see situations from a more reasonable perspective, and she can push him to make decisions more readily. This connection can be very romantic, stimulating, and fun-filled for a while, but in the long run, she may upset his sense of balance.

How He Relates to Air Sign Women
(Gemini, Libra, Aquarius)

The similar temperament in both partners will have a soothing effect on the communication in this connection. Both are cool, cerebral, and analytical thinkers. The air sign woman needs her space, and the moon in Libra man will both understand and respect that. Both are sociable, gregarious, and given to witty, clever conversation. The air sign woman seeks, above all, someone she can really talk to. During conflicted moments both will attempt to talk out their difficulties instead of getting stuck in an emotional morass that makes matters worse. This could be a very comfortable, stimulating, and satisfying romantic pairing.

How He Relates to Earth Sign Women
(Taurus, Virgo, Capricorn)

Basically, this is a neutral connection that has equal chances of success or failure. An earth sign woman is relationship-oriented, and with her the moon in Libra man will fulfill his basic need for love and security. However, the temperaments of these two are essentially different, and this could be cause for eventual communication problems. Being a cerebral air sign, he has a need for mental stimulation, while her earth nature makes her more focused on practicality and daily details. The earth sign woman requires closeness, while the moon in Libra man needs a certain amount of space. At times his approach to life may appear too cold and distant to meet her needs. In turn, at times he may find her needs too intense for him to take. However, this combination can also be mutually supportive for both signs and become the basis of a long and stable union. Or, through discord, the interaction can produce under-the-surface frictions that can erode the quality of the connection. Therefore, special attention should be put on keeping the lines of communication open and flowing.

How He Relates to Water Sign Women
(Cancer, Scorpio, Pisces)

The water sign woman may be a bit too emotionally enigmatic for the moon in Libra man. She is complicated, moody, and emotional, just the sort of female who sends him running for the nearest exit. He won't understand her, and she won't appreciate his cool, reasonable way. She needs emotional intimacy, while he can be perfectly happy in a shallow but beautiful partnership. There is potential here for much emotional misunderstanding, conflict, and fear. This partnership is one that is both difficult to build and to sustain over time.

The Moon in
Scorpio Man

Who He Is Emotionally

The moon in Scorpio man is often an enigma unto himself. Since Scorpio is the sign of sex, death, and regeneration, this is the most complex moon placement in the zodiac. Therefore, at various times, in response to various people, the moon in Scorpio man exhibits a wide variety of emotional responses. He can be cold, controlling, emotionally intense, but also very private, critical, moody, mysterious, indifferent, passionate, driven, compulsive, obsessive, compassionate, and completely distant. This is a very difficult moon sign to live with—for both him and his partner.

Control is key to the moon in Scorpio man's personality, and he will not only carefully control his own emotional response, he will control and manipulate his partner as well. Control makes him feel safe. It also makes him cut off from anything that deeply disturbs him—whether it is his own complicated emotions rising to the surface or a lover who has made him extremely angry. To be completely out of control is this man's nightmare, since his emotions can be so intense and engulfing that they can completely overwhelm him, leaving him feeling powerless. At his most emotionally chaotic moment, he is capable of intense passion, jealousy, violence, excruciating moodiness, and black depression. Even if he doesn't know his limits well, he has some idea of what he is capable of on the negative side, and it frightens him. He also knows that his survival is dependent on his ability to keep his feelings in check despite what he may feel like on the inside. Therefore, this moon sign encourages suppression and the sort of stiff-upper-lip attitude that appears to the world as cool, inscrutable, and invulnerable. This is a man who appears indifferent to his own pain and who thrives on performing under duress and coming out on top, even under the worst conditions. Many moon in Scorpio men are workaholics who throw themselves into their career or business with a compulsion that leaves little or no room for them to comfortably experience their own emotions.

Scorpio is the sign of power—power over others as well as power from within. Usually, men of this moon sign opt for power over others and themselves. These men feel a great deal of pride in their own sense of power and often don't grow emotionally until they are trapped in some life-changing situation that makes them feel completely powerless. There can be so much rigidity in this moon sign that often this man's emotional vessel has to completely crack open before he is able to face his strong feelings. As is most often the case, these men take great pleasure in their own willpower and invulnerability and will drive themselves hard in their chosen direction. They do this because they are frightened of the demons lurking in their inner landscape. Those men who are able to rise to the challenge of becoming more human, the men who are strong enough to face their own demons and not project them on their lovers, have the most extraordinary potential for wisdom, depth, emotional brilliance, and profound emotional healing. However, this option is only open to those men who have done deep psychological work. These are the men who drive themselves to be more than mere control mongers, having the laudable strength to face themselves and the complex forces that drive them.

How He Feels

Scorpio is a passionate and deeply erotic sign and certainly the man with this moon sign is capable of exhibiting both to the woman in his life. When deeply anxious about intimacy, he can be a fly-by-night playboy. However, his soul yearns for a much deeper connection, where he is able to respond with passion and intensity.

In general, this is one man who is not easy to know. He may seem extremely slow to someone who doesn't know him. This is because he has an all-or-nothing attitude to a romantic relationship. If a woman doesn't deeply click into his psyche, he can be extremely cold, detached, remote, and ambivalent. This is a man who is not only very complicated but who also tends to make matters complicated—in his own mind. Having a very calculating mind and a horror of any kind of vulnerability, he is deeply self-protective and would never venture forth in a romantic situation if there was a chance that he might get hurt. As much as he might like an intensely passionate, erotic relationship, he is not at all comfortable surrendering to it until he knows that he can either trust his lover completely or else control her successfully. This man knows this sort of surrender means possible loss of control and mental clarity, which is exactly what he needs for survival. Therefore, it is not uncommon to see moon in Scorpio men who are emotionally dead, living off their smarts and successes, carefully compartmentalizing the time and energy spent on a relationship, which, as a result, becomes empty and meaningless.

Some men with this moon sign completely repress their feelings and project their own darkness and hostility onto their partner. In this case, it is the partner who either carries the weight or becomes the sole source of his emotional problems. Other men with the moon in Scorpio are very moody, and the darkness from their unconscious will leak through and bring them deadening bouts of depression. This man may attribute these emotions to any number of external factors but will usually never admit that they have anything to do with something inside himself.

It is not uncommon for a moon in Scorpio man to be so cut off from others and himself that he doesn't really know what he feels. Often his anger over a situation doesn't surface for days, and when it does, it shows itself in the form of a mood swing or depression. This is a man capable of great emotional extremes. On the surface he always seems perfectly in control. However, what is going on underneath the surface is another story. In the extreme, when pushed, this is a man capable of cold violence and emotionally vicious acts.

This is the sort of man whom you can ask "What were you feeling then?" and get the response "I don't know." It might be that he doesn't really know. It might be that he doesn't want to know, and it might also be that he does know and he doesn't want to talk about it. Emotionally, this man can be a very secretive, closed person who would rather put up a happy front than honestly reveal what he is really feeling.

The moon in Scorpio man is so uncomfortable with his own feelings that he holds them in and hopes they will magically disappear. Even if he is madly in love, he is often very distrustful and cautious about expressing himself. He plays his cards very close to his chest to maintain his safety. He is also uncomfortable around heavy emotional displays, gushing sentimentality, self-pitying behavior, and violent or hysterical anger. Instinctively, he knows the latter can trigger his own anger and violence, which is just waiting under the surface, should something or someone provoke it at the right time. Because he is not comfortable with his deeper feelings, he does not communicate them. He is intensely private and prone to pushing emotions further down so that he will be able to sustain and display a steely kind of control. Emotional vulnerability is what his suspicious mind fears most. Should he be brought to his knees through some emotional devastation, he will be very slow to recover or may never do so fully. Instead he may simply become more contracted, controlling, and suspicious over time.

How He Shows His Feelings

The moon in Scorpio man may be both passive-aggressive and very critical. However, when he trusts, he can also be passionate and talk from the depths of his soul. He is potentially a very deep person when he is not living through repression, control, and defense mechanisms. Perhaps the way that he is most comfortable expressing his feelings is through sex. His is a deeply sensual and erotic nature that craves the kind of stimulation that allows him to lose his mind to the act. Because he is so instinctively sexual, he can be a sublime lover with an erotic sensibility that is boundless.

When his anger is aroused, however, this man's emotional display is equally boundless and potentially terrifying. He is capable of cold withdrawal. He is also able to display the sort of vicious acting out that, chances are, will never be forgotten. From scathing verbal abuse to cruel, calculated manipulations designed to destroy the perceived enemy, this man's anger can be extremely painful. It is also highly effective. The moon in Scorpio man knows how to hit deep and hard and when he is angry usually won't be able to stop himself from striking out in any other manner. Having emotionally sadistic tendencies, he can derive a great deal of satisfaction from how horribly he can wound and destroy. This ability, which is as instinctive as his sexual prowess, makes him feel safe and separate from his own potential emotional pain. When operating from an unevolved level, this moon sign is a psychological killer. When evolved and operating from a spiritual consciousness, this man has great compassion and depth of intuition, intelligence, insight, and feeling. The difference is usually dependent on how much this man is willing to work on himself psychologically to truthfully and courageously face his own demons and grow into a human being who lives life more openly without the single goal of control.

His Dark Side

The man with a moon in Scorpio can be highly vindictive when his suspicions become true regarding betrayal or abandonment. He has a jealous nature and can be darkly suspicious and distrustful of anyone close to him. Many men with moon in Scorpio simply cannot love; they can only control and manipulate and often do, not even realizing the difference between these tactics and deep love. Subjective and self-righteous, they don't understand the dynamic of emotional give-and-take. Nor would they want to. Usually they find their own mode of operating gets them what they want, if only for a time. Paradoxically, quite often it also brings them what they most fear—abandonment from the woman they want most.

This is the moodiest of moon signs. Some men repress this side of themselves through strict regimens of control—disciplined exercise, hard-driven work behavior, and pastimes that far more resemble work than fun. All of these things can make them forget that they have feelings like the rest of the world, and in doing so, they often feel secretly superior. This moon sign is naturally dark. The man with it usually needs deep psychological work—preferably Jungian analysis, which works with the unconscious to transform that darkness into a more conscious and meaningful way of living where the shadow is more balanced with light. Transformation is a key to this moon sign, and until this man wants to change psychologically, instead of focusing only on changing his partner, he will create the emotional crises in his life that he most fears. Usually the bottom has got to fall out of his entire world, and he has got to be emotionally reduced to a powerless creature before this man can start to look at his life in a deeply intelligent and wiser way. Even then, he may pick himself up and resolve to retaliate in such a destructive manner that there is no room left in his existence for learning. His darkness can become so pervasive that it denies the light of consciousness, and without any of that, this becomes one lonely man doomed to live his life only in the company of his own demons.

His Bright Side

When he is evolved, this is a man of great emotional depth. The moon in Scorpio is the deepest and most complex moon sign in the zodiac, and that is why it also tends to be so problematic. The moon in Scorpio man can be very loyal and deeply loving. An evolved moon in Scorpio man who loves can be completely devoted, caring, and compassionate. Because this sort of man also tends to be highly intuitive, he can bring a deep awareness to his connections that is not to be found in more shallow moon signs.

This moon sign can also be extraordinarily intelligent, psychic, and sensitive to the pain of others. He can be a friend who will go to any lengths to help someone he cares about. However, usually he has had to go through quite a bit of emotional suffering himself before he loses that cool, distant aloofness that can make him seem so harsh and inhuman. Deep, deep down he needs love more than any other moon sign. However, often he is not really conscious of his needs and wants to think that he is above and beyond needing anything or anyone.

This man knows control; he knows deep inner loneliness; he knows moodiness; and he thinks he knows power. What he needs to know is the truth of himself, the truth of his own soul and shadow. His greatest challenge is to explore it so deeply and successfully that it brings him to his own light.

His Attitude Toward Relationships

Basically, a man with this moon approaches relationships in two ways. One can be that early on in life he will avoid real intimacy and commitment and simply engage in strings of superficial erotic connections. However, sooner or later the need for something deeper and lasting will surface, and he will most likely seek to satisfy that with marriage.

Because he is so controlling, critical, and uncompromising, the woman married to this man can find herself in a dismal state. The moon in Scorpio man can be highly judgmental and critical of ways of thinking that differ from his own and is painfully open about his lack of tolerance. Getting him to see the entire picture and to feel compassion for some viewpoint that is not his own is by no means an easy task. As with other tendencies he has, this man gets a sense of power in his attitudes concerning his way of seeing the world. Therefore, communicating with him over any issue that is controversial can be exhausting and draining. This is unfortunate since in any relationship that is vital, fulfilling, and meaningless, communication is crucial.

The moon in Scorpio man is also jealous and possessive, although it is likely that his fierce pride will not allow him to speak of this openly. However, secretly, his mind can be quite suspicious, and he can become completely obsessed with his fears. When deeply upset, he seethes under the surface with intense emotion and compulsively retraces his worrisome thoughts. Although his personality can be cool on the outside, on the inside his mind can be like a rat in a maze, making him feel increasingly anxious and, minute by minute, multiplying his feelings of acute discomfort.

In a relationship the moon in Scorpio man's greatest enemy is fear. This is compounded by the fact that he often has terrible problems handling his fears, sometimes inflating them, and sometimes completely suppressing them altogether. Instead he compensates for his fears through carefully wrought defense mechanisms. If he can just summon the courage to do some real soul-searching in which he can be honest with himself and honest with his partner, bringing the darkness into a professional psychological setting, he stands a real chance of living life through his heart and not his defense mechanisms. The problem is that his pride makes him think that he doesn't need help. Yet, if he can manage to get beyond his pride and understand that by growing emotionally, the entire quality of his life and his relationship will change for the better, he has the potential of transforming himself into a profound, wise human being. It is then that he will be capable of achieving the deep psychological and spiritual intimacy that he needs in his soul.

His Romance Factor

When passionately in love, this man can be both romantic and thoughtful. In fact, when he is enthralled in the grips of a great passion, the moon in Scorpio man is obsessive and probably thinks of his love many times a day. He can also be very secretly sentimental about passionate, erotic moments that have made him feel intensely alive. This man needs passion. Passion makes him come alive, lose control, and forget his fear. However, the sort of woman who would also arouse his most passionate response might be wilder than he can handle and a true threat to his emotional comfort zone.

His Reality Factor

Although this man is very smart and highly functional in the real world, in his private intense emotional world, he can be something else altogether. There is a very strong tendency in him to deny his feelings or problems and to project them onto his partner. Although he may operate in the objective world in the most brilliant way, he sees his own emotional world through something of a distorted lens. This is a man who benefits from a lot of self-scrutiny and self-analysis. He needs to hear himself and see himself as he actually is, not as how he would like to be perceived.

His Fear Factor

The moon in Scorpio man has deep-seated fears of abandonment and betrayal, and all of his defensive behavior stems from this. Consequently, he is jealous and suspicious and can easily imagine the worst that can happen in any situation. Sometimes his imagination gets the better of him, as does his behavior, which brings about those situations of lonely powerlessness that he fears the most.

How He Relates to Fire Sign Women
(Aries, Leo, Sagittarius)

The moon in Scorpio man will be intensely attracted to a fire sign woman, precisely because of her fire, spirit, aliveness, and capacity for passion. However, since fire sign women are highly independent free spirits who can be very headstrong, these women will simultaneously make him very nervous. Of course he will try all his control tactics that this woman will outright refuse to tolerate. The moon in Scorpio man will not understand that it is precisely these emotionally underhanded control tactics that will eventually take his woman from him. In the end, it is the fire sign woman's freedom, independence, and ability to control her own life that is the most important thing to her. Should that be severely compromised, she will walk away, and the moon in Scorpio man may never really recover.

How He Relates to Air Sign Women
(Gemini, Libra, Aquarius)

Air sign women can be very detached and analytical. In fact, they can be so detached that they are capable of analyzing away or finding a method of tolerating this man's weird and domineering behavior. Their friendly, easygoing manner also does not pose the threat of the temperamental fire sign woman who can be more than challenging. However, at the same time, air sign women lack the emotional intensity and passion that are so important to this man. They can make great friends, but unless there are other Scorpio planets in her chart, this connection just might feel too cool for comfort to the moon in Scorpio man.

How He Relates to Earth Sign Women (Taurus, Virgo, Capricorn)

Earth sign women can be very sensual and erotic. They also offer the sense of stability that will make this man feel secure. Earth sign women will show him patience. At the same time, they also offer the physical and sensual intimacy that is so necessary to his psyche. It is most likely that they will not understand his moods, but they will tolerate them and not antagonize him further with fiery episodes. This could be a match that has the potential to last a very long time.

How He Relates to Water Sign Women (Cancer, Scorpio, Pisces)

Water sign women will intuit his feelings and have the potential of drawing the moon in Scorpio man out of himself. However, should he persist with his controlling, emotionally tyrannical ways, the water sign woman will withdraw and probably make him suffer, using a wide array of passive-aggressive ways. There is a basis here for a deep sensual, intimate contact. However, whether it would last would depend on what this man would choose to do with it. If terribly unhappy, a water sign woman may not leave, but she will withdraw sexually, leaving him steeped in intense resentment. However, for the mature moon in Scorpio man, this could be a very intimate and fulfilling connection.

The Moon in
Sagittarius Man

Who He Is Emotionally

The moon in Sagittarius man is freedom-loving and full of humor. A natural optimist who never tires of journeying in new directions, he loves life and looks only at the big picture.

Adventurous, curious, restless, and full of anticipation for what may be around the next corner, he likes to keep moving, exploring, and experiencing life on many levels. Whether philosophical, intellectual, or more interested in the great outdoors, this man is at his best when covering new ground. Having a natural zest for life and learning, he loves to travel and take on new people, countries, languages, and foods. The moon in Sagittarius man will try anything once and knows how to make the best of a bad situation. Seeking to live life to the fullest, he hates to feel fettered by any situation. As soon as something gets boring, he is bound to move on.

Whether he has a philosophical/spiritual/ecological world view or a self-indulgent appetite for the forbidden, this is a man who must follow his inclinations, even if they take him into dangerous territories. He could be a philosopher, a humorist, or a full-time libertine, but whatever he does, he does it to the max. John Belushi and Krishnamurti shared this moon sign as did EST founder, Werner Erhard. All traveled in different ways and in different directions, but all followed their chosen path to the extreme.

The rule of the moon in Sagittarius man is that he wants to enjoy everything he does, and he wants everything that he does to take him somewhere exciting. Idealistic and interested in all life's possibilities, he is a positive person who takes things as they come. The need for discovery spurs him on and gives him a peripatetic appetite for the truly unpredictable paths. He may be difficult to pin down for very long, but hanging around him is always a learning experience.

Sometimes flighty, irresponsible, and feckless, his behavior can be unreliable and immature. He is one to be charmed, not tamed, and even then his attention span can be short. Impatient and preoccupied with many things at once, he wants to know how they'll all work out. In the meantime, some things never get finished and fall inevitably by the wayside. Airbound, he's off to his new journey, country, religion, planet, romance, or over-the-edge experience. The moon in Sagittarius man will not be contained or controlled. He will break free of all boundaries even if the risk is a big one. Sometimes his wanderlust will lead him into dangerous places that can be insidiously self-destructive.

How He Feels

Inspirational and enthusiastic, this man has lofty aspirations and flights of fantasy that may never get grounded in reality. He often longs for the intangible as his heart soars skyward. The soaring experience is what he likes best, and whether he is in love or living for some ideal, he never wants to come down. He finds the earth too dark and depressing.

The moon in Sagittarius man moves fluidly through his feelings. He easily lets go of the negative and moves on to a new positive outlook in record time. However, because his feelings are so mutable, he often doesn't dive very deeply beneath the surface of any situation, encounter, or relationship.

He can be something of a butterfly who moves from flower to flower. He can also turn emotions into abstractions that have philosophical weight and seemingly eternal value. In distancing himself from all darkness, he often loses track of the feelings of others and can be terribly insensitive. The moon in Sagittarius man can be more impatient than sympathetic. In general, he needs a lot of thinking and breathing space and can be more detached than emotional, depending on his personal plans and how consumed he is by them in the moment.

When bad times do besiege him, he doesn't stay down for very long. He will think things out and try to find some silver lining. Before long, he can be seen bouncing back and is once again soaring above the clouds. The moon in Sagittarius man cannot tolerate negativity and prolonged depression, whether it's in himself or someone else. Therefore, he'll do his best to turn a dark situation around and gain something positive from it.

Impulsive and having a tendency to live in the moment, he can fall in love in about fifteen minutes and out of love in about four. Therefore, it's no surprise that Casanova was a moon in Sagittarius man. His youthful exuberance can often be a magnet to many women. However, should he find his best friend and true soul mate, he will transform into a man of staying power who will probably put his love on a pedestal and stick around for a lifetime.

The moon in Sagittarius man thinks in superlatives and wants all his experiences to be peak ones. The little significant moments and subtle feelings fly by him until he learns to slow down and really listen.

How He Shows His Feelings

Open and honest, he holds nothing back. The moon in Sagittarius man often speaks before he thinks and shows everything on the surface. His is a no-holds-barred sort of style. Throwing caution to the wind, he is capable of sharing his heart and mind with all his friends as well as the general public. This man is not at all frightened of his feelings.

Positive and open-minded, he will often express himself through his sense of humor, which can also be an armor against fear. Affectionate and filled with enthusiasm, he will embrace everything around him. The moon in Sagittarius man is very self-expressive and leaves little to the imagination. He loves to bare his soul and, in the process, set the world on fire. Generous, outgoing, and wanting to befriend the world, he can bring a lot of light to a lot of people and in the process provide himself with the sort of higher-minded satisfactions that his heart desires.

His Dark Side

Seldom dark himself, the behavior of the moon in Sagittarius man can bring darkness into the lives of others. When immature, he can be flighty and irresponsible, forgetting commitments that he never really meant to keep. He can sometimes live life on a shallow level that leaves little room for others' feelings.

He can be a ladies' man who doesn't show very much feeling for anyone in particular. When self-indulgent, he can go through many women and end up losing himself to the god of pleasure.

The moon in Sagittarius man can take a long time to grow up and follow a solid plan of action. He can be scattered and so focused on the big picture that he completely loses sight of all the important details. In order to find a fulfilling balance in his life, this man needs to concentrate on becoming grounded. Only then will he make the most of himself, his visions, and his ideals.

His Bright Side

This man can have a brilliant mind and shine like a bright light in a crowd of people. The moon in Sagittarius man can be charming, witty, and winsome and often has a captivating personality and a sense of humor that can win over almost anyone.

Positive, optimistic, and forward-thinking, he can be inspiring and intellectually influential. The moon in Sagittarius man has an enthusiastic, curious mind that gives him a thirst for knowledge and often makes him an interesting, clever conversationalist.

When in love, the moon in Sagittarius man can be both wildly generous and imaginative. His impulsive, ebullient ways can make all the tedious, mundane aspects of daily life seem to disappear. Full of a zest for life, this man has a spirit that can ignite sparks in a lot of souls and leave a trail of joy behind.

His Atittude Toward Relationships

The moon in Sagittarius man is a free spirit. He cannot be fenced in or pushed into someone else's plan for the rest of his life. Fearing entrapment, he may avoid relationships altogether and choose to spend his time exploring many people, ideas, philosophies, and countries.

Often ruled by his wanderlust, he doesn't feel the urge to settle down like some people. However, that doesn't mean that he never will. The moon in Sagittarius man needs a woman who is both a best friend and a playmate. The perfect soul mate is as independent, freedom-loving, and adventurous as he is. She is also someone who has such a full life herself that she would never think of tying him down.

The thing to remember about the moon in Sagittarius man is that he is often allergic to responsibility. If he feels someone is waiting in the wings and trying to make him feel guilty for being so free, he will decide that she is best forgotten, the flame will die out, and she will find herself sitting by a silent phone.

His Romance Factor

The moon in Sagittarius man is romantic about life and all its inherent possibilities. This enthusiasm can fuel a relationship, as well, providing it is with the right woman.

Given to grand gestures, this man will be impulsive, exciting, and imaginative in his response to his special woman. When not totally involved, he tends to be detached, dismissive, and so full of his own personal plans that he forgets nearly everything else. While he has the ability to be romantic, it's usually not his first priority. The moon in Sagittarius man hates to feel that certain behavior is expected of him. His first priority is to be free and true to his dreams.

This is a spontaneous man who needs constant stimulation. Change and variety are high on his list of lifetime requirements, and this can apply to his women. As has already been noted, the infamous lover, Casanova, was a moon in Sagittarius man. This sort of man can treat women as a series of passing adventures. However, should he find the woman of his dreams, she will star in one ongoing adventure.

His Reality Factor

This man is far more idealistic than pragmatic and lives in his own chosen world without too much interruption from the real world. He doesn't allow it. The moon in Sagittarius man can easily leave mundane responsibilities behind while he travels on to his next challenge, curiosity, subject of study, or long-term trip.

This man can busy himself with so many activities that he can become completely out of touch with his feelings. Therefore, his reality can be based only on his own subjective needs, and his behavior can be completely insensitive. Although on a philosophical level, this is a man who might dedicate his life to the search for truth, on a personal level what he chooses to see as truth is a matter of convenience. The moon in Sagittarius man likes life to fall sweetly into place all around him. Sometimes it does, and when it doesn't, he might move on.

His Fear Factor

He is frightened of anything or anyone who would threaten his freedom and need for complete independence. The moon in Sagittarius man must have his space, both physical and psychological. His terror of being trapped or tied down will make him behave in ways that are selfish and insensitive. This is not a man who can be molded, manipulated, or pushed around. He moves to his own music, and the more that he feels he's allowed to move, the more generous and pleasant he will be.

How He Relates to Fire Sign Women
(Aries, Leo, Sagittarius)

The freedom-loving fire sign woman is just his style, especially if she is a Sagittarian herself. Much psychic energy will be kindled between the two, and the excitement it will produce can be endless. Since the fire sign woman is spontaneous, impulsive, and loves the challenge of a great mind, she will show the enthusiasm and energy that this man requires. He will feel comfortable with her self-possessed, independent ways and respect her fiery spirit. She will feel simultaneously stimulated and entertained by him, and that just happens to be her favorite feeling.

How He Relates to Air Sign Women
(Gemini, Libra, Aquarius)

The cerebral and often intellectual air sign woman is turned on by new ideas and the thought of someone interesting to talk to. She will adore this man's mind and his sense of adventure. In turn, he will connect with her intelligence and feel inspired by her warm and intelligent responses. A freedom-loving woman herself, the air sign woman will respect his space and never try to entrap him. With her, he will feel that he can be himself and share parts of his mind and spirit that are very special and exciting.

How He Relates to Earth Sign Women
(Taurus, Virgo, Capricorn)

The security-minded earth sign woman will try to ground the moon in Sagittarius man and ensnare him. She will want to know his whereabouts at all times and where he might be headed in the future. She may also see some of his far-flying ideas and philosophies as foolish and impractical. Just by showing up, she will provide the sort of prison he wants to flee from, and he most likely will run.

How He Relates to Water Sign Women
(Cancer, Scorpio, Pisces)

The emotional water sign woman may scare him off with her need for closeness and intimacy. Emotional security is something that he really doesn't understand and also doesn't want to. She may find his mind challenging, but his behavior will bore right into her vulnerabilities. Deep down, she has a fear of being abandoned, and she will probably sense that this might be the man who will make her fears come true.

The Moon in
Capricorn Man

Who He Is Emotionally

There are basically two types of moon in Capricorn men—those who are defined merely by their ambitious drives and those who have evolved to value more than the material world. The moon is in detriment in this sign, which means that this man has a problem expressing his deeper feelings. Most moon in Capricorn men need to grow into themselves emotionally, and some never do because the drive for success and power is so overwhelming that it stifles their connections with their souls. The need for material security can also stunt this man's ability to express love.

Certainly, this scenario is most common in young men of this moon sign where the goal-oriented, enterprising nature gives rise to a never-ending list of more goals and more mountains to be climbed. Feelings take a backseat position to the burden of responsibilities that pave this man's road to financial security and, ideally, affluence. The moon in Capricorn man is ambition personified. This drivenness can cut him completely off from his feelings, as can be seen if we look to the lust for personal, political, and financial power displayed in many moon in Capricorn men, namely Adolf Hitler and Napoleon. However, Abraham Lincoln and the Dalai Lama are also men who share this moon sign and have the highly developed traits it has to offer. The difference in the men of these two groups is evolution. The values of Abraham Lincoln and the Dalai Lama are values that transcend money, power, and the material realm.

However, as a general rule, money is extremely important to this moon sign and is a strong motivating factor influencing the behavior of those born under it. Essentially, money represents security, both psychological and financial, and the typical moon in Capricorn man is very insecure. He won't show it, of course. As a matter of fact, he might go to extreme lengths to deny it. However, way down under his cool, controlled facade lie a vulnerability and fragility that he is always running from.

He will run from them with all his might and, with steely determination and extraordinary discipline, drive himself up all the mountains he wants to conquer until he owns each one. Many moon in Capricorn men believe above all in ambition and success. Loving is something that he thinks will only slow him down, and he often doesn't allot quality time for it until the last half of his life—if then. In many ways, this man can seem old at a very early age, often born striving, and becoming a businessman, even as a boy. The moon in Capricorn man has a natural, shrewd business acumen. He also has a need to be financially independent and is prepared to do whatever it takes to accomplish this, including making huge personal and romantic sacrifices.

To this end he will sacrifice personal time. He will also sacrifice love. That is not to say that he won't marry or form a relationship. However, the connection he sustains will sit on the back burner of his bigger goals, and his wife may easily become a widow to the duties and responsibilities of his truly pressing desire: financial freedom and/or power in the world at large.

The moon in Capricorn man tends to be pragmatic. He can also be ruthless and cold and marry only for the sake of a prominent social or political connection. However, he does not always have to stay in this shallow place and there are those born under this moon sign who do move beyond it. Those who do, begin to question life's larger meaning and sense a void within themselves that financial investments, political office, or workaholism can't fill.

Unfortunately, many men with this sign hide behind their self-created castles of achievement or work-related responsibilities. This is a highly self-protective moon sign. It is also one that is very private, especially about such deep-seated anxiety-producing thoughts as fear of failure or rejection. There is great pride to be gained by this man in being able to be beyond it all, beyond human vulnerability and fear. Therefore, the moon in Capricorn man will often submerge his emotions and assume a stiff upper lip or extremely positive attitude to save himself from his own fear. Over time, he will often become very good at putting a lid on the feelings that might betray him. In this respect, he can be his own worst enemy, although he might never see this. What he would choose to see is his own control and how successfully he wields it.

While some men need control over others, the moon in Capricorn man needs control over himself and the hidden demons within him that might deny him a fragile moment. He is so facile at the game of control that he often also ends up in a position where he has control over other people. Because our society usually hugely rewards this kind of behavior, this man usually does not attempt to go to deeper dimensions within himself. However, they are there, should he ever choose to explore them.

The moon in Capricorn man is capable of much more emotional depth than he usually allows himself to consider or discover. He is not a shallow man. However, he does tend to live as a mirror of society's material values. When and if he begins to transform and become aware of the need to find his own personal, emotional, and perhaps spiritual values, there is no end to his ability to love and care for others in the deepest way. It must be said, however, that his own depths scare him. Somewhere along the road of life he probably has really been hurt, and he has not taken it lightly. It is likely that with all his will, he will try to close the opening to that pain that he knows deep down he could still experience. However, if he is really lucky and not merely materially successful, maybe sometime in his life something or someone will come along and open it up again.

How He Feels

The typical moon in Capricorn man sublimates his feelings. His denial of emotions fuels him in his avid quest for wealth and power. This is a man who feels he must always be busy, and the more that he is consumed with constant enterprising activity and the world on the outside, the less he feels on a deeply emotional level.

Although he has the capability of depth, this man tends to live in the shallow end of his emotional pool, taken up with the world at large. If he can get beyond the mad clamor of daily life, he might find he is capable of compassion, based on his ability to relate to some suffering of his own from his past. However, his emotional thrust usually leads him in the more comfortable direction of some activity. Activity in general and activities in particular can take on a ritualistic value in that they lend him a sense of structure, productivity, and emotional escape.

Deep underneath his surface lies a vulnerable side protected by a web of psychological and behavioral defenses that may make him seem averse to love. As a matter of fact, he deeply needs it. However, somewhere in life he has been burned, and he knows that with the possibility of opening himself up to love comes the risk of deep emotional pain.

The moon in Capricorn man has to feel safe, secure, and on steady ground before he will allow himself to form a substantial romantic connection. Furthermore, his self-control and sense of discipline will allow him to quickly erect barriers that may become entire roadblocks, should he feel endangered by the relationship at any time. All earth sign moons want everything to be put neatly in its place, even emotions. That is why they can be so frustrating and perhaps boring when it comes to romance, which often requires some spontaneity and whimsy. The feelings of the moon in Capricorn man need to be drawn out slowly so that he doesn't feel engulfed with the emotionally ominous threat of the unknown.

Like all earth sign moons, this man has a strongly sensuous, tactile nature and tends to feel a great deal through his body and his senses. The proper scent can bring him down from his goal-oriented tower and get him in touch with feeling. Physical displays of affection are also essential, and a sexual relationship that is deeply sensual can ground him and get him deep inside himself—at least for a while.

How He Shows His Feelings

The moon in Capricorn man tends to suppress his feelings and not communicate openly. Nevertheless, no matter how much they are suppressed, painful feelings can affect him for a very long time. This is a man who sees himself as a survivor in a potentially dangerous world. He, therefore, does not open up easily. He can even be called distrustful and at times paranoid. He plays every move out in his head from the perspective of retaining power or retaining self-preservation versus pain.

The moon in Capricorn man has a serious problem expressing anger, and at times this can cause him to suffer from depression. Wanting order and control in all situations, he is thrown in the lurch by emotional situations that he can't put aside in a tidy little pile and forget. When deeply affected, he can take to brooding, withdrawing and becoming quite dark. This might be seen from the outside as startling emotional coldness. However, this man is usually experiencing deep introversion and is so much at the mercy of his own profound feelings that his connection with the surrounding world seems to disappear.

When it comes to love, this man may need a bit of drawing out, as well as a lot of emotional reassurance before he is comfortable revealing the deeper parts of himself. Even then, only a combination of time, magic, and chemistry will determine how much he will be willing to open up.

His Dark Side

Underneath his cool, efficient facade, the moon in Capricorn man can be dark, depressed, moody, and fearful. He tries to escape from these feelings through work, new projects, demanding enterprises, athletics, and perhaps travel. Fear and the need for security fuel him and can make him cold, distant, and perhaps a little boring at times. However, he is not a game player, nor is he deliberately cruel by nature. He can simply be difficult to get close to, although the irony is that deep down inside he needs intimacy perhaps more than anything else. The problem with the moon in Capricorn man is that he doesn't realize how he is denying his own life by living strictly by discipline and hard work. Sometimes life is kind to him and creates an opening to greater depths with the appearance of a woman who could bring meaning to his life. However, whether he will allow himself to trust it and how far he will go to meet it is a mystery. A key factor in unfreezing him is time.

His Bright Side

When the moon in Capricorn man is mature and strong enough to stand on his two feet without his defenses, he can be a deeply loving individual. He is also loyal, supportive, compassionate, and caring. When he is mature, he reveals and shares the many joys and fears he holds in his depths instead of trying to run away from them. When deeply involved, he is also deeply committed. He is not only serious about his relationship, he is protective of it and the person he loves.

The moon in Capricorn man is a highly responsible person upon whom you can depend in a crisis. There is a wealth of feeling deep within him that extends to friends, family, and especially the one closest to his heart.

His Attitude Toward Relationships

The moon in Capricorn man has an all-or-nothing attitude toward relationships. If he is very busy, he can exist without them. However, he often yearns for more than a full schedule in time. Nevertheless, this man's search for meaning can sometimes not take place until later in life. In the meantime, his focus will be on being efficient, productive, and financially secure.

When he does form a serious relationship, he is a

one-woman man. He is committed, responsible, and completely faithful. In turn, he expects the same. When he can trust, the moon in Capricorn man thrives on closeness, intimacy, and loving kindness. What's most wonderful of all about this man is that the fragile little boy in him is deeply appreciative of this kind of contact. Maybe he can't put it into words, but his day-to-day actions and the kind of consideration that he is capable of showing can spell a love that is genuine and comes straight from the heart.

His Romance Factor

When he can take the time away from work, the moon in Capricorn man can be quite romantic and able to create a great evening. Highly discriminating by character, he also tends to have great taste and is entirely open to romantic evenings anywhere—in trendy restaurants, at home, on the beach, in the bedroom. When deeply in love, he also has something of a secret sentimental side that is touched by tender moments.

Essentially, the moon in Capricorn man has to grow into himself before he can get to a level where he is capable of seriously loving. When he reaches that level and can manage to trust another deeply, he will try to make the time he does spend with his partner meaningful. He can be very caring, and when he is mature, he can offer a lot from a profound emotional depth. However, for him to do this, the connection must be something that he really wants and needs. Otherwise, he can be cold and put a woman on hold while he devotes himself to his work.

His Reality Factor

The moon in Capricorn man is a realist who sometimes has a hard time taking creative leaps. His inherent sense of pragmatism makes it easy and comfortable for him to put business before pleasure, which always takes its toll on his love life.

To protect himself, this man will also try to take a hard look at the entire picture in order to prepare himself for any negative outcome he might have to face in the future. There can be a kind of ruthless quality to his practicality when it pushes emotions to the side in order to function efficiently. Duty, discipline, and responsibility can easily edge out feeling in this man's life, and it may happen without him even knowing it. Often, the priority in his mind is to have the upper hand in his success scheme, regardless of what he may have to sacrifice in the moment.

His Fear Factor

The emotional realm is this man's source of fear, and it is something that he really needs to work on. The moon in Capricorn man can be both calculating and defensive to compensate for the fears that make him so uncomfortable. His need for control can dominate a great deal of his personal choices, making him detached, preoccupied, and permanently busy.

In the area of love, the moon in Capricorn man must come to terms with his inner world. The problem with this challenge is that he is preoccupied with the outer world, which is where he feels safe. This is a man who can turn an idea into a multimillion-dollar business and rise to the top of any challenge he seriously decides to take on. However, his greatest challenge is in learning to live meaningfully in his own feelings, a task that can be quite a formidable undertaking.

How He Relates to Fire Sign Women
(Aries, Leo, Sagittarius)

Fiery fire sign women can be challenging to the moon in Capricorn man. Their impulsive, independent ways can pose quite a threat to his need for emotional security. First of all, impatient fire sign women do not like to be put on hold and have threatening ways in which they let the moon in Capricorn man know this. A partnership between these two can be a wonderful learning experience in which both learn to listen to the needs and fears of the other. However, should the moon in Capricorn man put up a wall with his iron-clad defenses that persists for too long a time, the fire sign woman will want out. Should she want to try to stick it out for the potential meaning of this situation, she will have to show patience, sensitivity, and loving kindness. All three combined just might help the moon in Capricorn man forget his work and find his heart. In the meantime, the fire sign woman may become more in touch with the depths of her own heart.

How He Relates to Air Sign Women
(Gemini, Libra, Aquarius)

For a long time the detached air sign woman may fit in perfectly with this man's work schedule. Needing her own space, she may not even notice that he is rarely at home. Both will go their own ways and do their own thing. However, in time the moon in Capricorn man may find that what was once a convenient situation has become empty and superficial. In turn, the air sign woman may find something mysterious missing, the deeper emotional content that every woman wants. Neither should allow their own schedules and personal preoccupations to put the quality of relatedness in the backseat of the relationship. For this to work, the air sign woman has to become more conscious of her own emotional needs as well as those of his that he may not be expressing. As a woman, she has to draw him out and facilitate his deeper feelings. This is something that is not in her nature to do since she is usually so detached from her own deeper feelings. However, the ultimate success of this connection will depend on it as well as on how far he is willing to stretch to become warm and human.

How He Relates to Earth Sign Women
(Taurus, Virgo, Capricorn)

Here, the moon is in its own element and this works well for stability, security, and financial matters. Of course, how this match would ultimately turn out would depend as well on the placement of this man's sun sign. However, in general, these two would be in agreement about day-to-day matters and details. This connection would be more predictable than brimming with excitement, and it would encourage both to maintain the status quo rather than working on growing and sharing new experiences. If the moon in Capricorn man's sun sign is in Gemini or Aquarius, eventually he may get bored and restless and want more from the relationship than the shallow routine that this sort of connection tends to generate. However, if his sun sign is especially in an earth or water sign, this match has a good chance of lasting a lifetime.

How He Relates to Water Sign Women
(Cancer, Scorpio, Pisces)

The sensitive, intuitive water sign woman has the capacity to be patient and nurturing to the moon in Capricorn man, making him feel secure and loved. However, her emotional needs may get in his way and make him feel compromised on the work front. She will want to spend more time with him than he has time for. In turn, she may feel rejected and resentful of his rather rigid workaholic ways. This is a connection that may need work; however, that work and conscious consideration of each other could bring both people closer together, making this a growth relationship that both will benefit from.

The Moon in
Aquarius Man

Who He Is Emotionally

The moon in Aquarius man is the most emotionally detached of the twelve signs. Independent, freedom-loving and something of a rebel, this is a man who most wants to live life on his own terms.

Emotionally restless and intellectually free-spirited, the moon in Aquarius man is often ahead of his time. He dances only to his own beat and is best off when immersed in his own internal music. Many controversial philosophers, radical thinkers, and progressive public figures share this moon, such as Timothy Leary, Jean-Paul Sartre, and Albert Camus. Although this is a moon sign often seen in political reformers and activists, it is interesting to note that it is also unusually prevalent with psychopaths and serial murderers such as Charles Manson and the Son of Sam killer, David Berkowitz.

Although the moon in Aquarius man is superficially friendly, he can also exhibit profound emotional detachment in this sign. Men with this moon sign tend to be cut off from their deeper feelings, frightened of any degree of emotional intensity and ready to flee in the face of any sort of emotional constraint. They have a deep anxiety and sense of dread at the thought of being tied down to anything or anyone and only come to a relationship slowly and even then always seem to have one foot out the door.

Often more interested in ideas than people, the moon in Aquarius man gravitates toward the unusual in both. Valuing his own freedom and individuality above all else, he is also attracted to others whose wild ideas, statements, and attitudes define them. The moon in Aquarius man usually has a very challenging, rebellious attitude and can frequently be seen daring any sort of constraint to defy him. In the extreme he could be a Hell's Angel or a bomb thrower, a criminal who lives beyond the fringe of society or someone who repeatedly commits destructive acts and simply doesn't care. Whether it be positive or negative, what always seems to be associated with this sign is some sense of the extreme. When taken in a positive direction, this tendency can produce a powerful political figure who is out to change society for the better, such as Woodrow Wilson. However, it is also associated with more than its share of powerful political dictators who believe the end completely justifies the means, even at the sacrifice of countless innocent people. Fidel Castro and Lenin are two such examples of moon in Aquarius men.

Cool and sometimes downright cold, this is not a

man suited to a conventional relationship. Platonic connections suit him well, and his ideal in a lover is someone who is first and foremost a friend. Like all air signs, he is most attracted to someone exciting to talk to. Easily bored by anyone or anything too "normal," he is often attracted by someone who seems to offer a lot of surface or intellectual excitement. Usually cut off from his feelings, he neither understands nor appreciates the feelings of others. His style is to keep everything light, friendly, and not delve too deeply into any intense personal or emotional territory. Too much emotional intensity will feel overwhelming and confining, and confinement of any sort is just the thing to make this man take flight.

How He Feels

The moon in Aquarius man is emotionally shallow, so he tends to exist in a world of ideas or superficial activity. When called upon to evaluate what he might be feeling in a given situation, he needs a long time to process and think things out. What tends to affect him emotionally is what he thinks about a person or a situation. Never given to direct, visceral emotional responses, a man with this moon sign can be curiously unemotional and tends to talk away what little feelings he does acknowledge.

Often he can be emotionally changeable and unpredictable in strange and disturbing ways. Seemingly out of the blue he can coldly break off a relationship, walk out on a project or job or sever some other long-lasting commitment, leaving without a backward glance. These puzzling, inexplicable reactions that enable him to leave the past behind with such complete detachment can make him a rather risky friend or lover. All air signs are capable of losing feeling in what appears to be a flash; however, the moon in Aquarius can be the most emotionally erratic. It has often been noted that this moon sign is commonly associated with a childhood history of a broken home or is the product of a childhood situation indicative of some type of turmoil, separation, or instability. The correlation between this moon sign and an early development of detachment and extreme independence does often seem to bear itself out in the moon in Aquarius man.

How He Shows His Feelings

The moon in Aquarius man can talk endlessly about feelings, especially if he happens to be unhappy. However, even you might sense that he is strangely detached from himself.

Often this man doesn't know what he really feels, or he truly feels nothing. This moon sign can be very empty in the soul and the person born with it compensates for this vacuousness and disconnection through such things as a strident commitment to a cause, a self-destructive rebelliousness, drugs, alcohol, a compulsive breaking of rules, or a compulsive lack of commitment to creating anything lasting and meaningful.

The moon in Aquarius man tends to repress deep old painful moments and often has inappropriate emotional responses as an adult. He may be amazingly cold in a situation that calls for some human compassion. He may suddenly erupt in anger or violence at some misperceived slight, and he may appear strangely detached over something that would cause someone else emotional upset. Often when he talks about some emotional experience, you might get the odd feeling that it is some story he read somewhere in passing.

The positive side to his detachment is that it allows this man to function in disturbing, high-stress situations such as an emergency room or a battlefield. It can pose a lot of problems, however, in personal relationships where more is required than human efficiency.

His Dark Side

When the moon in Aquarius man is really dark, he is also really dangerous. He can be completely cruel, emotionally cut off and even sociopathic. He can suffer from chronic depression where he is emotionally dead and doesn't even know that he is depressed. He can also erupt into mood swings where he instinctively projects his darkness onto someone else.

Less extreme moon in Aquarius behavior reveals a person who can be cruel through omission. He can also be completely selfish and emotionally insensitive, completely cold and indifferent to the pain of another person. A dark moon in Aquarius man gives off an emotional chill that can be felt by anyone who is sensitive and emotionally attuned. He is often a very detached person who dissipates his energies through destructive or inconsequential acts. He is also very difficult to get close to and puts up a wall against real intimacy.

His Bright Side

Like all air signs, the man with a moon in Aquarius can be bright, witty, sociable, and very friendly. He can also be a lot of fun to be with. Because he tends to be so intellectually curious and interested in the open-ended, he himself can also provide interesting, stimulating company. The moon in Aquarius man can be very easy to talk to, and depending on how developed he is, he can also be a good listener.

When evolved, he can be a very good friend who is there in a crisis with a calm, supportive manner. Idealistic and imaginative, he can be a seer who is far ahead of his time and fully prepared to put his ideals into positive action. Often possessing humanitarian or high-minded philosophic values, this man can be a forward-thinking leader who changes society in powerful ways.

His Attitude Toward Relationships

The moon in Aquarius man is freedom-loving, independent, and committed to his own path, ready to go wherever it may take him. Although he is friendly on the surface, in reality he is close to very few people and puts up a lot of walls to prevent anyone from moving in too closely.

Restless, cerebral, and often in search of something intangible, this man needs a lot of space in which to roam. Having unconventional attitudes, he would never come near a traditional marriage unless he found in his lover a best friend. Even then, he might be slow committing and may take years making up his mind as to what he's going to do.

The moon in Aquarius man seeks a lover who is a friend and ideally a soul mate. If he doesn't have that, he is perfectly happy with connections that are platonic. Having a need for excitement and stimulation, not emotional security, he may drift around in limbo, never loving anyone, always looking for some unspoken and perhaps unconscious ideal.

Should he find his soul mate, this man will settle down and be faithful. However, he still needs to have his psychological space respected and acknowledged. Often the moon in Aquarius man is confused about his feelings and the issue of commitment, never really finding the right person and sometimes making an ambivalent effort in some direction. When this happens, it is not uncommon that one day he will just run cold, losing all interest and leaving his lover stranded. Unless this man is committed to his eternal soul mate, there is no telling what he will do. He himself doesn't know. His behavior is dependent on the mystery of his own unconscious feelings.

This man needs in a woman something of a challenge. A woman in search of emotional security is a horror to his sensibilities. Some moon in Aquarius men have relationships with someone married, someone living in another country, or someone so emotionally compromised that they aren't really present. This satisfies his need for distance and can be very reassuring to this man, who tends to be so deeply frightened of intimacy.

His Romance Factor

The moon in Aquarius man is romantic about his own ideas, philosophies, and personal freedom. With a lover who shares his ideas and ideals, he is friendly and enthusiastic but not conventionally romantic.

If truly involved, his style might be to take off on an impulsive trip or provide a little surprise that might turn out to be both winsome and unusual. This man can be unpredictable and ready to jump into action on the spur of the moment. He doesn't like to feel duty-bound and that things are expected of him. At all times he has to feel that he is free to do things in his own way, and that includes gift-giving. It is not uncommon for the moon in Aquarius man to give the gift no one would ever want. All he knows is that in the moment he chose it, it appealed to him, and that's all that seemed to be important.

Birthdays and anniversaries are a terrible bother to him. They mean pressure and obligation. Even if he tries to come through, it is likely that he will get so distracted that he will forget that he was even trying to remember that special occasion. The moon in Aquarius man has many rebellious little ways of saying that he can't feel forced into anything. He wants every move he makes to be an act of free will. Otherwise, he will so compromise the effort that in the long run it won't be worth it.

His Reality Factor

The moon in Aquarius man lives in a world of his own making and quite often this bears little resemblance to the world at large. He can be an idealistic dreamer who doesn't want to come down to earth. Often highly intelligent and ahead of his time, he can have a cutting edge sort of mentality that allows him to see beyond earthly limitations. He also doesn't blindly buy into society's values and decides for himself the way he sees things.

This man can be a hopeless rebel and completely out of touch with anything but the way that he wants things to be. His values determine how much he is willing to come to terms with a situation. Aquarius is a fixed sign and can be very stubborn and rigid. Therefore, the moon in Aquarius man tends to hold on to his own way of thinking and is not particularly open to another conflicting point of view.

His Fear Factor

Many men with moon in Aquarius fear nothing consciously since they are so out of touch with their own feelings. They also have little concept of fear since they so implicitly trust their own ability to cut and run, should anyone or anything get too close for comfort.

On a deep level these men fear intimacy, being confined and being suffocated. Of all the moon signs, this is a man who has the deepest problems forming close relationships. He may not be conscious of this, but his ambivalent and distance-producing behavior will be the indicator. This is a man who can only feel comfortable with a woman who is so cerebral, independent, and caught up in her own consuming interests that she barely has time to fit him in.

How He Relates to Fire Sign Women
(Aries, Leo, Sagittarius)

Since the restless fire sign woman is essentially freedom-loving herself and also requires a certain amount of excitement, this could be a mutually stimulating connection. She will love his mind and his unique way of looking at the world. His moon will challenge her emotionally and intellectually, and her independent, fiery temperament may just be the thing that wakes him up to some feeling.

How He Relates to Air Sign Women
(Gemini, Libra, Aquarius)

Emotionally detached herself, and needing a lot of mental stimulation, the air sign woman will be a natural match for this man lost in his own thoughts. Both are curious, communicative, and in love with learning. Clever, witty conversation is how they find a way to their feelings. Life may become one long thought, and to both of these signs it will feel like love.

How He Relates to Earth Sign Women
(Taurus, Virgo, Capricorn)

The earth sign woman wants to settle down while the moon in Aquarius man needs to keep moving. Her security needs and groundedness will suffocate him in a second. In turn, he will so confuse her and make her so insecure that she may find herself in a constant emotional crisis just trying to stick around him. He wants to explore the great beyond while she wants to stay in the same place and own it. The lack of communication here insures that nothing between these two will probably last for very long.

How He Relates to Water Sign Women
(Cancer, Scorpio, Pisces)

The emotional needs of the water sign woman will drown this distance-producing, freedom-loving man. She requires intimacy; he can't bear the word. The emotional closeness that she needs will terrify him. In turn, his coldness will completely turn her off.

The Moon in
Pisces Man

...The moon in Pisces ...is a ...'s individuals...

Who He Is Emotionally

The inner world of the moon in Pisces man is an emotional conundrum characterized by a variety of moods,
feelings, empathies, fantasies, and secret longings. At
times his moods make him a mystery unto himself. At
other times he is a vessel of pure intuition. Then there
are the times when he doesn't even know what he's
feeling. Sometimes a sense of apathy surrounds him,
and his first thought may be escape.

This is a sign that runs the gamut from great creative artists such as Michelangelo and Leonardo da
Vinci to alcoholic and drug-addicted people such as
Elvis Presley. In between are to be found psychics,
healers, and psychologists. Pisces is a mysterious, psychic, intuitive sign that is changeable, fluid, and closely
connected to the unconscious.

There are moon in Pisces men who are completely

cut off from their feelings. Some sublimate their nature wisely, while others live at the mercy of their own emotions. In general, this sign is a psychic sponge. It picks up the psychic and emotional contents of other people quite consciously and can be deeply affected by others' moods.

Often sensitive, compassionate, and caring, men of this moon sign have to wrestle with having a feminine, receptive sensibility in such a strongly masculine culture that denies the validity of men's feelings. Sometimes men with this moon sign unconsciously compensate by developing overly masculine attitudes or by cutting off from their feelings altogether. However, they will find their moods usually do rise to the surface, and when they do, they sometimes cause problems such as bouts of apathy or depression.

The moon in Pisces man can be highly intuitive. He can also be highly fantasy-oriented and become so involved with his inner life that he can become emotionally deluded and end up living in a dreamworld. Whatever the case, he usually has an imagination that is boundless. It can conceive of the best and the worst of what life has to offer. It can produce far-reaching vision, and it can produce a free-floating fear. This sensibility is one that needs to be channeled and directed in order to make the best of itself. In such a case, it has great creative and empathetic possibility. Otherwise, it can lead to aimless daydreaming and general dissipation of energies.

The moon in Pisces man is emotional. He is also romantic, and his vision of romance has phantasmagorical possibilities. Sensitive and psychically attuned to people and situations around him, he can often magically pick up on other people's vibrations. When he tunes in to his lover, he can leave behind the world and offer her a little piece of heaven. Whatever he shares, it comes from something deep inside him, and he will be prepared to sacrifice something of himself to make the picture perfect.

What he yearns for is a soul mate. What he wants is to merge beyond ego boundaries and enter a perfect world that is like a poem. This need for color and the intensification of life can also lead him to escape it. All sorts of escapist tendencies are common in this sign, from drug and alcohol addiction to deep denial.

The moon in Pisces man is always searching for something elusive, whether that be large or small, significant or the smallest, fleeting fantasy. Creative and often spiritual, he can find many constructive ways to express this soulful urge. However, often a sense of deep longing still exists somewhere inside him that he can't seem to satisfy. Many moon in Pisces men try to fill this hole through sex, which can lead to compulsive promiscuity and eventual dissipation. However, some very spiritual moon in Pisces men know how to go inside themselves to find themselves, or at least a deeper part of themselves that will add to their sense of meaning and make their life that much richer.

How He Feels

He is emotional and sometimes moody, experiencing fluctuations of feeling that he often finds inexpressible. The moon in Pisces man can be sensitive and sentimental. He can also be highly intuitive and emotionally tuned in.

Impressionable and easily influenced when his emotions are appealed to, the moon in Pisces man can be led in a lot of directions. Easily seduced by everything that appeals to his senses, he yearns for the divine highs of life, sometimes regardless of the cost. Sensual and searching for something more than a limited earthbound existence, he is most at home in his soul in some creative or spiritual capacity.

Dreamy, changeable, and known to vacillate emotionally, he can be an enigma unto himself. The composer Maurice Ravel was a moon in Pisces man and so much of his mysterious, impressionistic music reflects the deeply sensitive and soulful nature of this sign.

Because this sign is so connected to the unconscious, it can take this man a long time to process emotions and know what he is really feeling. For example, sometimes he may not realize he is even angry at someone's actions, only to be besieged a day later with a bad mood.

From time to time he needs to tune the world out and have some time alone to emotionally regenerate. Without even realizing it, he can absorb the negativity that surrounds him and suffer through subtle depressions and periods of apathy.

The moon in Pisces man lives in his own world. He is not open about his feelings. It is not that he is intentionally secretive, it is just that they often change so rapidly that they leave him confused. His emotional style is to go with the flow from moment to moment, never really certain of where that might take him but being open to all that comes his way.

How He Shows His Feelings

While at times this man may be curiously quiet and elusive, he is at others open and expressive. There is a strong element of unpredictability to this man. Emotionally subjective—sometimes sad and sometimes happy for no apparent reason—his emotional landscape is constantly changing.

He can be tender, caring, and compassionate. He can also be confused and not able to get in touch with his elusive inner feelings. At times he can be as sympathetic and empathetic a man as you'll ever find. At other times, he can be detached, preoccupied, and caught up in a world of his own.

A confluence of emotions, feelings, and impressions run through him at any given time period. Therefore, sometimes the moon in Pisces man is not in touch with them because he is confused by the changing nature of them. It is not uncommon for him to also be blocked because so much is going on inside of him that the contents of his mind are like a psychic stew that is bubbling over.

His Dark Side

The moon in Pisces man can be moody, depressed, and apathetic. He can also be indecisive, self-deluded, and lack determination. Having strong escapist tendencies, he can live in intense denial and be given to addictions to drugs and alcohol.

Strongly impressionable, he can be emotionally deceptive and unfaithful, falling in love with some new face in about five minutes while there is someone who simply adores him waiting at home.

Being able to imagine the worst in a situation, he can get emotionally caught up in his fears, which he blows out of proportion. Sometimes seeing situations through a distorted lens, he is capable of being very emotionally destructive when he acts on these feelings. When he is too consumed by his own inner world, the moon in Pisces man loses touch with the reality of the outer world.

His Bright Side

He can be brilliantly intuitive and instinctively intelligent. The moon in Pisces man can make a devoted, empathetic soul mate who will be affectionate, caring, and wonderful to talk to.

Creative, imaginative, and often uniquely artistic, he usually possesses an abundance of talent that flows through him like a brilliant light. Very compassionate and often spiritual, he can also be psychic, a healer, and a wonderful psychologist. Whatever direction he goes in, this is a man who can be deeply soulful.

His Attitude Toward Relationships

Wanting to see the world through rose-colored glasses, the moon in Pisces man most wants a relationship that reflects his phantasmagorical ideal. Great romance, drama, and perhaps a bit of sacrifice and longing will leave him very happy. The idea of a great love or an ultimate soul mate with whom to share his life is his ideal, and he will be prepared to give himself totally to it.

This man needs closeness, intimacy, and a deep rapport with a lover. Otherwise, he will feel lonely in a place deep inside himself. When connected to a woman who can share with him on this level, the chances are very strong that he will be faithful.

However, along the way, in his life there will usually be a string of false starts that have left him disappointed or disillusioned. The moon in Pisces man sees women as he would like them to be ideally, not necessarily as they really are. Therefore, it is not uncommon for him to go through a lot of growing pains in his love life, being attracted to the wrong women and being really in love with longing.

His Romance Factor

The moon in Pisces man could have invented romance. It's in his blood, his soul, and his psyche. In a larger sense, he has a romantic vision of the world that can be mystical, spiritual, or beatific. He wants to live beyond the earth, above the clouds; he wants to own a little piece of heaven and to have the joy of that become not only lasting but timeless.

Ideally, he wants a life full of beauty, sensuality, romance, and bliss where mundane responsibilities don't interfere. Having a tendency toward excess, he will bring that to the experience of his love relationship. When in love, he will love to the fullest. When making love, he will leave the world behind and perhaps even his body. The moon in Pisces man wants to lose his waking consciousness to the act of loving—as much and as long as he can.

He can love spiritually or he can love in a way that is addictive. He can also love in a kind, caring, compassionate way that evokes the deepest response from another's soul. When in love, he will know how to make moments magical. Champagne, candlelight, firelight, and lots of little surprises are some typical romantic gestures. However, also being a man who can be very unpredictable, there is no telling what he may think up.

The moon in Pisces man often elevates romantic love to an ethereal domain. Love and romance have great value to him. Ideally, he would love to meet his perfect love and merge with her spiritually and soulfully forever.

His Reality Factor

Fantasy-oriented and living in a private world, the Pisces man is often dreamy and self-deluded. With his tendency to be self-absorbed and sometimes supersensitive, he is not known for his sense of realism and objectivity.

Impressionable and often at the mercy of his emotions and the manipulations of others, the moon in Pisces man can be tossed about in a sea of feelings that lead to confusion, distortions, and blockages. He needs to learn how to work consciously with his intuition and psychic processes to sort things out and get a clear view of the world and his place in it.

His Fear Factor

The moon in Pisces man can be unduly suspicious and even paranoid. In love, he can be jealous and possessive, even though he is not always to be trusted himself.

The Pisces imagination is such that it can picture all possibilities in a situation, from the best to the absolute worst. In his mind these images play themselves out, depending on the emotional weight of the situation. The moon in Pisces man can be very irrational and when he is irrational, his distorted lens can lead him into very dark places where dreams can turn into nightmares.

How He Relates to Fire Sign Women
(Aries, Leo, Sagittarius)

He will be attracted to her sparkle and sheer zest for life. She will be impressed by his intuition and his sensitive, perceptive conversation. Both need romance and want life to be ever larger and more colorful. This is a mutually exciting combination that could offer both what they are looking for on many levels. There is a possibility here for a great deal of communication, passion, sensuality and the sharing of fantasies.

How He Relates to Air Sign Women
(Gemini, Libra, Aquarius)

The air sign woman is too cool and detached for the moon in Pisces man's sensibilities. She is rational, cerebral, and can be somewhat distant and distance-producing. The moon in Pisces man needs intimacy and a deeper, more intuitive kind of communication. The air sign woman will find his intelligence stimulating; however, he may find her reductive logic too simplistic. He sees life in terms of the open-ended. She tries to pin things down and define them. Essentially, they have two different ways of viewing the world, and these will always collide.

How He Relates to Earth Sign Women
(Taurus, Virgo, Capricorn)

The earth sign woman, with her down-to-earth, pragmatic outlook, has no patience for Piscean dreams. She won't understand his intuitive way of operating in the world or his sense of timing, which he may not understand himself. Her possessiveness and need to impose her reality as she sees it will completely confine him. Her need to make everything concrete can bring out the worst in this man, and his tendency for silent retreat will make her exceedingly insecure.

How He Relates to Water Sign Women
(Cancer, Scorpio, Pisces)

Since Pisces is a water sign, this pairing denotes perfect compatibility of nature, temperament, and emotional needs. Both are intuitive, sensual, romantic, and require a deep emotional rapport. Both are searching for the ideal soul mate, and they just might find it in each other.

Conclusion

Handling emotions can be a major task for all of us. For men this can be most difficult. As you have seen, there is a negative and positive expression to the moon sign, which affects instinctive emotional behavior. Because we are all flawed human beings, all cracked pitchers in our own way, we have a tendency to gravitate to the negative side and must always struggle to consciously integrate the positive into the negative. In our society men are not usually taught to value and explore the feminine side of themselves reflected by the moon. But they can benefit greatly from their feminine side. One of the ways is to become more emotionally aware and receptive. This, in turn, can help them create a life for themselves that satisfies the desires that drive them and the needs that otherwise, going unattended, will leave them empty and yearning for a meaning that remains persistently out of reach.

The moon sign reflects old habits and is often the place of least resistance within ourselves. This is the habitual, reflexive response to situations that our moon-ruled depths drive us to before we even have a chance to think, analyze, or evaluate. We all have to be aware of the moon sign's influence because if allowed to rule in its negative aspects, it can get us into trouble through a lot of destructive behavior.

Very slowly there is a polarization of consciousness taking place now: women are taking on men's roles and men are becoming more consciously in tune with their feminine side. When men are more aware of their emotional impulses and try to live through the more positive side of their feelings, their ability in relating to others is completely enhanced. When men are not willing to do this, when they are afraid and choose to repress the feelings they don't understand, they blindly and unknowingly project their own wounds onto their women and destroy their ability to form a strong, vital, fulfilling union.

There was an astrology client I once had who was highly intelligent, intuitive, ambitious, and successful. He was also very emotionally difficult, moody, unhappy, and driven by demons from his past. He never tried to change himself, to address old fears and the hurts they caused. His wife, who was a very upbeat person and who loved him very much, did everything in her power to accommodate him. She bent over backward to make his world a better place. She carried the load and he let her. However, she didn't have the power to free him from the past. Each one of us alone has the power to do that and needs the courage to face our torments and transform them. This is the mission of each one of us in this life.

When it came time for his reading, I said to him, "I want to get straight to the point. I'm not here to talk about all your wonderful qualities and you have some. I'm here to talk about the changes you have to make. You have a big old wound that controls every move you make or don't make in your life. Your wife has carried it for a very long time, and I don't think she's going to be able to carry it any longer, and that's good. Your marriage is under severe stress right now and might end, but that ending could be the opportunity for you to start to have a relationship with yourself that you've needed your whole life. And until you start to have that relationship, you will never have a real relationship with any woman because you can't love. In your present state, you can only absorb love."

This man told me that two weeks before his wife had served him papers for a divorce and sure enough said she was running on empty. There was nothing left for her to give, she said. This man was completely devastated. This divorce had very complex ramifications and was going to turn his entire life upside down. Of course, he didn't see it coming, and he could and should have. He told me that he told his wife that he had always done the best that he could. I looked him straight in the eye, and I said, "NO, YOU HAVEN'T. That is just one more lie you are feeding yourself." Then I tried to make him see that his time had finally come and that it held great possibility as well as pain. It could be a meaningless, deadening pain or it could be pain that brought him great meaning and transformation. He had a choice. He needed to take responsibility for his own feelings. He needed to work with his unconscious, and he probably needed the help of Jungian psychoanalysis. I explained that through this rupture he could begin to build a positive relationship.

He could begin to have a life of meaning as opposed to a life of meaningless routine. At the time this man seemed so eager to try anything and so I referred him to a highly acclaimed psychoanalyst. However, when I saw him a few months later, he had done nothing. He seemed to want to talk about nothing but his pain and the selfishness of his wife for being firm in her decision to end the marriage. At one point he confessed to me that he was seriously considering shooting himself. So many men in a typical situation will readily consider doing something completely destructive rather than looking at the truth and getting help.

I have a friend who is a psychotherapist who tells me that when he does couple counseling, without fail, the women come in burnt out and miserable, and the men think that there's nothing wrong except for the fact that their wife continually causes problems. This is a classic example of men not owning and taking responsibility for their emotional predicament.

This book was something I wanted to write because I see all the time that people, especially men, need help addressing these issues. Women can help by knowing the moon sign of their men and letting them know its significance. They can also help their men and themselves by refusing to take on the burden of their men's emotional loads and attending to their own. The moon sign is powerful and its realm complex. However, it is possible to be conscious of how it will tend to operate in situations and relationships. With knowledge of this, we can build an awareness that can be enhanced continually through reflection and communication.

I cannot stress enough how important the moon sign

is in a man's chart and the power his understanding of it holds for his success in a meaningful relationship. I know many, many women now who are all miserable within their relationships because their connections are shallow, meaningless, and give them nothing emotionally. Knowing a man's moon sign and how it affects him in relationships can be a powerful tool for women to use. Using the insights the moon sign has to offer, we can open up a communication with our men that can be potentially constructive, growth-producing, and conducive to a deeper meaning. A deeper meaning in relationship with men is often no simple task. However, the first step is awareness and communication. I hope this book will allow some food for thought that will be the beginning of a successful and interesting journey.

About the Author

ROBIN MACNAUGHTON is the author of twelve books, including *Power Astrology, Robin MacNaughton's Sun Sign Personality Guide,* and *Goddess Power.* She has written for *Cosmopolitan, Playgirl, Harper's Bazaar, New Woman,* and *Glamour.*

Explore the Powers of the
⭐ Mind and Beyond ⭐

DEVELOP YOUR PSYCHIC ABILITIES
by Litany Burns 70138-X/$6.50

FULL CIRCLE:
The Near Death Experience And Beyond
by Barbara Harris and Lionel C. Bascom;
Commentary by Bruce Greyson, M.D.
68616-X/$5.99

ANGELS OF MERCY
by Rosemary Ellen Guiley 77094-2/$5.50

THE 100 TOP PSYCHICS IN AMERICA:
Their Stories, Specialties—And How To Contact Them
by Paulette Cooper and Paul Noble
53401-7/$6.99

Available from Pocket Books